Short Stories
in the Classroom

" Short story as a
NET to catch a
timeless human reality "

Short Stories in the Classroom

Edited by

Carole L. Hamilton
Cary Academy
Cary, North Carolina

Peter Kratzke
American Thought and Language
Michigan State University
East Lansing, Michigan

National Council of Teachers of English
1111 W. Kenyon Road, Urbana, Illinois 61801-1096

Staff Editor: Kurt Austin

Interior Design: Doug Burnett

Cover Design: Jenny Jensen Greenleaf

NCTE Stock Number: 03995-3050

Library of Congress Cataloging-in-Publication Data

Short stories in the classroom/edited by Carole L. Hamilton and Peter Kratzke.
     p. cm.
     Includes bibliographical references (p.   ) and index.
     ISBN 0-8141-0399-5 (pbk.)
     1. Short stories, American—Study and teaching. 2. Short stories, American—History and criticism. I. Hamilton, Carole L., 1951– .
II. Kratzke, Peter, 1960– .
PS374.S5S48   1999
813'.0109'0071—dc21   99-20716
                                                              CIP

To our students, who teach us more than they know

The novelist may juggle about with chronology and throw narrative overboard; all the time his characters have the reader by the hand, there is a consistency of relationship throughout the experience that cannot and does not convey the quality of human life, where contact is more like the flash of fireflies, in and out, now here, now there, in darkness. Short-story writers see by the light of the flash; theirs is the art of the only thing one can be sure of—the present moment.

Nadine Gordimer, "The Flash of Fireflies"

Contents

Contents

Foreword: What Is a Short Story, and How Do We Teach It?

Often prescribed for students in introductory literature courses are textbooks crammed with readings divided into three sections: prose, poetry, and drama. Prose, exemplified by short stories, typically comes first because it is, presumably, easier to study. However, the short story's apparent simplicity is elusive: characters are not so "fleshed out" as in longer narrative forms; scene is refracted through what may be changing points of view; and plot, often beginning *in medias res*, may suggest more than it tells. The short story, in other words, is a genre caught between the lyrical possibilities of poetry and the concrete actions of drama. By its very brevity, it leaves much untold, and its readers may remain unfulfilled if they do not delve beneath the story's surface. But this challenge, as Edgar Allan Poe famously argued about the "short prose narrative," is also what makes the short story great: its *"Truth"* derives from a narrative *"totality,"* a focus on "a certain unique or single *effect*" (1446, Poe's emphasis). As Americans, we are Poe's descendants. Or are we?

Between Poe's world and today's classroom, something has happened. Poe's University of Virginia—then something closer to Jefferson's "academical village"—is now inhabited by a different kind of student reader. Mark Edmundson, a professor at today's UVA, describes students as "informed consumer[s]" (39), for whom "strong emotional display is forbidden" (41). The result, says Edmundson, is that "students . . . [are] sweet and sad, hovering in a nearly suspended animation" (43). Vanishing, in such a world, are passionate learners, replaced by efficient ones who have their consumer eyes on their consumer futures. How did the academy, once so beautifully formulated by Philologia and her seven handmaidens, the liberal arts, come to this state of affairs? Reader-response critics like Louise Rosenblatt partially blame New Criticism, a movement that discounted the reader's emotions by rallying around William K. Wimsatt and Monroe C. Beardsley's "affective fallacy." For Rosenblatt, the consequential triumph of "efferent" over "aesthetic" responses (i.e., the need to acquire information over the desire for private, "lived-through" experience) undermines what makes a text literary in the first place.

This book responds to the increasing consumerism of high school and college attitudes, its contributors united in breaking their students' "suspended animation." Although its organizing principle is sympathetic to reader-response philosophy, the essays collected here are in no way shackled by a single approach to teaching. Indeed, contributors discuss issues as wide-ranging as technology in the classroom, the academy's formation of canon, definitions of race and culture, and, of course, generic expectations. In the process, they have their eyes on increasing their students' competence as readers and writers—on their students becoming, in literary critic Stanley Fish's term, "informed readers."

The Short Story's Appeal

More than longer prose, drama, or poetry, the short story is an eminently *teachable* genre. Longer prose can be unwieldy, and discussion can lose the level of scrutiny that truly builds critical acumen. Dramatic texts, often compared to the mute notes of sheet music, are detached from theater. Poetry remains an intensely personal experience. In fact, so private can reading poetry be that, when we teach it, we mainly resort to what New Critic Cleanth Brooks dismisses as "the heresy of paraphrase"—retelling a poem in one's own words. The short story is different, its world flickering with multiple and changing perspectives that are perfect for the classroom.

Reading short stories is a special way of learning about life, a way of feeling experiences without actually living them. While maintaining a reflective distance, readers, Wolfgang Iser comments, "live through" fictional experiences in an "as if" reality (269). In today's increasingly technological world of cineplexes and interactive virtual games, this feature is crucial because, unlike visual media, it demands that the reader create a mental world by using textual codes. It is a problem of translation, with answers available to anyone willing to read carefully. We might even say that the short story—once relegated by Virginia Woolf to the stuff of middle-class, "common readers"—now speaks to and for all classes, a genre uniquely positioned to serve society as can nothing else.

In their assessment of writing short stories, authors offer different ideas with different reasons. Echoing Poe, the early twentieth-century writer Elizabeth Bowen praised the "heroic simplicity" (256) of a well-written short story, suggesting that its sparse, streamlined form dramatically foregrounds its subject and theme. In the same vein, Julio Cortázar speaks of the "sphere" that "should somehow be there before the story is even written down" and equates writing a short story to "modeling out of clay" (qtd. in Head 21). Nadine Gordimer is more visceral: "A short story *occurs* in the imaginative sense. To write one is to express from a situation of the exterior or internal world the life-giving drop—sweat, tear, semen, saliva—that will spread an intensity on the page; burn a hole in it" ("Selecting" 117). Short stories, Raymond Carver no less dramatically summarizes, can "send a chill along the reader's spine" (273).

Despite the short story's power, it is not without limitations. Frank O'Connor was pessimistic about the form's social influence, describing short story writers as "outlawed figures wandering about the fringes of society" (19). True to that profile, short stories do not demand long periods of attention; instead, they whisper from the sidelines their brief, often quirky observations of the world. For today's consumer student, that limitation can become the genre's strength. Students, if nothing else, are intuitively shrewd, recoiling when literature veers toward either didacticism or self-indulgence. The short story is remarkably good at avoiding both. In fact, Gordimer says, the short story amounts to the "flash of fireflies." Sometimes, it would seem, startling students is a good place to begin.

Critical Perspective

Fifty years ago, Rosenblatt tried to persuade English teachers that their objective was not merely to build skills that would promote reverence for literature; rather, their job was to reap insights into human nature. This book continues in that spirit, its contributors refusing to fall into the trap of teaching students their personal view, preferring instead to motivate students to discover their own readings and, more important, to apply them elsewhere. When that happens, students find the potential to revise more than their knowledge—they begin to revise their view of the world and their place in it.

Regardless of our particular philosophy or teaching strategy, recognizing how we orient ourselves to textual codes etches the cultural boundaries of our classrooms. How we approach reading, then, compels us to take a stand on how we direct students as social beings. At the same time, taking a stand may mean personal change, and that prospect can be uncomfortable. For students, it can be downright frightening. The public classroom, as a meeting place for readers, can pit one view against another. Instead of brawling over differences, contributors here believe, students can be led to agree to disagree—in other words, to argue and, by arguing, to learn and grow.

Overview of Chapters

At one point in this project, a professor asked one of us what was the point in compiling so many essays on teaching short stories. "When I decide to teach a short story, I already know what method I will use," he proclaimed, "and it is the same for every story." While there may be comfort in the professor's approach, there is also the kind of sadness that Edmundson sees in his Virginia students. The teachers here offer an antidote, readily acknowledging that not all students come to the classroom sharing our enthusiasm for reading, nor that their reactions match our expectations. The resulting teaching strategies, grounded in the relationship between text and reader, not only accept but embrace the implication that students are, simply, unpredictable. Just as important, these teachers accept that students—without sounding a note of melodrama—can be readers as legitimate as anyone else. Our job, then, is to temper that legitimacy with greater competence.

The organization of this book tracks how teachers use short stories to connect their students to imaginative fiction (Part One), to slow the reading process and thereby take a closer look (Part Two), to analyze generic aspects of structure (Part Three), to encounter alternative readings (Part Four), to hone critical methodology (Part Five), and to increase literary discrimination (Part Six). Of course, the essays themselves are by no means so focused as are the arrangement of these chapters, for each contributor addresses the full range of the reading experience in making reading personal, informed, and profound. To such teachers, no text is so simple and no reader so intuitive that a caring and experienced guide cannot point the way to different sources of learning. Indeed, with issues ranging from gender, class, race, and agency to style, structure, and history, there can be no single, pre-mapped "way in," nothing that is "the same for every story." Every text is a kind of encounter, and the classroom becomes a place to discover subtleties and create cohesive meaning while, at the same time, encountering other interpretations. This meaning-making allows us, in turn, to engage the world sympathetically and productively. With that, we come full circle: when we become better citizens, literature can be *useful* to its consumers.

Finally, while the contributors here encourage aesthetic reading, they do not ignore rigorous analysis. In order to foster that analysis, they choose texts that both speak to students and challenge them (Fish calls these sorts of text "dialectical"). The result, summarily stated, is that teachers help students toward both self-reliance and social responsibility—the very stuff, to return to Poe's era, of Ralph Waldo Emerson's "Man Thinking." Emerson's words from *The American Scholar*, in fact, are as true today as when he inked them: "There is . . . creative reading as well as creative writing. When the mind is braced by labor and invention, the page of whatever book we read becomes luminous with manifold allusion. Every sentence is doubly significant, and the sense of our author is as broad as the world" (1533–34). Good thing: the world is where students must go out and live.

Works Cited

Bowen, Elizabeth. Introduction to *The Faber Book of Modern Short Stories. New Short Story Theories.* Ed. Charles E. May. Athens: Ohio UP, 1994. 256–62.

Carver, Raymond. "On Writing." *The New Short Story Theories.* Ed. Charles E. May. Athens: Ohio UP, 1994. 273–77.

Edmundson, Mark. "On the Uses of a Liberal Education." *Harper's Magazine* Sept. 1997: 39–49.

Emerson, Ralph Waldo. *The American Scholar.* 1837, 1849. *The Heath Anthology of American Literature.* Ed. Paul Lauter et al. Vol. 1. 2nd ed. Lexington, MA: D.C. Heath, 1994. 1529–41.

Gordimer, Nadine. "Selecting My Stories." *The Essential Gesture: Writing, Politics, and Places.* New York: Knopf, 1988. 111–17.

———. "The Flash of Fireflies." *The New Short Story Theories.* Ed. Charles E. May. Athens: Ohio UP, 1994. 263–67.

Head, Dominic. *The Modernist Short Story: A Study in Theory and Practice.* Cambridge: Cambridge UP, 1992.

Iser, Wolfgang. "Towards a Literary Anthropology." *Prospecting: From Reader-Response to Literary Anthropology.* Baltimore: Johns Hopkins UP, 1989. 262–84.

O'Connor, Frank. *The Lonely Voice: A Study of the Short Story.* Cleveland: World Publishing Co., 1963.

Poe, Edgar Allan. "A Review: *Twice-Told Tales.* By Nathaniel Hawthorne." 1842. *The Heath Anthology of American Literature.* Ed. Paul Lauter et al. Vol. 2. 2nd ed. Lexington, MA: D.C. Heath, 1994. 1444–49.

Rosenblatt, Louise M. "Retrospect." *Transactions with Literature: A Fifty-Year Perspective.* Eds. Edmund J. Farrell and James R. Squire. Urbana, IL: NCTE, 1990. 97–107.

I Making It Personal

Narratives should not be primarily packages for psychological insights, though they can contain them, like raisins in dough, which feed the storytelling appetite, the appetite for motion, for suspense, for resolution.

John Updike, "Interview with Charles T. Samuels"

One basic premise underlies the essays in this book: that productive teaching of short stories can begin only when students make valid, heartfelt responses and connections. These personal connections to the self include idiosyncratic sympathies, quirky affinities, and sudden touches to the soul that enable readers to question values and beliefs, to seek new depth in understanding motives, longings, and secrets. Put another way, we all know how words can surge through our pens (or word processors) when we have need to complain, plead, or emote—that is, when we care. As teachers, we aim for the same sort of energy in our classrooms.

Meaningful connections imply that readers move beyond passive consumership of stories to active engagement and response. Readers who seek only validation of preformed, static judgments are consumers of fiction, not readers. Story consumers grimly hold onto their intuitive first responses, knowing what they like, validating and liking what they know. Real connections, on the other hand, shake the reader's soul. For their part, teachers challenge students to care, widening the tiny cracks in their students' intellectual and emotional armor and opening the way to deeper insight. The short story provides the perfect occasion to do that, for it resists facile assumptions, presenting an enigma, not an explanation. The short story demands contemplation and rewards interrogation, offering up its sweetest secrets to those who probe it in earnest.

Because reader consumership resists personal growth, the classroom must provide a hothouse atmosphere that nurtures change and growth. The climate must be composed of a sense that initial responses may be revised, that readers offer their interpretations tentatively. Indeed, Robert Probst cites tentativeness as one of five necessary conditions for response-based teaching (25). The process of sharing insights and findings in an atmosphere of acceptance and tentativeness transforms the class into a community of reflective thinkers who dare to plumb their own psyches as they study a story. For teachers, the goal is to shift attention away from finding the "right" interpretation to setting the right climate. By accepting this condition, says Jane Tompkins, "teachers can foster and safeguard an atmosphere of caring, careful attention." That way, teachers can "be there with them [students] in a human way, take the temperature of their feelings, find out what [is] really on their minds, give them an opportunity to take control of the material for themselves, let them run with it and see how it [feels]" (604). Tentativeness in reading honors that each reader may find a unique personal meaning, while at the same time it does not deny the validity of the text itself—the reader supplies the meaning; the text shapes that meaning. Tentativeness, in this light, is the optimum condition for the mind to accept new learning.

In the essays that follow, a bargain has been struck between New Critical adherence to the rigors of textual scrutiny and reader-response acknowledgment of the reader's meaning-making role. The classroom that honors tentativeness fosters personal connections and personal growth by accepting Wolfgang Iser's premise that "no reading can ever exhaust the text, for each individual reader will fill in the gaps in his own way, thereby excluding the various other possibilities" (55). As readers fill the gaps of an open text and see how others fill the gaps differently, they are freed to change their initial readings, to change their minds. The teachers here seize on this instability, using it to move students toward thoughtful, directed analysis. Initial reactions are used as stepping-off points, opportunities to discover pathways to deeper insight and personal growth as well as broader awareness of the peculiarities of the short story genre. In particular, in her view of Tim O'Brien's "The Things They Carried," Susanne Rubenstein bridges the generation gap between American soldiers in Vietnam and students born a generation after those soldiers were forgotten. Janet Kaufman leads her students through choral readings of Toni Cade Bambara's "Raymond's Run" to views beyond their judgmental first impressions of the story's main character. Sara R. Joranko capitalizes on her students' misinterpretation of the narrative voice in Graham Greene's "The Destructors" to lead them to a better understanding of narration. Last, Judy L. Isaksen's students use Zora Neale Hurston's multivalent

"How It Feels to Be Colored Me" as a springboard to explore their own multiple selves. For each teacher, the principle remains that personal connections should be made, explored, and reshaped.

Works Cited

Iser, Wolfgang. "The Reading Process: A Phenomenological Approach." *Reader-Response Criticism: From Formalism to Post-Structuralism.* Ed. Jane P. Tompkins. Baltimore: Johns Hopkins UP, 1980. 50–69.

Probst, Robert E. *Response and Analysis: Teaching Literature in Junior and Senior High.* Portsmouth, NH: Boynton/Cook, 1988.

Tompkins, Jane. "Comment and Response." *College English* 53 (1991): 601–4.

1 Shared Weight: Tim O'Brien's "The Things They Carried"

Susanne Rubenstein
Wachusett Regional High School, Holden, Massachusetts

Interviewer: If you were to give advice to a young writer, what would you tell him?

Elie Wiesel: First, to read. I never taught creative writing courses. I believe in creative reading. That's what I am trying to teach—creative reading.

1978 interview in *Writers at Work: The* Paris Review *Interviews*

They come into class burdened with books and bags and backpacks. I watch as they deposit all the paraphernalia of adolescence about their desks and feet. Matt sighs hugely.

"My locker's waaay on the other side of the building," he says, dropping his gym bag in the aisle. "I gotta carry all this stuff till fourth period."

I smile. I couldn't ask for a better opening. "Really?" I say, tapping my fingers on the cover of Tim O'Brien's novel *The Things They Carried*. "So tell me about the things you carry."

It doesn't take us long to amass a list of items that many of my twenty-two New Literature students carry. Chemistry books and calculators, Walkmans and water bottles, baseball caps and computer disks. Today Erin's got her senior pictures, Rosemary her art portfolio, Ken three detention slips. Christina produces a banana gone slightly brown ("I've been carrying it since Tuesday," she says sheepishly), Laurie a field hockey stick, and Pete a *Time* magazine. Their arms are full. When we've filled half of the blackboard with a list of all the stuff that they have spread about them, I stand back and survey the list. "What shall we call it?" I ask.

They barely hesitate.

"Necessities," says Rosemary.

They all nod in agreement, and I print the words *Necessities of High School Life*. Thinking that the game is over, they look at me expectantly, sure that "real" class is now about to begin. I see the look of surprise in their eyes when I tap the blank side of the board. "So that's it then?" I say. "That's all you're carrying?"

"Nope," calls Andy from the back corner, "but you don't want to know everything I've got!"

"Probably not," I agree, amid the laughter, "but maybe I'd like to know a little more. Who's carrying something that's hidden?"

"I am," says Erin. She rummages in her pocketbook. "These are my worry dolls. I don't go anywhere without them." She opens the little straw box and produces three tiny brightly dressed figures.

"My journal?" offers Cheryl, pulling from her backpack a worn blue book, ticket stubs and photographs jutting from its pages.

"Butts," announces Andy, tossing the pack of Marlboros up in the air and deftly slipping them back in his jacket.

I grab the chalk and we begin another list, this one of the items that line the dark recesses of their pockets and their purses. When the side of the board is full, we study the list. "What shall we call this?" I ask.

"Our secrets," says Matt.

"Our symbols," says Christina.

"Our selves," says Erin.

A few minutes before the bell rings, I hand out copies of Tim O'Brien's *The Things They Carried*. The students ruffle through the pages, certain that we have left the lists behind, sure that now we're on to more serious work. I give them a brief introduction, tell them that this semi-autobiographical novel, published in 1990, is a powerful exploration of the experience of war. A veteran of the Vietnam War, O'Brien describes, through a series of interlocking stories, the horror and complexity of war, and he carries his readers to a geographical and emotional territory they will never forget. For tomorrow, I ask the students to read the title story. They leave, bags, backpacks, and books in hand, while I hope that they carry with them the connection I have tried to draw between the baggage of their lives and that of Lieutenant Cross's men.

In "The Things They Carried," O'Brien uses the simple device of the list to organize his story and to make the reader begin to understand the terrible weight young soldiers carried in the jungles of Vietnam. We read of assault rifles and grenade launchers, radios and rations, flak jackets and flares. Dave Jensen "humps" three pairs of socks and foot powder, Kiowa a *New Testament*, Henry Dobbins canned peaches in heavy syrup. Someone carries comic books, another tranquilizers, a third a thumb cut from a VC corpse. The pounds mount up, the load increases, until suddenly we realize that the heaviest burden comes not in boots, binoculars, or bars of chocolate but in the weight of all that can't be measured: "They carried all the emotional baggage of men who might die. Grief, terror, love, longing—these were intangibles, but the intangibles had their own mass and specific gravity, they had tangible weight" (20).

"Cool story," Andy announces the next morning, tossing his tan backpack on the bookcase. The others are nodding, their words tumbling together.

"But why'd Sanders cut off the thumb?"

"Did guys really die the way Lavender did?"

"Could they really carry all that stuff?"

And a wail from Erin: "But why, oh why, did Jimmy burn those love letters?"

I know then the class discussion will take care of itself. O'Brien, with his brutal and beautiful honesty, has carried my students to a place they have never been, a place where, if they are a lucky generation, they will never have to go—to the heart of war where young soldiers

> plodded along slowly, dumbly, leaning forward against the heat, unthinking, all blood and bone, simple grunts, soldiering with their legs, toiling up the hills and down into the paddies and across the rivers and up again and down, just humping, one step and then the next and then another, but no volition, no will, because it was automatic, it was anatomy, and the war was entirely a matter of posture and carriage, the hump was everything, a kind of inertia, a kind of emptiness, a dullness of desire and intellect and conscience and hope and human sensibility. (15)

Just for today, though, I want my students to go to Vietnam, to a war that they need to understand, to feel, if they are to grow into young men and women who will make decisions about peace on our planet. O'Brien's writing takes them there, to "Vietnam, the place, the soil—a powdery orange-red dust that covered their boots and fatigues and faces . . . the humidity, the monsoons, the stink of fungus and decay . . ." (15). O'Brien makes them witness the death of Ted Lavender "zapped while zipping" (17) and feel the horrible guilt that Lieutenant Cross bears, "something he would have to carry like a stone in his stomach for the rest of the war" (16). And, as my students march with Lieutenant Cross's men, they too shoulder the weight of canteens and code books, moccasins and M&M's, ghosts and the ultimate loss of love. It is a lot for them to carry, but, I tell them quietly, they have surely all had training; one does not have to be in war to carry heavy burdens. Then, I want them to go one step further. I want them to go inside themselves to discover all the baggage that they carry.

I hand them each a piece of paper, announcing, "Yesterday we made lists of all the tangible items you were carrying. Today let's deal with the intangibles."

"Like Lt. Cross's love for Martha?" Laurie asks.

"Like his love for Martha," I say.

"Like the guys' memories?" asks Pete.

"Like their memories," I say.

There is silence for a moment. Then Andy speaks.

"Like the soldiers' fear of blushing?"

I nod.

They begin to write. I listen to their pens scratch across the pages, but I am watching their faces, and, in the movement of their eyes and the twisting of their mouths, I see that they are maneuvering weight. When I ask them to stop writing, they do not. It is only when I ask for responses to fill the board that they look up. Their faces tell me that they are reluctant to speak. It is one thing to share the things that fill your arms; another those that fill your heart. I wait, allowing them to decide if these are burdens they can bare.

Erin breaks the silence. "Divorce," she says. "I'm carrying my parents' divorce."

In the murmur of "Me too"s, their silence ends. Suddenly their words come fast and furious; my fingers fly across the board, struggling to keep up.

"College applications," someone shouts out.

"College rejections"—a quieter voice.

"Not being who my father thinks I should be."

"Not being who I want to be."

"Being shy."

"Being alone."

"Being afraid."

"Fear of AIDS."

"Fear of death."

"Fear of life."

Making the basketball team, making the honor roll, making the grade. Getting a diploma, getting a job, getting a life. Their words reveal all that lies under the buoyancy and brashness of their adolescent demeanor, and I am reminded that they are brave soldiers.

When the last words are spoken, there is an almost palpable sense of relief in the room. The students seem to breathe easier. They have placed their burdens on the board and now feel almost weightless. But of course the things they carry can't be left behind that easily; perhaps they cannot be left at all. Like the guilt Lieutenant Cross carries, many of their burdens are simply a part of who they are, and the only way to make the load lighter is to find someone to share its weight.

They leave class that day, each planning a paper. The paper will take the form of a letter to someone "back home"—that is, someone in their lives with whom they can share the weight of something that they carry. Pete has already decided. He will write to his father to explain why his parents' expectations seem an overwhelming load. Cheryl is considering writing to her boyfriend to tell him that his possessiveness is too much for her to handle. Erin of the worry dolls wants to know if she can write more than one letter. And Andy, all cocksure and confident on the outside, pauses by my desk to say, "I got a lot to write on this one, but I don't want anyone but you to read it."

A terrible war was fought in the jungles of Vietnam. The losses and the lessons of that war are part of my own adolescent experience, but, for my students, the war seems a piece of ancient history. Reading Tim O'Brien brings them to the edge of the jungle and makes them care about the lives of those who fought there. O'Brien's soldiers are not military models; they are boys like Andy, Pete, or Ken—boys who, though they must carry all the necessities of war, also carry the pieces of their selves, all the things that make them human. It is there that the soldiers' lives intersect with those of my students; it is there that empathy begins. The reading, writing, and discussion we do around "The Things They Carried" is intended to help my students see that all of life demands courage and that none of us marches without a burden. We are all like O'Brien's men who "carried all they could bear, and then some, including a silent awe for the terrible power of the things they carried" (9).

Work Cited

O'Brien, Tim. *The Things They Carried*. New York: Penguin, 1991.

2 Being People Together: Toni Cade Bambara's "Raymond's Run"

Janet Ellen Kaufman
University of Utah

Fiction operates through the senses, and I think one reason that people find it so difficult to write stories is that they forget how much time and patience is required to convince through the senses. No reader who doesn't actually experience, who isn't made to feel, the story is going to believe anything the fiction writer merely tells him. The first and most obvious characteristic of fiction is that it deals with reality through what can be seen, heard, smelt, tasted, and touched.

Flannery O'Connor, *Mystery and Manners: Occasional Prose*

Toni Cade Bambara's short story "Raymond's Run" narrates the first-person account of Squeaky, an apparently tough girl with a squeaky voice who doesn't "believe in standing around with somebody in my face doing a lot of talking" (23). No matter her vocal tenor, Squeaky's voice is strong and clear. Reading this story with students invites careful attention to writerly voice and description; and the relationships between the characters invite an exploration of female identity, friendship and competition, and abilities and disabilities.

Squeaky is a runner. The only thing that gets in the way of her disciplined training is her brother Raymond, a vaguely sketched character who isn't "quite right." We never find out exactly what is "wrong" with Raymond, but "he needs a lot of looking after." For minding Raymond, "which is enough," Squeaky is relieved from any "work around the house" (23). Perhaps Raymond has Down's syndrome or a form of autism, but a precise diagnosis remains irrelevant to the story. What matters, instead, is Squeaky's recognition of Raymond's abilities. Her recognition becomes a catalyst for transforming her various relationships, including her relationship with Gretchen (her chief rival), with other girls in her neighborhood, and with running. Early in the story Squeaky reveals her cynicism when she tells us that the neighborhood girls tease Raymond and ask dumb questions; they talk like "ventriloquist-dummies" and "never really smile at each other because they don't know how and don't want to know how and there's probably no one to teach us how, cause grown-up girls don't know either" (27). However, by the end of the story, Squeaky wins the annual May Day race, Gretchen comes in a close second, and Raymond, having been portrayed as inept, runs right alongside both girls outside the fence. Squeaky's surprise at Raymond's running overpowers her thrill of winning the race, and she and Gretchen "stand there with this big smile of respect" between them; for Squeaky, "It's about as real a smile as girls can do for each other, considering we don't practice real smiling every day, you know, cause maybe we too busy being flowers or fairies or strawberries instead of something honest and worthy of respect . . . , you know, . . . like being people" (32).

How do Squeaky and Gretchen finally start being "real people" together? How do they traverse the territory of competition and betrayal so common to adolescent girls? Why is it that Raymond's accomplishment begins to bring Squeaky and Gretchen together? These are some of the questions I pose to my students at the beginning of our discussion; the exercises we go on to do enable them to respond to these questions.

Description: Show versus Tell

To begin thinking through the matter of "voice" in writing, we begin by focusing on the students' own writing. Reading closely and engaging in their own writing, the students prepare themselves to read the literary text more closely and to discuss more critically. First, I introduce the idea of "showing" versus "telling" by looking at Bambara's writing as a model. Squeaky, for instance, never labels Raymond; we cannot, therefore, simply dismiss his "condition," assuming we have understood him. Instead, she *describes* his behavior, revealing the contrasts of her frustration and her patience:

> I'm standing on the corner admiring the weather and about to take a stroll down Broadway so I can practice my breathing exercises, and I've got Raymond walking on the inside close to the buildings, cause he's subject to fits of fantasy and starts thinking he's a circus performer and that the curb is a tightrope strung high in the air. And sometimes after a rain he likes to step down off his tightrope right into the gutter and slosh around getting his shoes and cuffs wet. Then I get hit when I get home. (24)

When we read this passage aloud in class, students find themselves amused by Raymond's antics. Though Raymond is older than Squeaky, he is like a little brother—innocent and entertaining, yet a troublemaker who has to be watched every minute. He is Squeaky's sidekick; she takes him along, tolerating him while she runs, not minding his antics "so long as he doesn't run [her] over or interrupt [her] breathing exercises" (24). Only at the story's end do we discover, with Squeaky, that Raymond, all the while, has learned to run alongside her; her astonishment and pleasure in Raymond's run, not in her own, causes Squeaky to smile a "real smile" at Gretchen for the first time.

After we discuss Squeaky's description of Raymond, I ask my students to write a half-page description of someone in their families—parent, grandparent, sibling, dog or cat—without using any adjectives—no *funny, beautiful, generous.* Instead, I ask that they write what the family member *says,* what he or she *does,* how he or she *acts.* At first my students stare at me blankly. After all, they have learned that adjectives exist precisely to describe people, places, and things. But what does "beautiful" *mean,* I ask them? What is the difference, for instance, between one person's beautiful mother and another person's beautiful mother? Are their little sisters *annoying* in precisely the same way? I ask the students to write specifically in their own speaking voice, just like Squeaky, when she tells us that she is "a poor Black girl who really can't afford to buy shoes and a new dress you only wear once a lifetime" (20). They write drafts overnight; then, the next day in class, they read their drafts aloud, hearing each other's distinct voices and gleaning ideas for revising. Hearing and playing with voice in their own written language helps the students develop a sensitivity to creating and reading voice in literary writing. From this activity, we move back to "Raymond's Run," to the matter of interpreting voice.

Kinesthetic English and Character Interpretation

Through their descriptive writing practice, the students begin to appreciate Raymond's character; then we shift the focus to Squeaky. Some of the students see Squeaky's confidence and matter-of-fact assertions as "conceited" because, early in the story, she tells us that she is the "fastest thing on two feet," even declaring, "There is no track meet that I don't win the first place medal" (23). Unable to accept that Squeaky's attitude represents anything but arrogance, the students sympathize with the neighborhood girls in the story who resent her "attitude." So that they can begin to read Squeaky's character more sympathetically, we engage in "choral reading," an exercise to enter her character, hear her voice, and imagine the body language accompanying her dialogue.

Choral reading, designed and explained by Bruce Pirie in his article "Meaning through Motion," is inspired by classical Greek dance and drama. As Pirie asserts, teaching with kinesthetic activities assumes that "the body has its own kind of knowing that may tap into new levels of understanding" (46). In his theory of multiple intelligences, Howard Gardner identifies a "kinesthetic" or "bodily" intelligence and, as Peter Smagorinsky argues in "Multiple Intelligences in the English Class," unconventional "thinking" about texts using other "intelligences"— including kinesthetic, spatial, musical, interpersonal, intrapersonal, and logical/mathematical—can strengthen our verbal/linguistic intelligence. One of the students in my class, Erica, affirmed this when she asserted, "Through the choral reading I was able to dissect Squeaky and her character. I looked at the words on the paper and had to think, feel, and act like her character."

In his article, Pirie outlines basic steps of the choral reading; I have borrowed and adapted them to work with "Raymond's Run." As Pirie reminds us, the words *choral* and *choreography* share a common root; members of the *chorus* in Greek drama were both singers and actors. For this reason, the choral readings that the students prepare use both sound and simple movement to explore meanings and feelings. Students begin by dividing into small groups of four or five, and their first task is to create a monologue for Squeaky, which they derive by linking together four to six passages from her narration or dialogue. Identifying characterizing phrases and sentences, then, becomes the first reading skill they must practice for the choral reading. One of their monologues included the following four passages:

> I am not a strawberry. I do not dance on my toes. I run. That is what I am all about. (28)
>
> Every time, just before I take off in a race, I always feel like I'm in a dream. . . . (30)
>
> Then I hear Raymond yanking at the fence to call me and I wave to shush him . . . and it occurs to me, watching how smoothly he climbs hand over hand . . . that Raymond would make a very fine runner. (31)
>
> And I'm smiling to beat the band cause if I've lost this race, or if me and Gretchen tied, or even if I've won, I can always retire as a runner and begin a whole new career as a coach with Raymond as my champion. (32)

Having ordered these passages on a page to be read as a monologue, students practice reading them together, aloud, and then determine, as

Pirie explains, "carefully thought-out, expressive movements" to accompany their reading (47). They read and move in unison as a chorus, keeping the movements simple—a sweeping arm, a stamp of the foot, a big smile—so that, instead of trying to remember choreography, they can concentrate on qualities such as inflection, stress, denotative and connotative meaning, and feeling. After practicing their reading first and then adding the motions—with the teacher circulating among the students, encouraging them to stand up and practice together—the small groups present their choral reading to the class. In the presentations, the dramatic speech and the motions bring Squeaky's character alive. Furthermore, they bring the students alive to each other. Commenting on this process, one student, Michael, wrote,

> Before we read the sentences out loud with emotion we did not really get a sense for the story and how Squeaky would have felt and acted if we could see her. . . . The choral reading . . . gave everybody a chance to participate. I really like the fact that if somebody messed up nobody was critical of them, and I felt that I could enjoy what I was doing and not worry about a grade or my peers laughing at me. I found that we could all work at any pace we wanted to, and the suggestions of my classmates were very helpful.

As part of the process of preparing the choral reading, the students naturally negotiate their interpretation of Squeaky. For instance, they find themselves debating which words to stress and which tone to use for Squeaky when she asserts, "I'm ready to fight, cause like I said I don't feature a whole lot of chit-chat, I much prefer to just knock you down right from the jump and save everybody a lotta precious time" (26). They discuss whether they will gesture with a wave of the hand on the words *much prefer* or if they will make a punching motion on the word *knock*. Remarking on these deliberations, Sara wrote that "when you change [Squeaky's] voice, and her accent, and her speech, you think of her as a totally different person with a completely different personality." Becca, explaining how her understanding of Squeaky changes through the choral reading, summarized many of her classmates' initial interpretations:

> If you were to give [most people] this story to read and then ask them to describe Squeaky in one word, they would probably say, "conceited." At the beginning that's what I thought, too, but after we did the choral reading I had a different opinion. I don't think Squeaky is conceited; I think she is insecure, so when she found something she was really good at she wanted everyone to know. At the beginning of the story, Squeaky is very reluctant

about taking care of Raymond, and looks at him as a responsibility. At the end she sees him as a real person who really can do things well. He has a talent just like she does.

Before the choral reading, Roselyn felt that Squeaky was "just a fresh girl who thought highly of herself" but, through the choral reading, she realized "how much [she] could relate to [Squeaky]." Like Roselyn, Squeaky "felt it bothersome to take care of her brother, Raymond." However, Roselyn saw that

> when someone had something to say about Raymond, they had to speak to [Squeaky] about it and she would stick up for her brother. She was a very fresh and agile person when it came to talking and answering by using comebacks.

By relating to Squeaky through her own experience, Roselyn discovered another aspect of Squeaky's character—determination:

> Squeaky was determined to disprove people she disliked, determined to run, which would show a sport at which she was quite competent, and determined to help her brother Raymond. Squeaky was determined to show her brother what life and running were all about; she wanted to show that she was sure of herself.

As the comments of Sara, Becca, and Roselyn show, the students move from judgment of Squeaky to empathy for her. The characteristics that they initially read as arrogance and conceit became those of determination and persistence. They ultimately determined that Squeaky is "aggressive and bold, but kind, too." Amy admitted that she initially thought Squeaky was "really conceited and full of herself," but after the choral reading and discussion she wrote, "Now I'm not sure how much was real, how much was bravado, and how much was just the truth of knowing." Comparing herself to Squeaky, Erica reinterpreted Squeaky's arrogance as a show of both independence and insecurity:

> [The choral reading] made me realize how I act in comparison to Squeaky and what a different (in a good way), brave, independent person she was. I think she was a dreamer. At the beginning she dreamt dreams for herself, but, as the story and her views towards Raymond progressed, her dreams began to differ. First she dreamt about HER, and running. Then her dreams were filled of hope for Raymond and her dreams for him such as running. Squeaky thinks very highly of herself so it was very hard for kids her age to be friends with someone like that. She and Gretchen had a sort of rivalry towards each other. Personally I think they both like each other inside but didn't know it. The choral reading showed me that these girls were confused when it came to feel-

ings. They didn't know how to act so they acted mean. They thought everything was fake. . . . I think that once the race was over their feelings moved one step closer to friends.

Erica's first observation seems central to her interpretation: the choral reading enabled her to identify personally with, and in contrast to, the character. This identification then opens the door to further interpretation, and her comments seem quite accurate in identifying the change in Squeaky's dreams. Further, she comes to sympathize with the girls' confusion and their inability to express their feelings. She understands that they "move one step closer to friends" because they step away from being disingenuous and mean and greet each other "with this big smile of respect" between them.

Conclusion

Concluding her comments, Becca wrote that she "really got a feeling about how the characters were acting or thinking. . . . The choral reading really made me believe I was there." Once the students are *there*, it becomes easier to engage questions about character and plot because they feel, as Karina wrote, "a connection and bond with all the characters." As this connection occurs, it facilitates the task of teaching literary interpretation and writing; once students feel affinity to a text, they read with more depth and their writing becomes clearer and more analytical. Though the students quoted here are seventh-graders, these exercises succeed equally well with high school and university students. In this case, with "Raymond's Run," the students moved beyond their initial assessment of Squeaky to understand "how important running is" to her and that "she's not ashamed; she wants to give the impression of a tough person but deep down she's sweet." By the end of the story, when Gretchen and Squeaky are standing there "being people," the students were also "being people" together.

Works Cited

Bambara, Toni Cade. "Raymond's Run." *Gorilla, My Love*. New York: Vintage, 1972. 23–32.

Pirie, Bruce. "Meaning through Motion: Kinesthetic English." *English Journal* 84.8 (1995): 46–51.

Smagorinsky, Peter. "Multiple Intelligences in the English Class: An Overview." *English Journal* 84.8 (1985): 19–26.

Further Reading

Boal, Augusto. *Games for Actors and Non-Actors*. Trans. Adrian Jackson. New York: Routledge, 1992.

Gardner, Howard. "'Multiple Intelligences' as a Catalyst." *English Journal* 84.8 (1995): 16–18.

———. *Multiple Intelligences: The Theory in Practice*. New York: Basic Books, 1993.

3 Destruct to Instruct: "Teaching" Graham Greene's "The Destructors"

Sara R. Joranko
John Carroll University

In the sphere of psychology, details are also the thing. God preserve us from commonplaces. Best of all is it to avoid depicting the hero's state of mind; you ought to try to make it clear from the hero's actions.

Anton Chekhov, letter to Alexander P. Chekhov

No college teachers I know "teach" short stories, if teaching means requiring students to master and memorize the elements of short fiction, or to identify characters in daily keep-'em-honest quizzes. We want our students first of all to enjoy the power of controlled narrative to make us feel, to take us temporarily out of our immediate surroundings and, conversely, to take us inside ourselves and others. Nowadays we also use stories to tempt students to think, talk, and write about the social, political, moral, ethical, and always *human* issues. As Louise Rosenblatt claims in *Literature as Exploration*, literary exposure to other worlds, cultures, and people can provoke students to re-examine their own surroundings and lives, with the desired result being an enhanced self-knowledge. However, while Hemingway muses that "it's pretty to think" that we can use short fiction as the agent of such growth, all too often the reality is, as students would confirm, "Not!"

Classroom failures like the one I shall describe may be related to the problem of designing a syllabus in August, which is like buying a gift for a complete stranger. The very stories you choose as guaranteed to intrigue or engage your students are the ones that always seem to bore them. Sure enough, when I assigned Graham Greene's "The Destructors," about a group of boys who methodically and ingeniously destroy a house that survived the bombings of London, my first-year students produced perfunctory journal entries, sometimes politely covering their mouths to hide their yawns. All twenty-five dismissed the gang led by the story's protagonist, Trevor, as "punks."

Maybe it was the post-World War II setting. But Cy Knoblauch offers another likely explanation. Apparently the students of whom he writes are similar to those at the small Jesuit university where I teach. As members of the "dominant culture" (15), Knoblauch's white, middle-class young adults dismiss everything different from their "middle-class innocence" (17). As a result, multicultural readings like Greene's story have little or no effect. Knoblauch's—and my—students seem "socialized to presume that the meanings of stories serve to ratify [their] beliefs" (18). And, because "there is a powerful self-interest, rooted in class advantage, that works actively, if not consciously, against critical reflectiveness" (19), there's really no reason for them to change. In my case, the failure to produce such reflectiveness has a happy ending, although the plan that worked against the students' apathy evolved in response to it rather than being worked out beforehand. Like the boys in the story who destroy the house from the inside out, I had to dismantle my students' facile presumptions about their own superiority to "punks" who do bad things for no reason.

For me, preliminary to class discussion of any story is determining "vital stats"—students must answer the journalist's questions "Who?", "What?", "When?", "Where?", "Why?", and "How?" That way, at least we can agree on expository information like setting, the ages and occupations of characters, and so forth. The stumper is always "Why?" Why does Trevor lead the gang to destroy the home of an innocent old man? Moving students beyond the knee-jerk explanation that "that's just what 'punks' do" entailed some focused journal writing.

I asked students to read a brief excerpt from sociologist Max Lerner's "Growing Up in America." After briefly explaining Lerner's distinction between the "cultural self," which is a product of the environment, and the "identity self," which evolves independently of cultural influences, I asked the class to brainstorm in a different direction, this time listing all the influences on their cultural selves. As they called out suggestions, I recorded them on the blackboard: home (parents, siblings, relatives), ethnic background (traditions, holiday celebrations, foods), friends, work (employer, other employees), religion, social status, school (teachers, classmates).

After our initial brainstorming session, I asked my students to write in their journals for five minutes on one item from their lists of influences. I prompted them, "To what extent has that influence made you who you are?" Five minutes later, I told them to switch, instead focusing on that part of themselves *not* a product of cultural influences. In a third prompt, I asked them to sink into the character Trevor: using

"I," they were to repeat the previous writings—in a journal that Trevor might write. I have learned since that this last journal entry is best done as homework because it takes a little more thought and requires textual evidence.

In the next class, my students and I discussed Trevor's personality and motivation. Is he, according to Lerner's definition, a balanced individual? That is, has he resolved the split between his two selves? Or is he motivated primarily by one or the other? Moreover, is Lerner's "identity" self even tenable? The arguments that ensued differed so strikingly from the initial perfunctory responses, especially the consensus about gangs of punks, that I anticipated far stronger essays than those that my students would have written without the focused journal writing. It paid off. They had now read more carefully, had developed *informed* opinions giving them something to say in their essays, and had discovered a link between themselves and fictional characters. Each student even had a potential thesis—a unique theory about the formation of cultural or identity selves.

Benefits and Applications

"The Destructors" illustrates behavior that puzzles students. Often, rather than working to understand the characters' motivation, students take the easy way out by criticizing what the characters do. The exercise detailed above gets the students inside the characters and helps them relate personally to the story's theme, despite differences in time, place, and situation. As a side effect, it forces students to read the text more carefully. I don't insist that each student write an essay about character motivation in Greene's story (though it's an option), but the exercise does model one way to approach character motivation with personal or expressive writing, a model that leads to analysis and "critical reflectiveness."

Sometimes, it would seem, we have to tear down before we can build anew.

Works Cited

Greene, Graham. "The Destructors." *Literature: Structure, Sound, and Sense.* Ed. Laurence Perrine. 3rd ed. New York: Harcourt, 1978. 50–61.

Knoblauch, Cy. "Critical Teaching and Dominant Culture." *Composition and Resistance.* Ed. C. Mark Hurlbert and Michael Blitz. Portsmouth, NH: Boynton/Cook, 1991. 12–20.

Lerner, Max. "Growing Up in America." *The Young Man in American Literature.* Ed. William Coyle. New York: Odyssey, 1969. 11–22.

Rosenblatt, Louise. *Literature as Exploration.* 4th ed. New York: MLA, 1976.

4 Zora Neale Hurston's "How It Feels to Be Colored Me": A Writing and Self-Discovery Process

Judy L. Isaksen
Eckerd College

The short story makes a modest appeal for attention, slips up on your blind side and wrassles you to the mat before you know what grabbed you.

Toni Cade Bambara, "What It Is I Think I'm Doing Anyhow"

t merely astonishes me. How *can* any deny themselves the pleasure of my company! It's beyond me" (155). These words, delivered by Zora Neale Hurston in her 1928 essay "How It Feels to Be Colored Me," might sound arrogant or pompous coming from someone else, but, from the forthright Hurston, these words are anything but bombastic; they are endearing. In fact, they are much more than endearing; they demand our immediate attention, for Hurston holds a special place in literary history. Just as both Herman Melville and Emily Dickinson toiled "long and difficult years in obscurity" only to be recognized later as among the "great interpreters of the age" (Glassman and Seidel ix), so too did and is Hurston, a congenial figure fast becoming canonized as an important literary interpreter and link to our past. And, so, we simply must engage in her company. In fact, Alice Walker, in her powerful Foreword to Robert Hemenway's definitive biography, *Zora Neale Hurston: A Literary Biography*, demands that we engage, calling it a "duty" (xviii).

Some may wonder how Hurston's personal essay might fit in a book that focuses on short stories. Despite the different genre, her essay fits beautifully because it reads like fiction; it is a belletristic essay. Hurston adapts techniques of fiction writing, including first-person narration, descriptive settings, and character development. In addition, she uses the approach of anthropological writing (yes, she was a successful anthropologist who traveled, researched, and published regularly). Most important, not only is her essay compelling to read and to teach but it also asks readers to make personal connections that can develop into profound observations about themselves, literature, and life. To me, that is what teaching is all about.

At Eckerd College—a small liberal arts school in St. Petersburg, Florida—I teach writing courses to students ranging from first-year to senior-level. I've used this particular Hurston essay for the narrative section of a Writing Processes course as well as the analytical section of an Analytic and Persuasive Writing course. Teaching this essay and the accompanying writing project is, I feel, transferable to all levels of high school and college students because a key point of analysis is the consciousness of "selves"—and students of all ages need (and generally love) to discover all of their "selves"/roles/voices.

In teaching Hurston's "How It Feels to Be Colored Me" (which appears in *The Norton Anthology of American Literature* and *The Norton Anthology of Literature by Women*), I have students read the essay at home, after which I read it aloud before we open the discussion. (It's short enough, and its wonderful literary quality warrants the use of precious class time—besides, I find that students love to be read to—perhaps it harks back to their childhood days!) I also request that students come to class prepared with one quotation from the text that moved them personally. This personal connection will be their point of departure in discovering the major thesis of the essay. We use these quotations to spark discussion. Often the majority of quotations deal in some way with Hurston's color. However, by the end of the discussion, most students agree that Hurston moves beyond black and white issues; for her, it's *colors,* not *color* that matter—all colors. Indeed, there are at least fourteen references to color throughout this short essay. I ask students to look closely at these passages and consider Hurston's intentions for using such a motif.

At this point, it is a good idea to break into small groups to let students ponder Hurston's essay more closely. I was rather impressed when one group felt that Hurston didn't perceive herself as a victim of race caught between the worlds of black and white; rather, they said that Hurston wore her many "selves" like a multicolored robe. Bringing the class discussion back together, we consider all the "selves" that her mosaic of colors symbolizes. And with Hurston, there are many "selves" to consider. In reading "How It Feels to Be Colored Me," we come to love her as, to name a few, a "Negro" (152), a good-will ambassador, "a little colored girl" (153), a descendant of slavery, a student, a jazz lover, a feminist, and "an American citizen" (155).

Underlying my teaching of Hurston's essay is the search for differences and commonalities. Although my students' various points of view may seem incongruent, I want students to consider the possibility, as Hurston does, that tension is healthy. Most students concede that Hurston feels relatively comfortable around whites; I argue and offer my opinion that if we, as society, embrace only differences without recognizing commonalities, the likely result will be a vast number of separate groups—an unhealthy and undesirable result. Conversely, if we embrace only commonalities without differences, the result will be one unified group, and anyone who may have a difference would be marginalized and silenced—a notion Hurston refused to accept. Therefore, we need both differences and commonalities, and this is precisely Hurston's message in her final paragraph: she claims that we are a "bag of miscellany" (155) who share a common humanity, and our individual bags are different colors that provide our need for individuality. That we all hold different things in our bags is perfectly acceptable. In the end, though, Hurston affirms the equal need for commonality: in that bag of miscellany, "A bit of colored glass more or less would not matter" (155), she says.

Right now, I can almost hear the collective sigh of relief from my students as they realize that there need not be a struggle between points of view. This notion also helps to make Hurston's essay relevant to today's multicultural world. Our discussion leads to some engaging journal writings, as students launch into profound self-discovery.

After we are finished discussing Hurston's essay (which usually takes two fifty-minute classes or one eighty-five minute class), it is time to turn to the "selves" of students. To do this, I ask students to brainstorm individually on paper all their selves, their roles, their voices. In this generative exercise, I encourage students not to write adjectives that simply describe themselves but to devise a list of nouns—to reach, in other words, for concrete, substantive descriptions. After about ten minutes I ask students to stop, but I let them know it's acceptable to add to their list at any time. At Eckerd, I have the luxury of small classes, so it's possible for each student to write his or her list on the board. While no list is typical, one may look like this: Friend, Student, Optimist, Writer, Lover, Athlete, Nature Lover, Scientist, Thinker, Volunteer, Catholic, Democrat, Italian, White, Heterosexual. It's a wonderful opportunity for all of us to get better acquainted, and I too go public with my list. After having read and discussed Hurston's essay, you'll be surprised how deeply students will look into their "selves."

Of course, we do not stop with our lists. In fact, they become the foundation for a writing assignment that I have dubbed "The Meeting of the Minds." First, students consider their lists and select four or five of their most prominent "selves" and freewrite about each. Then I ask them to write stories that illustrate these selected "selves"—stories that have been told at various times around the family dinner table or that illustrate an embarrassing moment that they'd rather forget. Sometimes, they tell of their most shining moments or their saddest memories. I also ask them to freewrite about the different appearances these "selves" might signify. For example, how might their "selves" look when going to a nightclub versus, say, going to a church service? What about their attitudes and moods? I ask them to write a passage or two that conveys their value system. I suggest they write dialogues—both engaging and conflicting—among the "selves." When conversation flows between these multiple "selves," unconscious revelations can emerge. Rather than providing these generative prompts verbally, I like to create a handout of specific prompts. While the handout may contain about thirty prompts, I encourage students to freewrite in response to only those prompts that ignite a spontaneous impulse and to move on if the prompt creates no immediate reaction. I believe creating this handout is essential for the success of this project: it gives students direction and impetus; plus it's a ton of fun to create.

By the end of our prewriting sessions, most students have about ten to fifteen pages of raw material. This freewriting can be done either in class or at home; however, I ask that students abide by one rule: write/type on only one side of the paper. I also tell students not to worry if their freewriting is disjointed and chaotic or contains large gaps between their ideas. I want them to experience the uninhibited feeling of writing while the editor side of their brain is on hold. After all, in this part of the assignment my objective is for students to appreciate the value of effective prewriting—to realize that, if their initial invention of raw materials is rich, then their final product stands a greater chance of being rich too. I also want them to take the time to discover and rediscover their "selves" and, like Hurston, think not only about where their "selves" come from but also how each "self" interacts with the world.

After completing their extensive freewriting, students begin the second part of the assignment. My objective in this phase is to give students a way to accomplish deep, substantive revision. Unfortunately, for most students, a little surface touching-up is their idea of revision—they do not realize what Hemingway meant when he said, "I write standing up and edit sitting down." I want students to realize that it's time to roll up their sleeves and get to the serious, hard, and humbling work ahead.

Facing my students, who by now have a stack of freewriting pages and rather confused looks on their faces, I explain to them Peter Elbow's legendary technique of cut-and-paste revision (see Chapter 14 of *Writing with Power*). In this method, pen becomes secondary to scissors and paste. Students today are quite comfortable with the cut-and-paste feature on their computers, and they are amused to learn that Elbow suggested this method using old-fashioned scissors and scotch tape back in 1981. Even though nearly all students write their "selves" passages on a computer, I ask them to print out their freewritings and do the cutting-and-pasting with scissors and tape, for the computer screen limits students from having a global view of their writings, and the tactile component of this project enhances engagement immensely.

In the initial revision process, I ask students to read through their hodgepodge of writing and to look for lively passages that are dense with details. I next instruct them to cut away, literally, all the dead writing, keeping only the energetic prose. Don't be surprised if students protest, for this readily exposes the large amount of dead wood in their words; consequently, they are liable to judge their freewriting efforts as a waste of time. (I find it best to do this assignment after students have already written several papers; this is for two reasons: one, its unorthodox methodology can possibly intimidate those students who need to work within rigid parameters, and, two, there is an act of faith on the student's part to follow these odd steps—it's simply not fair to expect the trust involved in the process early in the semester.) After students, in Elbow's words, "get rid of everything dead and keep everything alive" (149), I ask them to "play with different sequences" (147) of the passages, looking for a thread of meaning that conveys their "selves."

At this point, the project becomes rather space-consuming, for the students spread their blocks of writing like Legos on the floor and now must piece them together into a whole paper. This is also a great time to instill the value of this cut-and-paste revision technique on any paper that isn't pulling together well. (In fact, Jeanne, whose excerpt you'll read later, subsequently used this revision technique to good effect on a research paper about alternative healing that she wrote for another course. Her paper was disjointed, and she felt as though she had tinkered it to death, so she cut it apart and taped it back together, solving the problem.)

After students have put their raw materials in some order, I permit them to take pen in hand in order to tighten and clarify. Often this step involves adding transitional expressions and paragraphs, introductions, and conclusions. I give a brief lesson on the use of framing devices to connect the "selves" in the story and to link their ideas together. I define framing devices as a story scaffolding or a recurring image or prop that is used to tie the sections of their writing together. The frame provides an overall shape to the story and makes it a more sophisticated piece of work. Students enjoy designing framing devices, for it gives form to their ideas. Some of the frames that my students have used include different styles of shoes, a road trip, the octaves on a piano, and talking face-to-face with God on Judgment Day. Finally, students will take their choppy, rough drafts, along with their framing devices, and revise several more times in preparing to share.

For those students who feel comfortable about going public with their work, we spend a class in peer-editing sessions. In addition to the typical peer-editing questions, I include on the draft workshop handout questions that go something like this:

> Among all the "selves," does the thesis emerge? Please summarize it.
>
> Specifically address all the "selves" that seem alive, and specifically address any "self(ves)" that appear more cardboard than alive.
>
> What suggestions can you make to bring that "self(ves)" to life?

And for those students who choose for personal reasons not to work with their peers, I confer with them to assist their revision efforts.

I suggest allowing plenty of time for this writing project—about two weeks—for students need time not only to draft but to discover their "selves." And now I delight in sharing some student writings with you. I have chosen these examples because they demonstrate how each student uses rhetoric to deal with his or her own issues—some of which are joyous, some confounding, some distressing.

The first student writing comes from Jeanne, a returning student who chose to describe her "selves" as the pieces of a puzzle. In her story, Jeanne celebrates life, and gives life to her writing with a discernable rhythm:

> Through all the intricate curves and harmonies of this life, perhaps the most enduring was the Family Piece. The love I learned in that circle was precious. But still I was alone. Then, as unobtrusively as all the rest, a new voice came to be with mine. This

new one added a distinct and profound unity. It gave continuity. I married this one. And a little while later, I became the teacher and guide of another voice. A smaller, separate, precious voice, filled with sunshine in every belly-laugh! During these times, I thought my heart would burst with happiness. How much love can be measured in a child's prayer, or a lover's kiss?

   Thus it is that I have come to this place. I have reviewed The Pieces carefully. They are not all bright and shining, though I would like them to be that way. They are, in reality, a reflection of the life of a person who has been privileged to learn from the world. And to savor, with love, every moment in it. I shuffle these little Pieces around every day, hoping to separate the chaff, hoping to get it right this time. Always thinking that the Piece I hold now is the best one. Isn't it?

This project allowed Jeanne, who has always been a confident writer, to soar, but I have also seen this assignment bring out great writing in those who did not start out as strong. Colby, for instance, always had wonderful ideas, but he struggled with clumsy phrasing. In this paper, however, his writing flows beautifully. Colby chose to write about his imaginative self, his gullible self, his competitive self, his curious self, and his sensitive self. Here's what he has to say about his sensitive self:

> The sensitive one is often emotional and rarely exposes himself. His overwhelming love and respect for humanity creates a sappy, heart-wrenching picture. He runs from the others afraid to be made fun of or trampled on. The fear he carries with him creates a locked door only to be opened on rare specific occasions.

Needless to say, this is rich and engaging writing. Colby experienced, and I believe for the first time, the joy of writing—isn't that what it's all about?

   Another engaging work was titled "The Brothers at Riverside Park: Me." Rod, who puts his internal thoughts in italics, encounters many of his "selves" while sitting on a park bench, and each offers Rod words of wisdom or calls into question Rod's intentions:

> *While walking down the sidewalk at Riverside Park, I saw a group of strange men sitting comfortably on a park bench. All of those men were unique figures in their stature and voice, but when they spoke, they all sounded like old friends at a card game. . . .*
>
> *[A] younger man who seemed to have it all together broke into the discussion. His grammar was impeccable, dress well ordered, eyes clear and focus determined. In his hands were pencils, papers, ribbons, and diplomas. Directly behind him was a long road which had been rough; it was now paved except for a few miles.* "There are good days in your experience as well." "And more are coming." "You are in school and making progress." "Remember the little boy in your past who

was so bright and curious?" "He had a teacher (a wicked stepmother of sorts) who tried to destroy that in him." "Remember how it seemed he had lost all academic footing?" "He was tracked in the slow classes; he was not even concerned about it." "He thought that there was nothing he could contribute or gain from the discipline of learning."

With a mystical wisdom about him, he looked gently at me and said, "How great has been the suffering of your consciousness?" "You walked around feeling like you were made for more but never going to know the joy of more." *"How do you know me?"* "Let's just say we share something in common." "We are bonded brothers." "I am what you are becoming each school day you read a stimulating book or get lost in the teacher's proclamation of some rich ideas." "As a student, you are learning to engage all of your readings, and you are only as good a student as the last completed assignment which means putting those big shoulders to the grinding stone of academic work and toil." *I thought to myself, those were the truest words he could have used. . . . I thought I was near nirvana.*

Near the end of the bench, I saw a very, very dark man. He was much darker in appearance than I am. He was more angry than I thought I was. He had a sign in his hand that said, Read The Bell Curve War *Every Day. I mean this guy was so mad he could spit truth at racism from 400 paces.* "I hear you talking 'bout being a spiritual man, a leader, an intellectual man, but I want to know whether you're watchin' my back Brother?" "The war is on and the bullets are flyin'." "I want to know are you as mad as I am?" *"I don't know."* *"Should I be?"*

"Punk, have you forgotten that your mother was a maid, and the white folks called her nigger at their good pleasure around the dinner table?" "Have you forgotten that your grandmother refused to drink from drinking fountains here in the south long before it became fashionable not to do so, and she forbade any of her children to do so?"

"Have you forgotten your own awful encounter with racism?" "Remember how the white kids in Panama used to throw your raincoats and books out of the window of the bus?" "What about anti-affirmative action and rebuttals against fair-voting districts?" "When are you going to take a stand?" "I mean a real stand." *"Well, I know about all of that stuff." "I want to fight those things." "I do stand against those things." "My question is do I have to wear a t-shirt to prove it?" "Do I have to sound a certain way to be down with the brothers and sisters?" "And, do I limit my concerns to people who look like me?" "Can I fight for all underdogs and marginalized people— even white women or rural farmers if I get the chance?"*

The dark, beautiful brother said, "You do have a point." "I guess I get too implosive sometimes." "I get just a little bit too color-coded. . . ."

These are intense writings—writings that stem from pain, confusion, and joy. But perhaps the last word, and perspective, should spin around Hurston. Notably, Alice Walker applauds Hurston's sense of "racial health—a sense of black people as complete, complex, *undiminished* human beings, a sense that is lacking in so much black writing and literature" (Foreword xii–xiii). In fact, says Walker, like Hurston's contemporaries Langston Hughes and Richard Wright (who would say that Hurston was not political enough) "we are better off if we think of Zora Neale Hurston as an artist, period—rather than as the artist/politician most black writers have been required to be" (Hurston, *I Love Myself* 3). My students—like Jeanne and Colby and Rod—couldn't agree more. It is Hurston, after all, who has provided them the catalyst to explore their many "selves" and to place those "selves" in some context. I would say that each student has grown from reading and responding to "How It Feels to Be Colored Me."

Works Cited

Elbow, Peter. *Writing with Power: Techniques for Mastering the Writing Process.* New York: Oxford UP, 1981.

Glassman, Steve, and Kathryn Lee Seidel, eds. *Zora in Florida.* Orlando: U of Central Florida P, 1991.

Hurston, Zora Neale. *I Love Myself When I Am Laughing . . . And Then Again When I Am Looking Mean and Impressive—A Zora Neale Hurston Reader.* Ed. Alice Walker. New York: Feminist Press, 1979. [Includes "How It Feels to Be Colored Me," 152–55.]

Walker, Alice. Foreword. *Zora Neale Hurston: A Literary Biography.* Robert E. Hemenway. Urbana: U of Illinois P, 1977. xi–xviii.

II Seeing What Is Really There

I like the short story as a form. The intensity of it, the swiftness. Assemble the ambulances. Something is going to happen.

Joy Williams, "Shifting Things"

Once students have made personal connections to short stories, their curiosity may push them out, as it were, onto some very spindly branches. As teachers, our job is to lure them away from hazardous perches and to catch them if they fall. In this learning process, students come to understand the importance of careful reading and writing. Once alerted, students find that characters are often not what they seem and that the digressions of the plot contain clues to comprehending the story. Indeed, while short stories are just that—short—they imply worlds. How to get students to see this larger scope is the focus of this chapter.

In the classroom, the teachers of this chapter do not want to undermine their students' intuition; rather, their common goal is to scrutinize initial, I-know-what-I-like responses by exploring how language creates drama. Drama may involve any number of factors, but, in the main, it is what makes characters alive and memorable. The manner of rendering drama—the particular details, the tone, the diction, the characters' style of speaking and thinking—contribute as much or more to the effect of the story as the events themselves. Teachers focus on points in short stories where drama is particularly evident, asking their students to re-experience key moments and to ponder why they respond as they do. Too often, readers allow stories to sweep over them like a wave; they passively accept the role of audience to the mental movie the story creates in their minds. Stopping students in their tracks changes the reading experience and paves the way to insightful questions about narrative construction (the topic of Part Three).

In stopping students, teachers often put the writing process to use, sometimes beginning with journal assignments developed from classroom discussion. The critical moment here involves *intelligibility*, a quality that demands real honesty with ourselves. We all know the feeling of facing a paragraph of scrambled thoughts and words. Editing, we believe, will clarify and shape. Sometimes, though, editing only exposes that we do not, after all, know what we want to say—perhaps that we have nothing to say at all. At the heart of the onion—shockingly enough—may be nothing! The process of reaching intelligibility is difficult, even painful, but the moment when we know that we do not know is an important step in learning. Because the short story is compressed, it serves as, again, the perfect occasion for teaching this lesson.

The teachers in this section use the students' initial responses and interpretations as stepping stones to greater comprehension. Sometimes they purposely disrupt the reading process to make their point. For instance, Charles May uses a specially formatted computer text file of a short story to interrupt students in their reading and ask them to consider such elements as figurative language. In doing so, May asks students to glance backstage during the unfolding of the plot and thus to observe the construction of a short story. The lesson has wide-ranging implications, for through these interruptions students are prevented from experiencing the story as an entertainment and are forced to think about it as a constructed work of art. It is not always easy to see the artistry in a story that does not entertain. Janet Gebhart Auten examines a short story that appears to have no plot or purpose, Sarah Orne Jewett's "The White Heron." Auten uses Jewett's quiet story to teach students to look again when it seems as though "nothing much happens." Kelly Chandler, on the other hand, starts with a story with a seemingly obvious plot and purpose, Alice Walker's "How Did I Get Away with Killing One of the Biggest Lawyers in the State? It Was Easy." Students often confuse the narrator with the author, and Chandler's method of correcting this assumption leads her students into the moral world of the story. We must also stay alert to what the story refuses to say; Carole Hamilton discusses one simple way to probe the unspoken in Gina Berriault's "The Stone Boy," to discover how authors manipulate narrative gaps and how readers, in their turn, fill them. Allowing students the chance to posit their own meanings before being swayed by a teacher's lead is an important heuristic exercise. Thus, James Tackach's approach to Melville's "Bartleby the Scrivener" cautions students to examine the narrator's motivations in order to ascertain his reliability.

5 Forcing Readers to Read Carefully: William Carlos Williams's "The Use of Force"

Charles E. May
California State University, Long Beach

The novelist may juggle about with chronology and throw narrative over-board; all the time his characters have the reader by the hand, there is a consistency of relationship throughout the experience that cannot and does not convey the quality of human life, where contact is more like the flash of fireflies, in and out, now here, now there, in darkness. Short-story writers see by the light of the flash; theirs is the art of the only thing one can be sure of—the present moment.

Nadine Gordimer, "The Flash of Fireflies"

The most significant contribution Edgar Allan Poe made to the development of the short story as a new genre in American literature was his creation of an alternative definition of "plot" in narrative fiction. Instead of "simple complexity" or "involution of incident," Poe returned to Aristotle to suggest a new meaning of the term: "that which no part can be displaced without ruin to the whole" (*"Night and Day"* 116). By this one stroke, he shifted the reader's focus on narrative from mimetic events to aesthetic pattern. Poe argued that, without the "key" of the overall design or plan of a work of fiction, many points would "become null" through the impossibility of the reader's comprehending them. However, once having the overall design in mind, the reader will find that all those points that might otherwise have been "insipid" or "null" will "break out in all directions like stars, and throw quadruple brilliance over the narrative" (121). This suggestion—that to understand a narrative readers must begin with the end in mind—has since been made by a number of critics who have argued that a knowledge of narrative's whole is essential to an understanding of any of its parts.

The reader's inability to grasp narrative meaningfully merely by following the progression of its events through time has also been suggested by C. S. Lewis, who says that, for stories to be stories, they must be a series of events; yet at the same time it must be understood that this series is only a net to catch something else. And this "something else," which, for want of a better word, we call theme, is something "that has no sequence in it, something other than a process and much more like a state or quality" (91). The notion of narrative as a net is in turn related to recent studies of the computer application "hypertext," for hypertext simulates the reader's mental reorganization of temporal events into spatial patterns. George Landow, the best known spokesman for the relationship between hypertext and contemporary literary theory, has pointed out the similarity between such theoretical assumptions of Foucault, Barthes, and Derrida that the text is a "network," a pattern of "lexias," or an "assemblage," and the suggestions by such hypertext pioneers as Vannar Bush, Douglas Engelbart, and Ted Nelson that technology can mimic the associational paths the mind uses to store and manipulate information and can objectify mental concepts so they can be visualized and manipulated. Robert Coover has suggested that with hypertext we are at last free of what E. M. Forster never imagined we could be free of—the "tyranny of the line." On the computer, Coover says, the line does not exist, "unless one invents it and implants it in the text" (24). What hypertext does is to make us aware "of the shapes of narratives that are often hidden in print stories"—which is of course what Poe wanted readers to be aware of 150 years ago when he insisted that by "plot" he indeed meant "pattern."

A hypertext application that I created to help my students grasp this central feature of short fiction uses several unique features of the computer to exploit the generic characteristics of the short story and to compel students to "slow down" their reading and therefore construct spatial nets out of the seeming temporal flow of the story. The way the application does this is to force students to pause at potential nodal points that thematically connect to other points of the story. Students are asked to consider questions about the structure, the conventions, the motivation, and the theme of the story at these points. Periodically, after students have paused and responded to these points, they are asked to pull these suggestions together and formulate some ideas about their relationship.

Of course this would all be clearer with a demonstration. But because that is not possible on the page, perhaps an example will help. William Carlos Williams's often-anthologized story "The Use of Force"

[handwritten marginal notes: "a net to catch a timeless reality / themes" and "Theme = a net to catch everything in a ss"]

nicely illustrates the problem of getting students to make the leap from perceiving the story as a series of events in time to understanding it as a net to catch some timeless human reality. If you ask students what the story is "about," they will tell you it is "about" a frightened and stubborn child trying to prevent a cruel and determined doctor from finding out that she has diphtheria. If you push them further to tell you what it "means," what is its "theme," they will talk about how children are often afraid of doctors and how doctors are duty bound to protect people from sickness no matter how afraid they are. Although the teacher could cut through this immediately by pointing out that the doctor uses his scientific duty as an excuse to exert brutal power and that the child feels she must keep some part of herself secret and inviolate, students will not truly grasp how the story structures this basic human conflict unless they discover it themselves.

As students read through stories that are formatted with hypertext, they use a mouse to click on small lightbulb icons in the margins at various points. When they click, a small window pops up on the screen and asks them to consider the implications of some aspect of the narrative at that point. For example, a window may pop up and ask them to consider the significance of such language the doctor uses as *eating me up, catlike movement,* and *savage brat*. A bit later in the story, a pop-up window asks them to consider why the child says, "you're killing me." At another point, the students are asked to describe how they react to the doctor's saying he could have "torn the child apart and enjoyed it." Another asks them to consider what the doctor means by the "longing for muscular release."

At each one of these pop-ups, students click on a button labeled "Notes" at the bottom of the screen, which links them immediately to a notepad where they can respond to the lightbulb questions by brainstorming and freewriting. Although the readers' responses to the lightbulb prompts may be free-form, at certain points in the story, after having responded to several such prompts, students click on an icon of a hand writing on a piece of paper, which takes them to another screen where a writing prompt asks them to pull together some of the brainstorming ideas and write one or two developed and organized paragraphs based on their brainstorming. For example, one writing prompt asks students to discuss how the doctor's motivation changes as the story progresses. Another asks them to consider the battle between the child and the doctor as a battle between basic human impulses and to discuss the most general level of the doctor's motivation to attack the child and the child's desire to keep her secret hidden.

Because they have been brainstorming these ideas on the Notes page throughout the story, they find it easy to synthesize the various brainstorming strands and develop hypotheses about the story's basic pattern and thematic significance.

In the four years I have been using a hypertext application in my short story class, over four hundred students have used it. I have been astonished at how much more carefully students read stories using the application and how much more thoughtful writing it generates than more conventional oral and written methods I have used previously. Each time I have used it I have administered a feedback response form at the end of the class, assuring students that their responses would have no effect on their grade and that I would not read them until grades had been turned in. What I wanted to discover was *why* students were more apt to respond in such depth and detail using hypertext—what was it about this format that encouraged such response? The following theses about the reasons for hypertext's effectiveness are based on my observation of student work, my reading of their computer notebooks and writing prompts, and their feedback responses.

1. Research indicates that reading text on a computer screen is less "efficient" than reading text in a book, that is, one cannot read as fast. As a result, reading text on a computer screen, by its very medium, slows readers down, not allowing them to skim hurriedly to the end of the story. Although reader slow-down may be undesirable when one is reading solely for content, to read narrative analytically one cannot read hurriedly.

2. Students with little experience in the analysis of texts associate reading with an informal, nonanalytical pastime. One student said, "I would have preferred reading these stories curled up in my bed with tea and a book," but grudgingly admitted, "the computer application made me think more carefully."

3. Research indicates that students who read text at a computer put themselves in a more serious analytical state of mind than when they read from a book. As William Costanzo says, whereas reading for pleasure is based on a "mechanical simplicity, the pleasure of being swept along in a stream of words with nothing more demanding than the turning of a page to interrupt the flow. . . . [c]omputer-aided reading makes people read more systematically. They become more conscious of the choices that they make as readers, since the computer makes those choices more explicit. As a processor, the computer draws attention to the

complex process of reading" (60). Reading narrative on a computer with hypertext, in which students are made to slow down, to stop, to think about what they are reading, forces them into an analytical mode. It makes reading a different kind of experience, one in which they get caught up in the analysis of ideas and techniques and seem quite willing to follow this up.

4. Students are apt to feel more "captive" to text on the computer screen and less apt to drift off to other matters than they are when reading a book. One student wrote, "Being on the computer made me focus more on the story. Once I started, I felt compelled to finish it. Questions in a book would have allowed me to procrastinate more easily." Another noted, "Responding to the questions on a sheet of paper just makes you want to answer the questions and get it over with. Hypertext prompts don't. I don't know why."

    The fact that students don't try just to "get it over with" using hypertext the way they do when responding to heuristic prompts in the book on paper is a curious phenomenon. Part of the reason may be the fact that Socratic questions embedded within the actual story rather than tagged on at the end help students to focus on key points in the story *at* those points. Some students did indeed suggest this reason. One noted, "The computer makes you read more carefully because it asks questions every couple of paragraphs, whereas questions at the end of the story allow the reader to summarize." Another suggested, "The computer makes it easier for some reason, maybe because you're typing and reading as you go along."

5. Students are apt to read stories hurriedly and casually if they think that they can come to class and get "answers" from the teacher. As one student put it, "Without the application, I would have relied on the teacher to spoonfeed us what the stories were about. The computer forced me to come up with my own ideas." Another said, "Without the computer version of the stories, I would have left all the explaining up to the teacher, but I liked figuring them out and knowing I could do it."

6. Students who do not know where to pause and reflect on stories are thus motivated to move quickly on to the end. One student said, "Rather than read the story like a newspaper article, the computer forced me to slow down." Another suggested that "if you skim the stories there is no way you can answer the questions." Suzanne Hunter Brown has noted, "The inclination to 'get on with' the story . . . is a strong one; readers need all the added resources of attention that

brevity can supply if they are to emphasize non-sequential connections instead" (243).

7. Students need to be encouraged to pause as they are reading rather than to reflect back on the story after they finish it. Embedding questions within the story makes the students more aware of the conventions of short fiction. John W. Harker has discussed a kind of "metalinguistic awareness" demanded of the reader, a consciousness of the particular and specialized conventions of printed language, suggesting that this consciousness is necessary for the reader to decode the text at increasingly higher levels of understanding (470).

8. Students need to learn how to transform the temporal nature of the story into abstract meaning. As Gregory Colomb has pointed out, tests to determine the difference between inexperienced and expert readers indicate that the former are stuck in the realm of particular details while the latter are able to discern patterns. Tests of expert performance indicate that the experts were able to see an abstract general problem and to subordinate all other issues to this problem, could state a general solution that also solved many subordinate problems, and could see a long chain of implications in their solution. On the other hand, novices gravitated to particular rather than general statements, found correspondingly particular solutions, ignoring subordinate problems, and saw few or no implications in their solutions (425).

9. Although I am sure that this will fly in the face of cherished humanist beliefs that there is something sacred about a bound book, students are apt to feel a closer sense of interaction with the computer than with a book. As one student said, "Because I was involved with the computer I felt a closer relationship to the story. When asked to consider an idea, I was by the nature of the interactive relationship with my computer more involved." Another noted, "With the stories on computer you feel you are more a part of the story because you are working within it. Without the computer I don't believe I would have felt as involved in my work as I have." Another said, "The pop-ups and prompts occur at the exact place in the story that your mind is most involved with a particular idea or concept. I doubt I would have done half as much thinking about these stories without them."

10. Students need a means by which to brainstorm freely about a story that does not threaten them with negative responses. Although the questions embedded in hypertext may be very similar to those a teacher might Socratically pose in a discussion class, embedded as they are in

the text, the student has no fear of making the wrong response and receiving a negative reaction from the teacher or the rest of the class. Part of the reason for this increase in the willingness to brainstorm lies in the relative ease of doing the reading and the responding in one seamless activity. One student noted, "It was easier to work on the computer because you didn't have a lot of materials to sort through. Everything was right there on the screen. You can read much more carefully on the computer because you don't have to worry about going from book to paper." And another student said, "I must honestly admit that if not for the computer version I simply would have read the story once and not given it another thought, regardless of whether or not I understood it. I would never have learned the value of brainstorming a story without it."

11. Placing a story on computer in hypertext format creates the illusion that it is the story, not the teacher, that is asking the questions. I know this may sound absurd, for, if pushed, students would admit that they knew someone had to program the queries and pop-ups into the story, but somehow when they begin working they forget that. This is a common phenomenon; computer users often refer to the computer itself as if it had some innate intelligence, and indeed some computer-assisted instructional programs encourage this illusion. This effect in hypertext is that students do not think that a teacher is leading them along to a preconceived conclusion, but that the story itself is trying to help them understand. As one student noted, "Without the computerized versions of the stories I would not have developed my own analytical skills; I would have learned only how you saw the story. This way, without your guidance I came to my own conclusions."

12. Students enjoy being able to "master" a story on their own, and they enjoy the sense that they are engaged in difficult, even profound, hard-to-discuss ideas. A hypertext application gives them this sense of mastery, and, if the questions are sufficiently provocative, the pleasurable sense of thinking profound thoughts. As one student noted, "Working with hypertext stories on computer built my confidence in reading deeper into stories, which is an enjoyable experience." Another said, "My learning experience would have been different."

13. Stories in hypertext format exploit not only our familiarity with video screens for providing information, but also the irresistibility of interactive "hot spots" or buttons on a screen as in video games. Although students may ignore interlinear questions in the margins of a

book page or at the end of the story, they do not ignore icon-linked hot spots. One student said, "I was always curious about what lay behind the light bulb or writing prompt symbols."

14. Students are able to transfer their experience with the heuristic prompts embedded in the hypertext format to stories outside that format. A number of students said that after a few hypertext assignments they found themselves anticipating the questions that were asked, guessing what they were before they clicked on the lightbulbs to pop them up on the screen's virtual page. After using hypertext stories for a semester, students were able to isolate the significant issues, focus on the meaningful nodes, link motifs in the story to related motifs, and generalize about these issues without getting bogged down in simple plot summary or the mere citation of specific details.

Although I created hypertext versions of stories with Hypercard on the Macintosh computer, a number of other alternative authoring programs can be used. HyperStudio, for either Macintosh or Windows, is a favorite hypertext program for public school teachers and is available on most public school campuses. Toolbook for Windows is one of the most popular hypertext authoring programs for Windows. Programs that will allow you to convert Macintosh applications created with Hypercard into Toolbook Windows applications are also available. Teachers might also like to explore the possibility of creating hypertext applications on the World Wide Web. However, they should only use stories in the public domain to avoid copyright infringement problems.

Reading stories in hypertext format illustrates the essential truth of Poe's original intuition that short fiction depends more on spatial pattern than on temporal succession. It also indicates that teaching students how to read short fiction is a matter of engaging them in that spatial pattern in such a way that they can make their own discoveries about the story's meaning and way of meaning. Although simple in design, hypertext versions of stories indicate that practical pedagogical value may be derived from a blending of old-fashioned literary theory and newfangled technology. I like to think that Poe would have been pleased by it.

Works Cited

Brown, Suzanne Hunter. "Discourse Analysis and the Short Story." *Short Story Theory at a Crossroads.* Ed. Susan Lohafer and Jo Ellyn Clarey. Baton Rouge: Louisiana State UP, 1989. 217–48.

Colomb, Gregory. "Cultural Literacy and the Theory of Meaning: Or, What Educational Theorists Need to Know about How We Read." *New Literary History* 20 (Winter 1989): 411–50.

Coover, Robert. "Hyperfiction: Novels for the Computer." *New York Times Book Review* 29 Aug. 1993: 8–10.

Costanzo, William. *The Electronic Text: Learning to Write, Read, and Reason with Computers.* Englewood Cliffs, NJ: Educational Technology, 1989.

Gordimer, Nadine. "The Flash of Fireflies." *The New Short Story Theories.* Ed. Charles E. May. Athens: Ohio UP, 1994. 263–67.

Harker, John W. "Information Processing and the Reading of Literary Texts." *New Literary History* 20 (Winter 1989): 465–81.

Landow, George. *Hypertext: The Convergence of Contemporary Critical Theory and Technology.* Baltimore: Johns Hopkins UP, 1992.

Lewis, C. S. "On Stories." *Essays Presented to Charles Williams.* Ed. C. S. Lewis. Grand Rapids, MI: William B. Eerdmans, 1966. 90–105.

Poe, Edgar Allan. "Review of *Night and Day.*" *The Complete Works of Edgar Allan Poe: A Study of the Short Fiction*, vol. 8: 114–33. New York: Thomas Y. Crowell & Co., 1902.

Williams, William Carlos. "The Use of Force." *Fiction's Many Worlds.* Ed. Charles E. May. Lexington, MA: D. C. Heath, 1993. 242–44.

6 "Nothing Much Happens in This Story": Teaching Sarah Orne Jewett's "A White Heron"

Janet Gebhart Auten
American University, Washington, D.C.

For me stories usually begin . . . out of some magical association between characters and their settings. There are some stories (I won't say which ones) which evolved almost entirely out of their settings, usually rural.

Joyce Carol Oates, *Conversations with Joyce Carol Oates*

As our reading lists are increasingly enriched by the inclusion of diverse voices and a variety of styles in short fiction, traditionally trained students—and their teachers—may find themselves disconcerted by unfamiliar styles of storytelling. In particular, the stories of everyday domestic life told by nineteenth-century women regional writers such as Mary E. Wilkins Freeman ("A New-England Nun"), Kate Chopin ("The Story of an Hour"), and Sarah Orne Jewett sometimes seem pointless in their scant plots and dull in their painstaking attention to detail. Even a "classic" such as Jewett's "A White Heron" may evoke the kind of reaction typified by one of my students who complained, in a journal response, about the "bland setting" and the fact that "there is nothing more than the characters when it comes down to it. . . . Nothing much happens in this story." Such a response suggests that we may need to help students find ways to connect to the human interest and intimacy that made stories like "A White Heron" popular in the first place.

Jewett's widely anthologized story introduces many students to regional realism, a form of short fiction that is particularly important to American literary history. In the story, a young girl named Sylvia encounters an ornithologist from the city who has come to find—and take—a white heron. The "plot" of this kind of tale turns on everyday epiphanies, the kinds of little dramas that ordinary people have: meetings and partings of old friends, slights and kindnesses, remembrances and reconciliations. Such stories are identified with a tradition in fiction that, as Elizabeth Ammons puts it, "most twentieth-century literary criticism and history have been eager to dismiss as unimportant, . . . a separate and predominantly female tradition, which coexisted with but remained in important ways largely independent of the masculine gospel of Great Works" that privileged plot over gradual layerings of detail (xx).

Jewett herself recognized that, by favoring details and atmosphere over exciting plot twists, her stories represented empathic rather than eventful reading. She even acknowledged that to students of her own time her fiction might seem static. In a letter of May 1906, Jewett consoled a Newton, Massachusetts, teacher who had sent her some critiques from his high school English class:

> My heart goes out to the young friend who complains that "there are a great many words but nothing seems to be *going on*" in one of the stories . . . I cannot help thinking that my stories must be difficult for girls and boys like these—they are so often concerned with the type rather than the incident of human nature. (Cary 163)

The way that student response from the nineteenth century echoes in my twentieth-century student's journal reminds us just how long-standing has been the focus of knowing what is "going on" in the story. When I teach Jewett, I alter that prescription a bit.

When "Nothing Much Happens": What Is There to Notice?

Whether in high school or college, students usually come to assigned reading with a school-sponsored definition of what constitutes "great literature," most of the time preferring plot over characterization, conflict over context. In challenging these preferences, I try to alert students to alternate ways that writers may tell stories and readers might read them. A useful first step is a journal assignment. Concerning "A White Heron," however, a traditional request for response and reflection is liable to prompt students to complain. As one of my students wrote, the story "doesn't seem to have a definite plot. It just depicts a conflict of values." In her unwitting discovery of conflict in this seemingly "plotless" story, the student revealed how my unimaginative assignment evoked equally unimaginative judgment and thus closed off significant insight. Needless to say, in subsequent journal prompts, I have aimed to steer students toward the strength of Jewett's work and away from their usual quest to see what "seems to be going on."

As I have revised my approach, I now ask two questions for journal response. The first directs my students' attention to the way Jewett uses significant detail. However, I can't expect to redefine students' reading habits simply by putting them on a treasure hunt. A focus on "vivid details" alone can lead students into trouble when they strain for thematic significance and struggle to draw clean conclusions by taking the mere measure of a story's pictorial, picturesque qualities. One of my students, for example, literally missed the forest for the trees when he wrote, "she describes the country with such great precision. Jewett mainly focuses on trees though. This probably is so because of her fascination with birds."

Journal assignments can prompt students to reflect on what Jewett is *doing* with details and ask them to identify particularly vivid details in the story. In reading a regional story like Jewett's, students soon discover that many of the most vivid details surface in setting. In turn, these details spin a complex web of meaning that many students are not expecting. Prompted to explain the importance of setting, one student decided that Jewett

> describes the trees and birds in detail mainly because they are part of the main character's existence. However, the most vivid description is the scene where Sylvia climbs the big tree, searching for the White Heron. This scene is the focal point for me. I feel as though I were perched quietly in the tall pine viewing the world through Sylvia's eyes.

Here, the student identifies a climactic moment through her personal response to Jewett's descriptive details. By doing so, she discovered how Jewett uses setting and character to help the reader apprehend ideas.

Examining the details of setting can send students in other directions as well. For instance, another student discovered a dark tone in the story when he examined his own response to such details, specifically those when Sylvia first meets the ornithologist. The student noted how "the author describes the awkwardness of his gun in those natural settings . . . [,] representing all that is not nature, almost destruction." Thus, the student's writing led him to see that nature and life are associated with the story's rural setting and that destructiveness and death are associated with city life.

Making Connections

In teaching stories like Jewett's, we need to help students connect not only with setting but also with characters. In another story about her "pointed firs" country, "William's Wedding," Jewett explains that such personal connection cannot be made simply through the efforts of the writer, for "those few words which escape us in moments of deep feeling look but meagre on the printed page" (559). Instead, readers must find "moments of deep feeling" for themselves. Using Jewett's insight when teaching "A White Heron," I ask students, in my second question, to pick the most memorable "moment of feeling" in the story. After they have done so in their journal, I divide the class into small groups and ask them to share their responses. Each group is to come to a consensus about which "moment" in the story makes the deepest impression. Not surprisingly, this consensus-building leads us to discuss what issues Jewett brings to our attention in these moments of connection.

In one particularly memorable class session on "A White Heron," our four discussion groups produced four different "most memorable" passages. The first group chose a passage that describes how the coming of the little girl, Sylvia, to the country "was a good change for a little maid who had tried to grow for eight years in a crowded manufacturing town, but . . . it seemed as if she never had been alive at all before she came to live at the farm" (687–88). The second group felt an emotional connection with the young girl's response to the male stranger, especially at that moment when, asked by the stranger about the bird, "Sylvia's heart gave a wild beat; she knew that strange white bird, and had once stolen softly near where it stood . . ." (690). The other two groups chose passages about the young girl's feelings for nature. One picked a spot that explains how Sylvia "was not often in the woods so late as this, and it made her feel as if she were a part of the gray shadows and the moving leaves" (688). The other chose a moment that focuses on the girl's perceptions after her climb up the tall pine tree—indeed, that very moment at which the girl's dilemma and Jewett's descriptive powers intersect in a "sea of green branches, . . . this wonderful sight and pageant of the world" (693).

Many students argue that the story, by depicting a conflict of interests, revolves around Sylvia's "heart." When they add how their own loyalties have been similarly strained and called into question, the story becomes even more meaningful. Some see "A White Heron" as not so much a story at all, but as an emotion-grabbing word painting. That term leads us to discuss the way we read plot elements of conflict and climax; the result is a deeper sense that character can be action. One student realized, "Jewett made a decision that exploring the detail and human nature is just as important as telling what activity characters are doing." That activity, said another student, engages us, too, for "we think along with [Sylvia] as she works through her moral dilemma."

Canons in the Classroom: Widening the Scope

A final consideration in teaching "A White Heron" is the way we define "great literature." To do that, I ask students to write about the labels that have applied to Jewett and other regional writers and to speculate on the way a term such as "local colorist" can both explain and limit literature. What qualities does it highlight or include? What qualities does it overlook or exclude? Students are quick to point out, as one wrote, Jewett's "knack for picking up the particular speech patterns of the country folks in New England." We talk about the positive and negative connotations of the adjective *local,* and the way it relates to *locale.* In discussing the word *color,* students usually affirm Jewett's ability, as one wrote in her essay, to "paint a picture in the reader's mind." Most students, I am glad to report, see the limitations of labels. One student commented, "I think Jewett got the label of local colorist because she simply described the everyday things that she saw take place in the small towns around her and she rewrote them even in the same dialect. [But] the purpose of this label is almost to downplay her effect as a writer."

This last phase of teaching "A White Heron" can lead to a wider discussion of the way regional fiction evolved from the travel "sketch" in American writing, a means of expressing a personal view of picturesque places. The literary sketch had roots in artists' drawings (a point that relates well to Jewett's ability to "paint pictures") and played an important role in the writing of such famous male literary figures as Washington Irving and Nathaniel Hawthorne (which brings up comparison and discussion of "alternative" literary modes). Moreover, this information may help students see the place of Jewett in the larger sweep of American literature. Just as important, it can open students' minds to the possibility that, even when "nothing happens" in a story, there is assuredly something going on that may, after all, be vivid and memorable.

Works Cited

Ammons, Elizabeth. Introduction. *"How Celia Changed Her Mind" and Selected Stories.* Rose Terry Cooke. New Brunswick, NJ: Rutgers UP, 1986. ix–xxxv.

Cary, Richard, ed. *Sarah Orne Jewett Letters*. Waterville, ME: Colby College P, 1967.

Jewett, Sarah Orne. "A White Heron." *The Story and Its Writer*. Ed. Ann Charters. 3rd ed. Boston: Bedford-St. Martins, 1991. 687–94.

———. "William's Wedding." *Sarah Orne Jewett: Novels and Stories*. New York: The Library of America, 1994. 556–66.

Further Reading

Renza, Louis A. *"A White Heron" and the Question of Minor Literature*. Madison: U of Wisconsin P, 1984.

Sherman, Sarah Way. *Sarah Orne Jewett, An American Persephone*. Hanover: U of New Hampshire by UP of New England, 1989.

Smith, Gayle L. "The Language of Transcendence in Sarah Orne Jewett's 'A White Heron.'" *Colby Library Quarterly* 19 (1983): 37–44. Rpt. In *Critical Essays on Sarah Orne Jewett*. Ed. Gwen L. Nagel. Boston: G. K. Hall, 1984. 69–76.

7 How Did I Break My Students of One of Their Biggest Bad Habits as Readers? It Was Easy: Using Alice Walker's "How Did I Get Away . . ."

Kelly Chandler
Syracuse University

When I write "I" in a story or a novel I do not mean I-myself. Some people have been disappointed that I am not any one or all of my characters.

Elizabeth Jolley, "Dipt Me in Ink"

It was one of those photocopied handouts that seemed to appear spontaneously in my file cabinet. I knew neither where it came from (my student-teaching mentor? my colleague Jon?) nor how I could find another copy quickly if I accidentally gave out the original to a student. I just had it—never mind how—and I'm glad I did. Even though it was less than four pages long, Alice Walker's short story "How Did I Get Away with Killing One of the Biggest Lawyers in the State? It Was Easy" packed quite a punch in English 10. Not only did it spark the most lively discussion of the year in my least talkative section, but it allowed me to chip away at one of my students' most ingrained misconceptions about literature: their identification of a first-person narrator as the author.

I originally included the story as part of a unit on justice that featured a half dozen short pieces—most of them nonfiction—about the law and whom it protects. I expected "How Did I Get Away" to raise issues about how race, gender, and class can affect the quality of justice individuals receive. The narrator, an unnamed African American female, relates the story of her affair with Bubba, a prominent lawyer and the son of a segregationist politician. After being raped by Bubba, the fourteen-year-old girl begins a relationship with him, exchanging sexual attention for money, clean clothing, and the promise of a college education. When her mother, a domestic who works in white people's homes, opposes the liaison, the girl, with Bubba's help, has her committed to a mental institution. The narrator's mother dies near the story's end, and something seems to snap inside the girl, who ends up killing Bubba in his law office, the scene of the rape. She is never charged with the crime.

I chose to read Walker's story aloud to my reticent sophomores, in part because this was my habit for many of the short pieces we dealt with and in part because the narrative seems to require it. The entire text is enclosed within quotation marks, as if to suggest that the narrator is talking to an unidentified listener. None of my students, a heterogeneous group by the way, initially noticed this unusual textual feature, although they all had copies in front of them as I read. Their oversight should have been a clue to me of what would follow, but I was too busy planning the discussion to notice.

After finishing my reading, I posed one of my prepared questions: "Was killing Bubba justified?" A number of students responded immediately and vehemently:

"He deserved it. He shouldn't have raped Alice."

"Well, I don't usually think taking the law into your own hands is a good thing, but nobody else was going to help Alice."

"Alice lost her mind when her mother died. She didn't know what she was doing."

As the students spoke, a fascinating pattern began to emerge in their comments, and it wasn't in their overwhelming sympathy for the narrator, although that was evident. Rather, it was the way that almost all of them had automatically identified the anonymous girl as "Alice."

In retrospect, I should not have been so surprised. I had repeatedly warned the students to be wary about assuming a one-to-one correspondence between narrators and authors; they almost always jumped to that conclusion when reading a first-person narrative text. For most of my students, especially those who hated writing fiction, the idea of a created narrator was counterintuitive. Only when we read Edgar Allan Poe's "The Tell-Tale Heart" did they separate the narrator's persona from that of the author. However, when the texts were less bizarre in nature or set in more contemporary times, most of the students collapsed the two categories. My best hypothesis is that years of biographical book reports had taught them to do this.

In the case of "How Did I Get Away," my students' merging of narrator with author severely limited their range of responses. Because they had identified Walker as the main character, they talked about character choices, not authorial options. It did not occur to them that the piece might have been written in another way, nor did they critique it in any other literary measure. Instead, they talked about Bubba and Mama and "Alice" as if they were guests on a daytime talk show.

While the students' investment in the story's plot and characters pleased me very much—especially because this particular group hadn't been invested in much that we'd read together—I was concerned by their inability to see the text as a deliberate construction by an author. When I reflected a bit, though, I had to admit that I'd partially set them up for this kind of response by asking questions that required them to pass judgment on the morality and ethics of the characters' actions without pushing them to examine the authorial stance as well. Indeed, as I listened to the students talk more about the story, I realized that the most interesting aspect of their discussion had nothing to do with justice and everything to do with narrative construction.

So, I threw out my list of probing questions about the legal system and its lack of protection for African Americans and followed the compass of my students' comments. Just after Ryan declared that he didn't think Alice should have put her mother in that institution, I broke in and asked a single spontaneous question: "How do you know her name is Alice?"

"Huh?" said the bewildered Ryan.

"How do you know her name is Alice?" I repeated. "Where does it say that in the story?" All around the room, kids started ruffling through the pages of their handouts, searching for the clue that would either save Ryan from scrutiny or condemn him to public humiliation. Students who hadn't glanced once at the text while I read aloud were now poring over paragraphs looking for vindication.

Meanwhile, with a hunted look on his face, Ryan was sweating it out, hoping that someone else would find the answer before I asked him another potentially embarrassing question. "Now, wait a minute," I said, when no one could find a direct mention of the narrator's name. "Ryan's not the only one who's been calling this girl 'Alice.' Why did the rest of you do that?"

At first they were defensive. Well, of course, it was the author. Who else could it be? When I insisted that they back up their assertion with some concrete evidence, they took up the challenge and began to treat the text—and the narrator's identity—as a puzzle to be solved.

Someone pointed out the poster of Walker that hung prominently in my classroom and noted that she was indeed a black woman. This established, they moved on to the birthdate—1944—that followed Walker's byline (something most of them had overlooked). Using the clues about Bubba's father blocking the schoolhouse door in defense of segregation, they estimated that the piece was set in the late 1950s or early 1960s—sometime after the Brown v. the Topeka Board of Education case, an event many of them had seen dramatized in a television movie.

"If it was 1958, Walker would have been fourteen, just like the girl in the story. That," announced Jason with some quick math, "could work."

"Wait a minute," countered Matt skeptically. "You think she'd be writing about this, if she really did it? Why would she confess it?"

"Well, maybe the statute of limitations ran out, and they couldn't prosecute," Jason shot back.

At this point, I was too excited about their close reading to lament that my students seemed to know more about the intricacies of the justice system than they did about either genre or point of view. Who cares? They were working hard to solve a text-generated problem, and they were actively reasoning using logic—something they often seemed to leave outside the door of my classroom, just as a family leaves its shoes in the mudroom. I couldn't have been happier.

After a few minutes, though, the talk died down. They realized that they couldn't prove the narrator's identity from the few clues scattered through the story. I waited and counted to ten a couple of times. Then Becky, who could usually be counted on to raise some provocative point or another, said, "Well, OK, we don't know that it was Alice, but it could have been. That sort of things happened to a lot of black girls in those days. It could have been true." Starting from Becky's insight, we were able to move into a deeper discussion of the events of the story and their grounding in historical context. We talked about many of the issues I had wanted to discuss in the first place:

> How does social class affect the way justice is meted out?
>
> What happens when morality and legality conflict?
>
> Have things changed for African Americans where the justice system is concerned?
>
> What part does gender play in the issue?

Only when my students let go their insistence on verisimilitude were they able to engage with these ideas as bigger theoretical questions suggested by, but not limited to, the story. Moreover, the theoretical questions came from them, not from the list I had scrawled on a yellow legal pad during my prep period.

Finally, Becky, still probing, asked the sixty-four million-dollar question: "Well, if it wasn't true, then why did she want us to think it was?" To address that question, we had to discuss the effect and limitations of a first-person narrative. One student said that she became immediately angry about the abuse in the story because she was convinced that it had happened to someone real. The first-person device had caused her to identify strongly with the main character. Another one suggested that we might not be able to trust everything that the girl said because we were only hearing her point of view (I filed this comment to use in a future discussion of unreliable narrators). And, finally returning to those unresolved quotation marks, Suzanne said that they made her wonder to whom and for what reason the narrator was revealing her crime: "It's kind of mysterious, you know." The interpretations and speculations were fresh and intriguing.

In the end, almost everyone was involved in the debate, even the class naysayer (the boy who, no matter what the text or the topic, always said, "You people need to get a life. You read too much into this junk. Maybe she just wrote it that way and didn't mean anything by it at all."). Because of the way the story generated critical inquiry and emotional investment, this eighty-minute period made me remember why teaching is so much fun. The vivid title, the sensational subject matter, and the lively discussion combined to make "How Did I Get Away" a touchstone for the students when they were tempted to fall back into their old habit of confusing the author with the narrator. More than once after that class, I heard students caution each other about assuming too much too quickly: "Remember that piece about the girl who killed that guy? This is a story. You don't know that's the author talking." And, more than this practical matter, the group began to understand the distinction that Tim O'Brien draws when he says that "story-truth is sometimes truer than happening-truth" (203). "How Did I Get Away" had touched my students in a profound way as readers and as people. They were beginning to learn that just because fiction isn't factually true doesn't mean that its effect is any less real.

Works Cited

O'Brien, Tim. *The Things They Carried*. New York: Penguin, 1990.

Walker, Alice. "How Did I Get Away with Killing One of the Biggest Lawyers in the State? It Was Easy." *You Can't Keep a Good Woman Down.* New York: Harcourt Brace, 1981. 21–26.

8 Reading between the Lines of Gina Berriault's "The Stone Boy"

Carole L. Hamilton
Cary Academy, North Carolina

The significance and complexity of motivation *may cover a vast range of intensity. If my leg itches, I am moved to scratch it. If Othello becomes suspicious of his wife, he is moved to resolve his suspicions and know the truth. But however important or unimportant the motive, we can hardly think of the action of a plot without acknowledging that it proceeds* through *the passionate decision of characters.*

R. V. Cassill, *Writing Fiction*

Recently, Amazon.com sponsored a contest in which cyber-respondents supplied the words for *Doonesbury* cartoon scenes. Teachers have long known that this kind of lesson—supplying missing pieces of information to that already known—exercises the imagination. By giving voice to what is not said, readers develop a lexicon for discussing the story. Gina Berriault's "The Stone Boy" is a short story that offers tremendous potential for practice in supplying missing ideas and information, for its moments of silence, deliberate gaps in expository information, and fragmented characterization force readers to create meaning where none is explicitly given. For eighth graders or college students, the analytical process of noticing how what is said may imply what is not said is an important exercise in critical inference. Moreover, when students become aware of the intellectual machinery behind these processes, the range of their interpretation is likely to grow as well.

In Berriault's story, the main character, Arnold, is interrogated by the sheriff after accidentally shooting his brother Eugie. Arnold cannot break out of his silence to explain his uncanny behavior after the accident, and the result is typical of Berriault's use of narrative gaps:

> "All right, that's what happened," said the sheriff. "But what I want to know is this. Why didn't you go back to the house and tell your father right away? Why did you go and pick peas for an hour?"

> Arnold gazed over his shoulder at his father, expecting his father to have an answer for this also. But his father's eyes, larger and lighter blue than usual, were fixed upon him curiously. Arnold picked at a callus in his right palm. It seemed odd now that he had not run back to the house and wakened his father, but he could not remember why he had not. They were all waiting for him to answer.
>   "I come down to pick peas," he said.
>   "Didn't you think," asked the sheriff, stepping carefully from word to word, "that it was more important for you to go tell your parents what had happened?"
>   "The sun was gonna come up," Arnold said.
>   "What's that got to do with it?"
>   "It's better to pick peas while they're cool." (348)

There are several levels of silence in this passage. One is Arnold's silence about why he did not or could not tell his father that he accidentally shot his older brother, whom he loved and admired. Another level is the silence of the father, who sits mutely after answering most of the sheriff's initial questions about the accident. The sheriff, too, is silent about his real reason for probing the young boy for an answer to his question. Because the narrator comments only on the observable behavior of the characters, there is also a narrative silence.

At issue in the dynamics of Arnold's taciturn family is what, exactly, makes Arnold so reluctant to reveal his fears and to own up to his reaction to the unexpected event. He alone knows that the gun fired accidentally. Why does he not explain how sorry he is to have made this innocent but devastating mistake and thus to begin mourning the loss of his only brother, his parents' oldest son? What makes this admission so difficult, especially when the others are interpreting his silence as a sign of his evil nature? In approaching these questions, we know all too well what Wolfgang Iser means when he says, "What *is* said only appears to take on significance as a reference to what is not said; it is the implications and not the statements that give shape and weight to the meaning [of the story]" (168).

As Berriault's story progresses, Arnold's family and neighbors find a meaning in Arnold's silence that differs from the reader's interpretation. When they use silence as a weapon against Arnold ("it was then he had felt his father and the others set their cold, turbulent silence against him"), the reader wants to shout the truth. At the wake, no one acknowledges Arnold. At meals he is virtually ignored, and the silence is filled with meaning. In my middle-school classroom, I want students to notice these moments, and to recognize how they, as readers, fill the silences with their own interpretations. To this end, after having assigned the story the night before, I begin by having the students write out one or two questions they have about the story, and we share them. Usually, their questions are variations on the central question in the minds of the sheriff and Arnold's parents, "Why doesn't Arnold tell anyone what happened?"

We are not ready, yet, to pose answers to this pertinent question. I tell them that first we need to understand the other gaps and silences in the story. I ask them to break into groups, and I give each group a blank "bubble thought" sheet to fill in, so that we can conduct a modified version of Rebecca Sanchez's "bubble reading" exercise (described in the December 1995 *NCTE NOTES Plus*). On the sheet, I have sketched three cartoon faces (representing Arnold, the sheriff, and his father, for example), and next to each face I have drawn a large "thought bubble" with lots of blank lines inside. Then, I ask the students to find a passage where silence is an issue and to brainstorm some thoughts that might be unspoken. These will go into the thought bubbles. I have them identify the faces with names and write in a sentence of spoken words from the text to serve as a place marker. To explore the possibilities fully, I ask the groups to work silently at first, each group member writing down his or her own ideas before sharing them. Then the group recorder writes into the bubble for each character as many different thoughts as the students can imagine. Once done, they discuss their ideas and try to arrive at some consensus while still keeping a variety of different thoughts in the bubbles.

After the groups merge back into the class, we talk about the significance of the different silences and the implied interior dialogues they have written. At this point the class may go in a number of directions. One class got interested in the "dysfunctional" aspects of Arnold's family, and we postulated reasons why the family climate discouraged open discussions. We looked at the interactions between Arnold and his father, and those between him and his mother. Some students had chosen the line in which his mother says to Arnold, "Is night when you get afraid?" to explore using bubble thoughts. For Arnold they assigned such thoughts as "Yes, mother, I am afraid. Of you and father," and, "Please don't be angry at me, I need you!" For his mother, they inferred thoughts the text only touched upon: "Son, just say you are sorry, and I will comfort you." I list their inferred thoughts on the board, and circle the key words in each phrase: *angry, sorry, comfort, need.*

Berriault is an author for whom gestures are highly evocative—her stories are like screenplays in the way she describes the characters' movements. The film version of the story, which stars Robert Duvall as the father and Glenn Close as the mother, follows the story very closely. Before we view it in class, however, we add to our growing lexicon descriptions of gestures and facial expressions, words like *halting, fearful, tentative, exploring, reaching out, yearning.*

In another class, we looked more closely at the narrator's voice. Someone pointed out that the narrator isn't exactly silent. The narrator offers reasons why Arnold does not join the family for dinner, including that they might not want to see him and that he doesn't want them to "go to the trouble of calling him." Yes, the narrator has supplied "reasons," but they are incomplete reasons. Once again, inferences are needed to flesh out Arnold's inner thoughts. Our lexicon in this case included such words as *shame, pain, exposure, burden, witness,* and *withhold.* We discovered that Arnold's reasons were complex and deep, not simply practical concerns about "troubling" the family. Clearly, the narrator oversimplifies the meaning of Arnold's silences, thus committing the same crime as Arnold's family—zeroing in on just one narrow aspect of the situation, ignoring deeper feelings. The reader, having fallen into the same trap, recognizes his or her own tendency to collapse complex relations into simplistic outlines. We have discovered one of the story's themes.

No matter where the discussion leads us, I stop before it loses its momentum. We have a board full of inferred inner thoughts and key words describing expressions and gestures—a lexicon for discussing the story's gaps. I ask them to choose six of these words, and especially to include those that seem to "fight" with each other, such as *withhold* and *burden, yearning* and *angry.* Now I ask them to write an answer to their original question—*Why* does Arnold act as he does?—using these six words in their answer. They are to use their six words and at least one scene from the story as evidence to support their claims. Their list of words provides a lexicon for describing and building their theories. In this way, they are poised to move from perceiving implications of a text's language to arriving at inferences about theme. Happily, the essays I have received after this exercise are remarkably thoughtful and eloquent. The inference and lexicon-building exercise helps my students to avoid the plight of "The Stone Boy," who had something important to say but no words to say it.

Works Cited

Berriault, Gina. "The Stone Boy." *Points of View: An Anthology of Short Stories.* Ed. James Moffett and Kenneth R. McElheny. New York: Penguin, 1966. 342–53.

Iser, Wolfgang. *The Act of Reading: A Theory of Aesthetic Response.* Baltimore: Johns Hopkins UP, 1978.

Sanchez, Rebecca. "Bubble Reading: The Active Read Aloud." *NCTE NOTES Plus* Dec. 1995: 9–10.

Further Reading

Marzano, R. J., et al. *Dimensions of Thinking: A Framework for Curriculum and Instruction.* Alexandria, VA: Association for Supervision and Curriculum Development, 1988.

9 Led to Condemn: Discovering the Narrative Strategy of Herman Melville's "Bartleby the Scrivener"

James Tackach
Roger Williams University

> *This crank narrator is an enraged petty clerk, or a starveling, or a genius, or a monomaniac, or any sort of crazy. His is not an especially adult voice.*
>
> Annie Dillard, "Contemporary Prose Styles"

Herman Melville's widely anthologized short story "Bartleby the Scrivener" has many uses in the classroom. The story can introduce students to more difficult Melville works like *Moby-Dick* or *Billy Budd*. When grouped with texts like Henry David Thoreau's *Walden* and Rebecca Harding Davis's "Life in the Iron Mills," "Bartleby" also works well to convey the deep suspicions of nineteenth-century commercial and industrial culture associated with writers of American Romanticism. And, just as effectively, Melville's tale of the homeless scrivener might also be included on the syllabi of the new service-learning courses that are appearing in high schools and colleges (for a discussion of such courses, see Cooper and Julier). Students who engage themselves in community-service activities involving the homeless might have particularly interesting comments on "Bartleby."

I find Melville's story especially effective for teaching students in introductory literature courses the difference between merely reading for plot and conducting the kind of close analysis that is expected in upper-division courses. (High school teachers might choose the story as a way of training students in this kind of analysis.) For many of my students, the meaning of the story changes drastically after a close second reading; hence, they learn the value of scrutinizing, in addition to plot, the story's setting, narrative strategy, and style.

First, a review. Melville's story is narrated by an elderly attorney who employs two scriveners to compose multiple copies of deeds, contracts, and other legal papers. When his business increases, he employs a third scrivener, Bartleby. At first, Bartleby works very diligently. After a short time, however, Bartleby ceases all work, responding to the narrator's various orders and requests with the polite but firm response, "I would prefer not to." After the narrator discovers that Bartleby is living in the office, he tries to rid himself of his newest scrivener. When offering Bartleby money to leave does not work, he relocates to a new office, and Bartleby is imprisoned for vagrancy. In prison, Bartleby prefers not to eat and dies.

When I assign "Bartleby the Scrivener," I ask my students to consider one question as they read: Does Bartleby deserve our sympathy or our scorn? I must say that, because our attention has been drawn to the plight of the homeless, I do have an increasing number of students who, on first reading, express sympathy for Melville's scrivener. Generally, though, a good majority of my students respond by asserting that Bartleby deserves our scorn: he is a lazy bum who decides not to work and gets exactly what he deserves. I am actually very pleased by this response, for it provides me the chance to teach the lessons of close, analytical reading.

I open to the first few paragraphs of Melville's story, generally spending the rest of the class session reading it. In the opening paragraph, the unnamed narrator identifies himself as a "rather elderly man" (1) who has had contact with a large number of scriveners during the course of his legal career. He goes on to explain that, of all the scriveners whom he has known, the one named Bartleby was the strangest. After reading the opening paragraph, I ask the students what makes Bartleby stick in the narrator's memory and what makes the narrator tell the story. Almost always, a student will respond that the narrator remembers Bartleby because he was so different from "normal" scriveners. Yes, that is certainly one reason, but are there others? Inevitably, one student, perhaps one who has indicated sympathy for Bartleby, suggests that the narrator remembers Bartleby because the narrator feels some guilt over Bartleby's death. "Should the narrator feel guilty over Bartleby?" I ask. "Did the narrator indirectly cause Bartleby's death?" Someone always offers a loud "no" in response to that question: Bartleby caused his own death by refusing to work and refusing to eat. Okay, I repeat, then why does the story stick in the narrator's mind if he is completely blameless for Bartleby's death? Sometimes a student will provide an interesting response to that question: we sometimes feel guilty over something even if we have done nothing wrong, like the person who misses the airplane that crashes and feels guilty for having survived. Fine, I say, but then I repeat the second part of my question: What makes the narrator tell the story? I receive some of the same responses: Bartleby was so strange; the narrator feels guilty; and so on. One particularly shrewd student once suggested that the narrator tells the story because he wants to convince us that he acted responsibly and professionally toward Bartleby; the narrator is a guilty man who is desperately trying to assert his innocence.

At this time, I tell the students that we must gather more information about this narrator, so we reread the story's second paragraph. In it, the narrator reveals more about his personality and character. He holds a "profound conviction that the easiest way of life is the best" (1); he is "one of those unambitious lawyers who never address a jury, or in any way draws down public applause; but, in the cool tranquillity of a snug retreat, do a snug business among rich men's bonds, and mortgages, and title-deeds" (2). He goes on to call himself "an eminently *safe* man" whose "first grand point" is "prudence" and second "method" (2). We analyze each of the details in the second paragraph separately. What is an "eminently *safe* man"? What kind of man prefers the "easiest way of life"? What kind of man would avoid the drama of the courtroom in favor of a "snug retreat" where he can perform easy but financially rewarding tasks? After rereading this paragraph carefully, my students start to become more critical of Melville's narrator. Someone will call him a selfish man who cares for no one and nothing but money. Another will call him a coward who is afraid to take on challenging work or risks that might disrupt his easy way of life. I am pleased by this kind of analysis, but the class works best when a student challenges this portrait, when someone raises her hand and points out that the narrator gives Turkey, one of the other scriveners, a winter coat, offers Bartleby money to leave, attempts to understand Bartleby's problem, and even visits Bartleby in prison.

After letting this kind of debate go on for a while, I turn the students back to the text. In the third paragraph, the narrator offers a complaint. He had once held a political appointment, Master in the Chancery, but his position—which had been "not a very arduous office, but very pleasantly remunerative" (2)—had been eliminated when a new Constitution was enacted. He complains that he "had counted upon a life-lease of profits" but "only received those of a few short years" (2). Usually, a student will react to this passage by claiming that the narrator is a man who shuns work but wants to be richly compensated.

I then ask if the narrator treats his scriveners the way he himself likes to be treated in the workplace. Do the scriveners have an easy task for which they are handsomely paid? No, their work is tedious, replies one student, and they receive the standard scrivener's wage of four cents per hundred words. Is it fair for an employer to have an easy, well-paying job and expect his employees to work extremely hard for minimal wages?

By this time, I have gotten the students to scrutinize the narrator, maybe to mistrust him, perhaps to become suspicious of his motives. I might mention the point that Robert Scholes and Robert Kellogg make in *The Nature of Narrative* about unreliable narrators: "A narrator who is not some way suspect to ironic scrutiny is what the modern temper finds least bearable" (276–77). Using this alternative critical lens, students who had considered Bartleby a lazy bum begin to see that their view of the scrivener has been shaped by a man of dubious motives. Perhaps they recognize the need for a more careful reading.

By the end of a first class session on "Bartleby," I try to cover the story's fourth and fifth paragraphs, in which the narrator describes his office. Its most dominating features are walls: walls separate the lawyer from his scriveners; a brick wall stands outside the window; the office is on Wall Street in New York's financial district. I ask how many students noted how frequently Melville uses the word *wall* in his story. Some students will have noticed, but others will have not. What meaning is Melville trying to convey through this symbol? Before my students head for the door, I tell them to read the entire story a second time, keeping in mind the portrait that we have drawn of the narrator. I urge them to take a particularly close look at any acts of kindness that the narrator extends toward Bartleby. Are the narrator's motives noble? Did the narrator fail Bartleby in any way? Does the narrator have any reason to feel guilty? I also ask them to reconsider their view of Bartleby. Why does he stop working? Why does he prefer not to live at the story's end?

After the students have had time to read the story again, I open discussion by asking whether or not the narrator is a fair and ethical employer. The overwhelming response is that he is not. He pays his workers poorly and erects walls around them. He gives them orders without ever saying "please" or "thank you." I try to defend the narrator by pointing out his random acts of kindness, like giving Turkey the coat. "Why doesn't he pay Turkey a decent wage so that Turkey can afford to buy a new coat?" one student suggests. I point out that, after Bartleby stops working, the narrator offers him a considerable sum of money to leave the premises, but a student likens that apparent gesture of generosity to our tendency to throw money at social problems without taking the time to understand the source of those problems and find permanent solutions. I identify passages in which the narrator seems to show an understanding of Bartleby's problems and a willingness to help him. When the narrator realizes that Bartleby is living in his law office, for example, the narrator exclaims, "Immediately then the thought came sweeping across me, what miserable friendlessness and loneliness are here revealed! His poverty is great; but his solitude, how horrible!" (21). But a student who has reread closely provides an earlier line that casts doubts on any of the narrator's acts of kindness. "To befriend Bartleby," states the narrator, "will cost me little or nothing, while I lay up in my soul what will eventually prove a sweet morsel for my conscience" (16).

In a last-ditch effort to defend the narrator whom my students have now turned upon, I summon the passage where the narrator, exasperated after his many attempts to rid himself of Bartleby, invites the scrivener to come to his own dwelling to take up residence. We carefully examine Bartleby's response to this offer: "No: at present I would prefer not to make any change at all" (41). A particularly observant student will focus on the words *at present*. Perhaps if the narrator had made the offer earlier, she says, Bartleby might have accepted, but the present is too late. When I can get students to recognize that the meaning of a passage can twist upon a single qualifying phrase like *at present,* I know that I am on the right track.

A second reading changes my students' estimation of not only the narrator but of Bartleby as well. One student will point out that the first two tasks that Bartleby refuses to do—proofreading texts and going to the post office—are jobs for which he will not be paid. "Why work if you're not getting paid?" the student will ask. "Proofreading and running errands take time from copying, for which he is getting paid by the word." Students also point to the alienating nature of Bartleby's work, to his lack of home, family, friends, and sufficient income. Instead of calling Bartleby a worthless bum, my students come to admire him for refusing to work in such an alienating, confining, and uninspiring atmosphere. "Bartleby is on strike!" a student once said. "He won't go along with the program; he won't conform," another stated. After a closer reading of Melville's story, my students' opinion of Bartleby usually turns from derision to sympathy and even to respect and admiration.

The interpretation of Melville's story that I am offering here is certainly not original. Many—perhaps most—Melville critics view the tale as a critique of mid-nineteenth-century American capitalism. As this argument goes, Bartleby is a victim of an oppressive workscape that alienates and ultimately destroys the individual worker. The lawyer represents the ruling class capitalist who, though not without sympathy, maintains his snug position by exploiting his workers. What I am offering here, rather than a fresh interpretation of the story, is a method for prompting students to read fiction closely and analytically, to scrutinize the story's narrative technique, style, and setting, and to discover how those factors shape the story's meaning. Melville's "Bartleby the Scrivener" is a perfect story to illustrate the importance of close reading because its meaning changes so dramatically when the students read it a second time.

Works Cited

Cooper, David D., and Laura Julier, eds. *Writing in the Public Interest: Service-Learning and the Writing Classroom*. East Lansing: The Writing Center at Michigan State University, 1995.

Melville, Herman. *"Bartleby the Scrivener."* New York: Penguin, 1995.

Scholes, Robert, and Robert Kellogg. *The Nature of Narrative*. New York: Oxford UP, 1968.

Further Reading

Bernstein, John. *Pacifism and Rebellion in the Writings of Herman Melville*. London: Mouton, 1964.

Bickley, R. Bruce Jr. *The Method of Melville's Short Fiction*. Durham: Duke UP, 1975.

Bloom, Harold, ed. *Herman Melville's "Billy Budd," "Benito Cereno," "Bartleby the Scrivener," and Other Tales*. New York: Chelsea House, 1987.

Inge, M. Thomas. *Bartleby the Inscrutable: A Collection of Commentary on Herman Melville's Tale "Bartleby the Scrivener."* Hamden, CT: Archon, 1979.

Kirby, David. *Herman Melville*. New York: Continuum, 1993.

III Perceiving the Story's Underlying Structure

I fancy much of what I value . . . escapes the observation of the great mass of my readers, who are intent more upon the story than the way in which it is told. For my part, I consider a story merely as a frame on which to stretch my materials.

Washington Irving, letter to Harry Brevoort

After stopping students in their interpretive tracks, teachers can next help students by exposing the rhetorical dimensions of the short story. In the process, students begin to consider the nature of genre, especially as genre involves their own expectations. In short, by seeing how their emotional response is *confirmed* in formal elements that, in turn, coalesce in rhetorical purpose, readers start on the road to that elusive quality best known as taste.

Although generic classification models can be helpful in approaching the *fictio*—the imagination—of the short story, these schemes at some level inevitably fail. Literature, after all, is a wonderful swirl of a writer's recollection and projection, thesis and hypothesis. Because such texts expose their writers as participants in the text, readers, too, become more active, closing the gap between their imaginative and real worlds. When they do, readers recognize their own lives as emerging stories. Indeed, one might say that, by understanding how fiction is pieced together, we can even shape how we piece together our own lives.

Understanding how lives are constructed informs, not surprisingly, the writing process. In identifying story structure through careful reading, students learn to write purposefully, discovering an arsenal of compositional options. Their awareness, ironically enough, is the start to engaging the world on *its* terms, and it is in that direction that the remaining chapters of the book tend. It is the start, in other words, to identifying not only what we know but how we know it and can use it.

As Emerson writes in *Self-Reliance*, "The Soul raised over passion beholds identity and eternal causation, perceives the self-existence of Truth and Right and calms itself with knowing that all things go well" (1550–51).

The relationship between life and art, upon which is arguably predicated all matters of genre, pertains to the essays of this section. Informed by art, we perceive order in life where previously we saw randomness. Grant Tracey shows his students how to discover the plot structure in Morley Callaghan's "All the Years of Her Life." In this case, the structure is a key to the meaning, which depends on epiphany, a significant element to the short story genre. Also at issue is the timeless relationship between the fuzziness of life and the coherence of art: while our lives, day-to-day, seem generically unfocused, stories about life involve plots that reveal purpose; while we cannot see our futures, most of the time the stories that we tell have a beginning, a middle, and an end. Brenda Dyer seizes this issue to teach stories that are about telling stories. Similarly, Tamara Grogan uses Virgina Woolf's "An Unwritten Novel" to show how short stories are "constructed objects, aware of themselves." Her objective is to familiarize her students with "the tricks of an author's trade" so that they can dream "somebody else's dream." Readers can, in Oscar Wilde's words, see that "Art is our spirited protest, our gallant attempt to teach nature her proper place" (673). In a reader-response view of that art, we learn to expect the unexpected. One consequence is that seemingly fixed meanings become relative ones, and upon this structuralist premise Linda L. Gill approaches Edith Wharton's "Roman Fever." Gill shows her students how the power relationships in the story are reflected in the physical arrangement of the action. Those relationships are constructed of binary concepts, usually one supplanting the other, "Like the sun to the moon, like aviators to gladiators, like mothers to daughters. . . ." In identifying these concepts, we see ourselves, too.

Works Cited

Emerson, Ralph. "Self-Reliance." 1841, 1847. *The Heath Anthology of American Literature.* Ed. Paul Lauter, et al. Vol. 1. 2nd ed. Lexington, MA: D. C. Heath, 1994. 1542–58.

Wilde, Oscar. "The Decay of Lying." 1889. *Critical Theory since Plato.* Ed. Hazard Adams. New York: Harcourt Brace Jovanovich, 1971. 673–86.

10 One Great Way to Read Short Stories: Studying Character Deflection in Morley Callaghan's "All the Years of Her Life"

Grant Tracey
University of Northern Iowa

A story, if it is to be a story, must have a psychological turning-point.
Elizabeth Bowen, *Early Stories*

A s an undergraduate studying literature in the early 1980s, I noted that professors treated short stories as warm-ups for themes more fully realized in novels. The demands of the short story, the structural rules of the genre to which even "great" writers adhere, were ignored.

But during my graduate years, as I wrote stories for Professor Ben Nyberg, I learned a great way to read short stories. In contrast to the traditional plot-driven approach to fiction (rising action, a series of conflicts, climax, falling action, and conclusion) that deftly draws out and illuminates the conflict between protagonist and antagonist, Nyberg's approach encourages students to analyze the narrative structure of a story through the prism of one character and how all events affect and change that single character.

Nyberg contended that most short stories have a built-in tripartite structure: exposition, deflection, and resolution. For Nyberg, the deflection was the key because fiction always focuses on something new happening, a turning-point experience that changes things (Nyberg 10–11). He explains the model with an illustrative diagram:

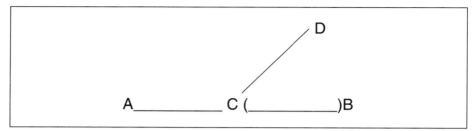

Figure 1.

According to this view, our imaginary character begins his day at point A and expects to reach point B. But during his quest something magical happens (C) that changes his route and deflects him to a new understanding of the self (D). If students understand the story's resolution (D), usually what the character feels about another person, they can work back to discover what deflected the character toward this understanding (C) and how the resolution was foreshadowed in the exposition (A).

I recommend this approach for teaching short fiction of the modernist era, especially the works of such diverse writers as Anton Chekhov, Guy de Maupassant, Ernest Hemingway, James Joyce, D. H. Lawrence, Bernard Malamud, Katherine Mansfield, Alice Munro, and Flannery O'Connor. Lay Nyberg's paradigm over various stories and ask students to locate the three phases. The repetitive practice enriches their understanding of the short story as largely character-driven and empowers them to realize the text's total effect. A good story to begin with is Morley Callaghan's "All the Years of Her Life" because it is deceptively simple, tightly plotted, and high school and first-year college students can relate to its theme of troubled adolescents needing love, understanding, and dignity.

In Callaghan's story, adolescent Alfred Higgins, who has been caught stealing toiletries from Sam Carr's mom-and-pop store, needs to grow up. The narrative moves him toward responsibility. When teaching the story, begin with the epiphany (D). What has Alfred learned? Look at the conclusion. Upon returning home, Alfred's mother, who had rescued him from Carr's anger, bitterly sends him to his room. He retreats, admiring how she handled things with his former employer: "'She certainly was smooth,' he thought. 'Gee, I'd like to tell her she sounded swell'" (6). Appreciative, he wants to thank her and walks toward the kitchen. Undetected, he watches as she sips tea, her hand trembling. Suddenly Alfred changes: "[H]e knew all the years of her life by the way her hand trembled as she raised the cup to her lips. It seemed to him that this was the first time he had ever looked upon his mother" (6). Through the distilled image of his mother's trembling, Alfred realizes the pain that he has brought his mother through the years.

By looking at the conclusion first, students discover that the story focuses on Alfred and his mother. Alfred recognizes his own guilt and reassesses the earlier opinion that "She sounded swell." The brave "dignity" Mrs. Higgins had shown at Carr's store, Alfred now realizes, was an act his mom staged to rescue him. Callaghan, through the suddenness of fiction, informs us that Alfred "looked upon his mother" for the "first time." Where else in the narrative did he look upon her? What deflected him (C) toward this compassionate feeling for someone outside himself?

To discover phase two (the deflection), encourage students to focus on Alfred's earlier feelings toward his mother. In terms of the plot, she appears at the story's middle, rescuing Alfred from Carr, who had threatened to phone the police over the petty thievery. But before she arrives, Alfred underestimates her. He assumes that "She would rush in with her eyes blazing, or maybe she would be crying, and she would push him away when he tried to talk to her, and make him feel her dreadful contempt" (3). Although he wants to be rescued by his mother, he is slightly embarrassed by her. However, his mother's arrival surprises him: "She did not look as Alfred thought she would look" (3). This moment is the story's deflection. When he marvels over how his mother carries herself with a "calmness and dignity," Alfred begins an ongoing process of (re)looking, reassessing her. Carr, too, is surprised. With a rapid switch in point of view, Callaghan indicates that Carr is a "bit ashamed" by her "understanding gentleness" and kind "patient dignity." Having previously enjoyed his power over Alfred, Carr is shamed by Mrs. Higgins's grace into refusing to press charges. Later, in his epiphany, Alfred's first reassessment undergoes further revision.

After you have established the story's resolution and deflection, turn to the exposition (A). Often when students analyze the expository phase of a story, they leap to a false deflection. In this case, they might contend that the deflection occurs in the opening paragraphs when Alfred is caught stealing. They may reason that he has never been caught stealing before; thus, this event deflects him from his presumed path from A to B: checking in, working, stealing some toiletries, leaving Carr's. Be sympathetic to these responses, but remind students that the deflection usually involves two key characters. Callaghan's story isn't about Alfred and Carr, but it is about Alfred and his mother (note the title). The act of stealing doesn't bring about Alfred's newfound understanding toward his mother and himself; instead, Alfred's change is predicated upon how well he understands his mother's differing responses to the petty crime—in the public sphere (Carr's store) versus at home (at the kitchen table).

Callaghan establishes several key character traits and the story's central theme in the pages leading up to Mrs. Higgins's arrival. Alfred is caught stealing. We discover that he had dropped out of school. His father, a printer, is rarely at home, and Alfred is the youngest of four children, the rest married (2). Moreover, he has been in trouble often. All of these bits of information provided by Callaghan establish a character who lacks male guidance and is irresponsible. Alfred's immaturity, his status between boy and man, is clearly hinted at by Callaghan as the youth wonders what Carr will do:

> "Just a minute. You don't need to draw anybody else in. You don't need to tell her." He wanted to sound like a swaggering, big guy who could look after himself, yet the old childish hope was in him, the longing that someone at home would come and help him. (2–3)

Alfred tries to appear tough and independent, to "swagger" off the problem, but he's still an in-between, trying to be grown up but desiring that others defend him.

The three-phase demonstration of a character-driven reading is now complete. Outline the chronological order for the students. A sensitive young teen is caught stealing from the store for which he works. He desires to stand alone against his accuser, but the childlike need for help is still in him. While he awaits his mother's arrival, he underestimates her by assuming that she'll arrive tearfully (A). Upon her arrival, the story's deflection occurs. She doesn't act the way he expected (B) but instead surprises him with her calm "dignity." Therefore, he reassesses her (C). Alfred's reassessment is further revised in the story's resolution as he watches her tremble while drinking tea. Callaghan's conclusion opens up the moment for the reader. Alfred's epiphany forces him to look upon his mother and, in a sense, what his irresponsible behavior has wrought: "He watched his mother, and he never spoke, but at that moment his youth seemed to be over" (6). As he watches his mother, we watch Alfred. His knowledge redeems him before himself and the reader, as he crosses into adulthood (D).

Works Cited

Callaghan, Morley. "All the Years of Her Life." *Morley Callaghan's Stories.* Toronto: Macmillan, 1986. 1–6.

Nyberg, Ben. *One Great Way to Write Short Stories: A Step-by-Step Approach.* Cincinnati: Writer's Digest, 1988.

11 Stories about Stories: Teaching Narrative Using William Saroyan's "My Grandmother Lucy Tells a Story without a Beginning, a Middle, or an End"

Brenda Dyer
Tokyo Woman's University

[The story] resembles a ballad or a sonnet and depends on a spontaneity that conceals its architecture.

V. S. Pritchett, quoted by Daniel Halpern in *The Art of the Tale*

It is not only the process of art that selects and sorts details; the process of living itself necessarily does the same to the innumerable sense impressions of reality. Our daily actions—parties, dinners, conversations—create and embrace an underlying order in life. Art comes from such actions, for, as T. S. Eliot says, it "give[s] us some perception of an order in life, by imposing an order upon it" (86). Indeed, life as a lived story, a true fiction, shaped by imagination and circumstance, is the focus of such twentieth-century prophets/story-makers as Ira Progoff and Joseph Campbell. In his "Intensive Journal Process," Progoff advises that journal writers consider what their lives try to be and identify the goals of their lives (206). Campbell, in the video *The Power of Myth* (1988), quotes Schopenhauer:

A version of this article was published in *English Quarterly* 26.4 (Summer 1994). This article is reprinted with the permission of *English Quarterly*. Copyright ©1994 Canadian Council of Teachers of English and Language Arts.

> When you reach a certain age, and look back over your life, it seems to have had an order, it seems to have been composed by someone, and those events that when they occurred seemed merely accidental . . . turned out to be the main elements in a consistent plot. Who composed this plot? Just as your dreams are composed by an aspect of yourself of which your consciousness is unaware, so your whole life has been composed by the Will within you.

It is important for our students to examine the ordering of fiction and life, "truth of fiction and the fiction of truth." For those students interested in the study of literature, fiction is a delightful window into the complexities of narrative. But there are even wider benefits to this kind of metatextual study. Evidence from Canada, the United States, and the United Kingdom suggests that young people think and worry a great deal about their apparent powerlessness in the face of imminent personal and global crises (Roald et al. 1988, Tizard 1985). Robert Scholes, in *Textual Power,* warns, "In an age of manipulation, when our students are in dire need of critical strength to resist the continuing assaults of all the media, the worst thing we can do is to foster in them an attitude of reverence before texts" (16). The greatest writers—writers like Chaucer, Shakespeare, Sterne, Woolf—have self-consciously and irreverently "played" with text. To view text critically, to establish the shifting lines of truth and fiction, and, most important, to use the tools of storytelling to empower and enrich our increasingly fragmented and discordant lives toward happier and truer endings—these are the goals of today's English classroom.

I have several favorite "stories about stories" that I have used with high school students: "Sleepy Time Gal" by Gary Gildner, "Snow" by Ann Beattie, "The Open Window" by Saki, "An Astrologer's Day" by R. K. Narayan, "Metonymy, or the Husband's Revenge" by Rachel de Queiroz, and "My Grandmother Lucy Tells a Story without a Beginning, a Middle, or an End" by William Saroyan. Saroyan's story is fun to teach—short and humorous, it is also a puzzle. Its internal narratives lend themselves to prereading activities, and its lack of closure to postreading discussion. In it, the narrator and Grandma Lucy are impatient with "plot and formula" and try to tell a story "for nothing more than the fun or sorrow of it." In both the narrator's and Grandma's stories, there is an apparent formlessness. The narrator is frustrated by the gaps and superfluities in Grandma's tale: "Is that the whole story?" he asks, "What happened to that part?"; "What about . . . ?"; "Haven't you forgotten some of the story?" In response, Grandma calmly insists that her story is "quite complete" and "good enough." The narrator, for his part, juxtaposes his Grandma's "pointless" tale with the rhetoric of Winston Churchill's speech to the U.S. Senate on December 26, 1941, which is heard on the radio in the background of Grandma's kitchen. He claims to have "put down the background for no reason other than its verity—I wanted to hear Churchill's speech and I wanted to hear Lucy's story. I heard both at the same time" (298). He "ends" his narrative with a laconic lack of closure in a statement that could be his own or Grandma's voice: "Things are changing in the world, there is no doubt about that" (299).

Prereading Task #1

In groups of three to four, students must create a short speech that could have been given by Churchill to the American Senate in December 1941. Students will need to use library resources (e.g., an encyclopedia) to establish what was happening in World War II, the status of U.S. participation, and the motivation for Churchill's speech. The speech should be a genuine attempt to persuade the United States to join the war effort against Germany. When students have completed preparing their speeches, ask for volunteers to be the Senate. The rest of the class presents their speeches to the Senate, and the most persuasive speech is chosen. The Senate justifies its choice.

The teacher guides class discussion regarding the most effective speech. Was the speech "true"? Was it somewhat fictionalized? How was it made persuasive? Was it well organized, with a beginning, middle, and end? Was it a "story"? Why/why not? What is a story? How about the "story" of World War II? When did it begin and end? For the Chinese, it began in 1932; for the Americans, in 1941: whose version is correct? If history is composed of narratives, is it a kind of fiction?

Prereading Task #2

Distribute the following excerpt (Grandma Lucy's story) from Saroyan's story, read it aloud, and have students discuss the questions in partners/groups.

> A man packed up and went to other countries. Before departing he was asked what city it was he wished to reach. The city without worries, he replied. He was told, When you get there, please see if you can do anything about my worries—my wife and children. My wife wants me to be a success, and my children refuse to believe that I am poor—they want things which I cannot give them.

On the way, the journeyer noticed an apple tree, beside which sat an old man. As other journeyers came to this tree, they plucked apples from its boughs, took one bite and threw them aside. The journeyer went to the old man and said, Why do they take one bite only and then throw them away?

Beneath this tree, the old man replied, is gold. The journeyer began to dig under the tree. He uncovered a great deal of gold. (297)

The following questions may be asked:

Is this a story?

If you say it is, what elements does it have that make it a story?

If you decide it is not a story, what elements of a story does it lack?

How is it different from Churchill's speech?

Small- and then whole-group discussion usually concludes that, although the passage has the makings of setting, character, plot, and theme, there are significant gaps. In small groups, students rewrite the passage so that it is a "story" to their liking, and then share these. The complete story is then distributed and read aloud, with two students taking the part of the narrator and Grandma Lucy.

Discussion

A flurry of questions arises. Is Saroyan's "story" a complete story? What makes it unusual? The narrator says there is no connection between Grandma's story and Mr. Churchill's speech. Do you believe him? How are the two pieces of discourse different? How is this ironic? How is fiction "true"? How is history "fictional"? Why did Saroyan write this story? What meanings does it have for you?

Essay

Discuss the following comment by Harold Rosen in terms of Saroyan's story:

The story is always "out there" but the important step has still to be taken. The unremitting flow of events must first be selectively considered, interpreted as holding relationships, causes, motives, feelings, consequences—in a word, meanings. To give an order to this otherwise unmanageable flux we must take another step and invent, yes, *invent*, beginnings and ends, for "out there" are no such things. Even so stark an ending as death is only an ending when we have made a story out of a life. (13)

The real author of a narrative is not only the one who tells it but the one who generates it, takes it from an idea to a verbal or printed text. And narrative is everywhere, "not to be regarded as an aesthetic invention used by artists to control, manipulate and order experience," says Barbara Hardy, "but a primary act of mind transferred to art from life" (1). Saroyan's narrator claims to present a narrative "without plot or formula," just for "the fun or sorrow of it." Yet the fun and sorrow of it is "made up" just, as Peter Walsh ponders in *Mrs. Dalloway*, "as one makes up the better part of life" (50). The fun and sorrow of it is the result of the reader's remarkable human capacity to *make* "plot and formula," to shape meanings in the very act of reading, and thus to re-make the story. It is impossible to read the story without making "a point" for it. Beginnings, middles, endings—let us empower our students as readers and writers of their own and other's stories, to realize with Schopenhauer that

> just as those people whom you meet by chance became effective agents in the structuring of your life, so you have been an agent in the structuring of other lives. And the whole thing gears together like one big symphony. (Campbell)

To recognize this symphony is to bridge the gap between text and life, opening the windows and doors of our classrooms.

Works Cited

Campbell, Joseph. *Masks of Eternity. The Power of Myth,* Part 6. Public Broadcasting System, 1988.

Eliot, T. S. "Poetry and Drama." *On Poetry and Poets.* London: Faber and Faber, 1957. 72–86.

Hardy, Barbara. "The Nature of Narrative." *The Collected Essays of Barbara Hardy, Vol. 1: Narrators and Novelists.* Totowa, NJ: Barnes & Noble Books, 1987. 1–13.

Rosen, Harold. *Stories and Meanings.* Sheffield, England: National Association for the Teaching of English, 1984.

Saroyan, William. "My Grandmother Lucy Tells a Story without a Beginning, a Middle or an End." *My Name Is Saroyan.* New York: Putnam, 1983. 296–99.

Scholes, Robert. *Textual Power: Literary Theory and the Teaching of English.* New Haven: Yale UP, 1985.

Woolf, Virginia. 1925. *Mrs. Dalloway.* London: Penguin, 1976.

Further Reading

Beattie, Ann. "Snow." *Sudden Fiction International: 60 Short Short Stories.* Ed. Robert Shapard and James Thomas. New York: Norton, 1989. 286–89.

Gildner, Gary. "Sleepy Time Gal." *Sudden Fiction: American Short Short Stories.* Ed. Robert Shapard and James Thomas. London: Penguin, 1988. 214–16.

Narayan, R. K. "An Astrologer's Day." *An Astrologer's Day and Other Stories.* Cambridge, England: Eyre and Spottiswoode, 1947. 1–7.

Progoff, Ira. *At a Journal Workshop.* Rev. ed. Los Angeles: Jeremy P. Tarcher, 1992.

Queiroz, Rachel de. "Metonymy, or the Husband's Revenge." *Modern Brazilian Short Stories.* Ed. and trans. William L. Grossman. Berkeley: U of California P, 1967. 27–32.

Roald, J., et al. *The Global Outlook of the Class of 1990.* St. Mary's, Halifax: School of Education, Dalhousie, 1988.

Saki. "The Open Window." *The Complete Works of Saki.* New York: Doubleday, 1976. 259–62.

Tizard, B. "Problematic Aspects of Nuclear Education." *Lessons before Midnight.* London: U of London, 1985.

12 The Story Looks at Itself: Narration in Virginia Woolf's "An Unwritten Novel"

Tamara Grogan
University of Massachusetts at Amherst

*The more sophisticated reader plays a deep double game with himself;
one part of him is identified with a character—or with several of them—
while another part holds aloof to respond, interpret, and judge.*

Robert Penn Warren, "Why Do We Read Fiction?"

Virginia Woolf's "An Unwritten Novel" takes us to no less a theme than the relationship between art and life. A rather uneventful story: a narrator riding a train, peeking over her newspaper at an older woman, imagining her life. That's it. In the end, the older woman gets off the train. She leaves the station with her son, to the consternation of the narrator, who had not imagined such a connection. Uneventful indeed, to the point of being plotless.

Yet in the space of this brief, real-time moment, Woolf grapples with essential, writerly questions. Where does inspiration come from? How does the creative process work? Where is "life" to be found—in large-scale, headline-news events? in microcosmic details of a single human experience? or in the imagination, the worlds created by language? It is a wonderful exploration for an honors class or a class of would-be writers, students who have something invested in these questions.

Woolf's story is important to read even for those without ready-made motivation, because, in its plotlessness, its parallel tracks of the real and the imagined, it has much to teach about stories as constructed objects that are aware of themselves. By subverting the seamless, continuous dream of most mainstream fiction, the story is almost provoking in its insistence on the mechanical functions necessary to the act of creation. First, we have an author, whom we usually don't see in other stories, constantly poking her head up, self-referential. Then we have the story, which the author treats alternately like a game ("Let's dodge to the Moggridge household, set that in motion") or like a reverie run wild:

> (as Minnie eats an egg and drops the eggshells in her lap) . . . fragments of an eggshell—fragments of a map—a puzzle. . . . She's moved her knees—the map's in bits again. Down the slopes of the Andes the white blocks of marble go bounding and hurtling, crushing to death a whole troop of Spanish muleteers, with their convoy—Drake's booty, gold and silver. But to return. . . . (354)

Then there is the "actual" ongoing life in the train (which is, again, constructed)—the banal, everyday stuff of life on a public conveyance, with people reading and yawning and pretending indifference to everyone around them. Woolf manipulates these three constructs in such a way that they interrupt each other, overrun each other, vie for the upper hand, and the story becomes a sort of house of mirrors, a metafiction, which, as John Clayton notes, is about "the process of fictionalization and the meaning of storytelling" (349). It is a useful story for becoming more sensitive to fictional devices and how they operate.

I approach this story—blatantly, aloud—as a hard one. This is not a piece simply to throw to students and see what they make of it. It is imperative that it be read more than once. First of all, there is much within it that is unfamiliar: cairngorms, aspidistra, commercial travelers, the sights and sounds of early twentieth-century England—these are strange to me as well as to my students. In their first reading (overnight), students get the general lay of the land and look for places that throw them: words used, references made, anything unfamiliar that can't be derived from the context. Thus, the next day we get discussion of truncheons and President Kruger, types of buttons—"peacock-eyed, others dull gold; cairngorms some, and others coral sprays" (354)—which would have a great deal more importance in a world without zippers and Velcro. We familiarize, try to breathe in the atmosphere and contextualize this world. An essential aspect of this process is biographical information on Woolf: the depressions she suffered after writing each of her novels, her suicide. The story gets along without these sidelights, but students feel empowered when they know something of an author's life and death. It makes the second read, and the narrator's talk of what life is—both its unhappiness and joy, her impassioned hymn to the world at the story's end—more immediate and compelling. We relate the misery of the woman she sees on the train, who says, "I can face it no longer," to some pain of the author's. We see

Woolf's interest in the thingness of this world, and in the creative life that creates thingness from nothing, as perhaps what kept her going for as long as she did.

By their second reading, students have a certain level of comfort with the story; they have had the guided tour, they know where they are going and can enjoy the trip. The class is divided into two groups for reading purposes (I let them choose whichever group they prefer to join).

Group One's job is to separate the action of the story into (implied) PRESENT WORLD and IMAGINED WORLD. These students are trying to decide what, in the story's terms, is really supposed to be happening. What is the narrator creating? Group Two is asked to look for evidence in the story of how a writer's process works: based on one particular story by Woolf (other stories by other authors may provide completely contradictory notions), what generalizations might be made? The reading for the second night's homework is thus directed, with the expectation that each group will discuss their findings the next day and try to reach some conclusions to share.

For Group One, the division of real versus imagined is at first simple. Woman on train people-watching; newspaper on her lap full of real events; peace between Germany and the Allied Powers; a passenger train at Doncaster in collision with a goods train. She folds and holds up the newspaper as a shield against the clear unhappiness in another woman's eyes. All passengers disembark except the two women. Left alone, one talks of "stations and holidays, of brothers at Eastbourne, and the time of year, which was, I forget now, early or late." The narrator replies, "Sisters-in-law," at which the first woman, pursing her lips, rubs at a spot on the window glass. The narrator suddenly feels herself suffused by something of the other woman's physical being: she, too, rubs the window glass, and feels a spasm pass through her, a twitch like the elderly woman's. Then while the narrator sits back in her corner, "shielding my eyes from her eyes, seeing only the slopes and hollows, greys and purples, of the winter's landscape, I read her message, deciphered her secret, reading it beneath her gaze" (351). At this point, the narrator is off, imagining the woman's visit to her sister-in law in such detail that she feels obliged to gloss over some of it: "But this we'll skip; ornaments, curtains, trefoil china plate, yellow oblongs of cheese, white squares of biscuit . . ." (352). From that point, the group's work is more about digging the "real" references out from the imagined—"A moment's blankness—then, what are you thinking? (Let me peep across at her opposite; she's asleep or pretending it; so what would she think about, sitting at the window at three o'clock in the afternoon? Health, money, bills, her God?)"—and gets complicated as the narrator's mind grows crowded with figures: Minnie, Hilda, Bob and Barbara, Moggridge, a President Kruger-type God (352). For instance, although we know Jimmy Moggridge is not real, that he is a character imagined by Woolf the author, we must wonder whether, in the story's terms, he is supposed to be an actual passenger on the train. Or is he a figure imagined by the narrator as a torment to self-conscious Minnie, an inevitable fixture in the domestic scene that has been sketched, the commercial traveler dining on Thursdays with the Marshes, one who must "emerge . . . if the story's to go on gathering richness and rotundity, destiny and tragedy, as stories should, rolling along with it two, if not three, commercial travelers and a whole grove of aspidistra" (354).

Group One's assignment forces close reading, looking for those details that indicate when the narrator has soared off on an imaginative flight: "The flicker of a hand—off, up! then poised again. Alone, unseen; seeing all so still down there, all so lovely. None seeing, none caring. The eyes of others our prisons; their thoughts our cages. Air above, air below. And the moon and immortality . . ." (354). Or, perhaps, they might find that moment when she has grounded herself, forcibly returned to the initial setting of the train: "Oh, but I drop to the turf! Are you down, too, you in the corner, what's your name—woman—Minnie Marsh; some such name as that?" (354). The point here is not some tidy dissection of halves, real versus imagined, from which satisfaction is derived, but a clearer sense of the two strands of this story and how they intersect, how the real gives birth to the imagined, which turns back upon the real and alters the narrator's (and the reader's) perception of it. Group One is responsible for discussing and presenting this split in the story, all of which takes roughly half an hour. They give the rest of the class a way to see it.

Group Two's reading focus is on the writerly process. Because Woolf's story is a metafiction, highly aware of its own tricks, Group Two approaches it almost as if it were an essay about writing, which it can very well be considered. In view of Woolf's other work, "An Unwritten Novel" could be taken as either a story or an essay. The first thing students typically notice is Woolf/the narrator trying things as she goes, accepting and rejecting notions of character, toying with bits of description ("A crime. . . . They would say she kept her sorrow, suppressed her secret—her sex, they'd say-the scientific people. But what flummery to saddle her with sex! No—more like this" [352]). This story allows them a glimpse backstage, and makes them aware of writing as process. Stories are not born full grown—they have to be built a piece at a time, nursed, cared for. We see difficulties: Minnie has nothing to look at when the lights go out in the building opposite and the narrator is forced to divine her thinking, first deciding what Minnie might think about, and then envisioning it, having to build from scratch such weighty thoughts as Minnie's God (he is a surly gentleman in a frock coat wielding a truncheon, with a cloud or two for effect). Students notice the narrator's constant decision-making about what to leave in, what to leave out, her awareness of herself as a writer, her own tics and tendencies ("Rhododendron would conceal [James Moggridge] utterly, and into the bargain give me my fling of red and white, for which I starve and strive; but rhododendrons in Eastbourne—in December—on the Marshes' table—no, no, I dare not" [354]).

In the main, students become aware of how characters reveal themselves to an author one piece at a time, how each decision necessitates other decisions, and how, ultimately, characters start to take on their own lives. For example, at one point the narrator's crescendo of thoughts has Minnie in an associative reverie, assuring her that inanimate objects have meaning and are speaking her name: "—placards leaning against doorways—names above shop windows—red fruit in baskets—women's heads in the hairdresser's—all say 'Minnie Marsh!'"; suddenly, Minnie thinks, "'Eggs are cheaper!'" The narrator's own thoughts were heading this character "over the waterfall, straight for madness, when, like a flock of dream sheep, she turns t'other way and runs between my fingers. Eggs are cheaper." The Minnie Marsh created so far by this narrator is "Tethered to the shores of the world, none of the crimes, sorrows, rhapsodies, or insanities for poor Minnie Marsh; never late for luncheon . . . never utterly unconscious of the cheapness of eggs. So she reaches home, scrapes her boots" (353). This character has already become strong enough, incarnated enough, to reject ill-chosen notions about her. It is a mysterious thing, this issue of who has the upper hand between a character and an author. Of course students know that Woolf has written every word of the story. They know, realistically speaking, that Minnie Marsh is only Minnie Marsh because Woolf has allowed her to be, has simultaneously envisioned a narrator, an observed woman, and a life for the observed woman. And yet, Woolf rails—imagining James Moggridge's wife, a retired hospital nurse—"for God's sake let me have one woman with a name I like!" as if she had no choice in the matter, as if this nurse, once her relationships and station in life have been established, sets briskly about the business of creating herself (355). Students may view this as one of Woolf's metaphoric comments for what happens during characterization, or may see it as this narrator's own particular delusion. Whatever their slant on this moment in the story, they can't help but be alerted to the constraints of building a character.

This group looks for other metaphors as well, ways in which Woolf encapsulates the creative process in an image. The story is rich with them: "the unborn children of the mind, illicit, none the less loved, like my rhododendrons"; "How the mud goes round in the mind—what a swirl these monsters [characters] leave, the waters rocking, the weeds waving and green here, black there . . ." (355, 350). One particularly appealing metaphor for students is the narrator who comes

> irresistibly to lodge myself somewhere on the firm flesh, in the robust spine, wherever I can penetrate or find foothold on the person, in the soul, of Moggridge the man. The enormous stability of the fabric; the spine tough as whalebone, straight as oak tree; the ribs radiating branches; the flesh taut tarpaulin; the red hollows; the suck and regurgitation of the heart; while from above meat falls in brown cubes and beer gushes to be churned to blood again . . . (355).

This evocation of what an author is doing by "getting inside" a character is sudden, brash, and physical—up to this point in the story, characterization has been a matter of names, in-laws, jobs, religious leanings, and table manners. Here we find ourselves splashing around in James Moggridge's stomach juices! It seems, well, improper, scatological, and it also makes students laugh to think that this is what it takes to know a character adequately. It is not enough to say, "The man was a traveling salesman"; there must also be, figuratively, knowledge of spine and flesh and the alimentary canal, even with a character such as Moggridge, who doesn't linger.

Group Two is also responsible for sharing their insights with the rest of the class. Their task is, admittedly, somewhat harder than the one faced by Group One, a fact that might suggest more judicious division. However, by dividing the labor, you can take advantage of differing levels of ability in your class, and everyone gets exposed to and takes responsibility for some major issue of the story.

If you have more time to spend, here is a final, more hands-on approach that can be done as an in-class assignment. Ask students to write a short creative piece—a page or two—based on a picture. This works best if everyone is using the same picture, and if the picture has a person in it, to approximate more closely the conditions of the story. What is that person seeing, thinking, feeling? Where is he going? Why?

What led him to stand in the middle of the street? What are his face and body saying? Before students begin to write, ask them to divide their pages in half with a line down the middle. They should write down the left side of the page, using the picture for inspiration, trying at the same time to be aware of other voices sneaking into their thoughts as they write, from the self-deprecating, "Well, that's pretty stupid," to the metafictional, "It will be more interesting if I write from this picture-person's voice" to the unrelated "This wart on my thumb—will it ever go away?" They should write these "other" thoughts, as they occur, on the right side of the page, close to the place where the ongoing, narrative thought process was interrupted. (Another idea might be to have students write across a page normally and, as other thoughts occur, to write them down within the flow of the creative text, bracketed by parentheses). They may need a little time on this; it is not an easy thing, at first, to corral your less-focused thoughts when you are supposed to be writing an assignment for class. Tell them to think of it as a sort of freewrite, where everything related to the picture—things they might include in a scene—ends up on one side, and everything else ends up on the other. A lot can be done with this: reading aloud; taking home and working up more polished pieces that incorporate both the scene and the thinking; having pairs of students read one student's piece, with the ongoing scene read in one voice and the other thoughts read in another voice. It gives students a chance to participate in the thinking behind this story, to attempt for themselves, on a small scale, the hard alchemy that takes life and makes it literature.

Metafiction is important for shaping students' thinking, early on, about what they read. It rejects the notion that a story appears, beautiful and coherent, from an author's fertile mind. It teaches vigilance toward the tricks of an author's trade and facilitates creation of the "double mind" necessary for close reading: that of the questioner, the critic, as well as the consumer, the dreamer of somebody else's dream. "An Unwritten Novel" may be challenging and less accessible than contemporary work, but it is worth the effort if students gain a new way to think about what they are reading. By doing so, they manage to feel a bit for themselves how hard and interesting it is to create the three-ring circus of the metafiction.

Work Cited

Woolf, Virginia. "An Unwritten Novel." *The Heath Introduction to Fiction.* Ed. John Clayton. Lexington, MA: D.C. Heath, 1996. 349–58.

13 Structuralism and Edith Wharton's "Roman Fever"

Linda L. Gill
Pacific Union College

Interviewer: *What comes first, the plot?*

John Cheever: *I don't work with plots. I work with intuition, apprehension, dreams, concepts. Characters and events come simultaneously to me. Plots implies narrative and a lot of crap. . . . Of course, one doesn't want to be boring . . . one needs an element of suspense. But a good narrative is a rudimentary structure, rather like a kidney.*

1969 interview

The ideology of liberal humanism, which places great value in the individual and posits a human essence that transcends history and society, underpins the New Critical idea that the literary truth or theme is already there in the text, and thus it is our task to crack its code and pluck out its theme—like the meat from a walnut. Certainly, this is the way most high school and college students approach texts, and just as certainly it is an approach that continues to be useful, valuable, and enriching. However, this ideology and approach are based upon certain premises that need to be questioned rather than assumed. In particular, liberal humanism assumes that we—the subjects reading the text or life—are both central and essential; it assumes that meaning is something we uncover or discover in both a text and in life; and it assumes that, because truth is something that is stable and transcendent, the meaning of a text is stable and transcendent. Structuralism, as formulated by Ferdinand de Saussure and put into practice by Claude Levi-Strauss, introduces a radical rethinking of the way things mean what they mean, for it decenters the human subject, posits meaning as relative, and refuses, therefore, to allow for any transcendent meaning of a text, life, or, for that matter, our own identities.

A wonderful opportunity to teach the alternative vision of structuralism is Edith Wharton's "Roman Fever." Indeed, it is immediately obvious that, in this story predominantly about a power struggle between two women, each woman has meaning only in relationship to the other and, to a lesser degree, to the things around her. The boundaries these women draw in their self-determination and the construction of truth through which they view life are thus possible only in the context of the other. Furthermore, without the other against whom each constructs her identity and her way of seeing life, not only would each woman cease to have any coherent meaning, but there would be no story to tell; Mrs. Ansley and Mrs. Slade would have no biography.

Before teaching a structuralist perspective of "Roman Fever," I introduce students to a few basic tenets of structuralism and suggest why it is such an effective tool for reading a text and, by extension, our own lives and ourselves. Structuralism insists that

1. Transcendent meaning is in the structure of language, or *la langue*, and not in what is communicated, or *la parole*.

2. The basis for this structural meaning revolves around binary oppositions—the relationship that renders relative meaning possible and remains consistent despite variants in particulars.

3. Binary oppositions always experience mediation; that is, binary oppositions are rendered meaningfully coherent through the bridges that connect them.

The practical application of structuralism is to bracket what is said (content, or *parole*), to examine relationships between elements (structure, or *langue*), and, thereby, to isolate the underlying set of laws by which signs are combined into meaning. In short, it determines meaning as a function of relationships. Taking a cue from Levi-Strauss's study of myth, I present the God-Jesus-man relationship as a ready example (most students are familiar with the Christian myth—if they are not Christians themselves). God and man can be seen as binary oppositions. Jesus, simultaneously both God and man and neither God nor man, is the mediator between the two extremes. It is only in the relationship between the three particulars that each has meaning. "But," a student will undoubtedly ask, "What about Literature [capital "L"]?" Why is structuralism a *literary* theory? Does it have any idiosyncracies that make it particularly appropriate for Literature? At this point, we have the first opportunity to apply structuralism to Literature (again the capital "L"). After asking students to list the books they consider—or have been taught to consider—as great or canonical, we discuss the often hidden criteria that inform our lists. Usually we generate a lot of value-laden words (e.g., *good, beautiful, inspiring*) that do not have obvious objective meanings. Such words have meaning only in the context of other corresponding words like *bad, ugly,* and *dull.* And, when we consider their lists of canonical texts relative to those texts that have been left out of the canon, we discover that the canon is predominantly composed of white-Anglo-Saxon-Protestant authors who write of predominantly patriarchal values. In other words, the canon articulates our culture's dominant ideology. By moving us out of our easy complacency in that ideology, structuralism forces us to question how we come to assume the fundamental premises by which we determine who we are and what life means.

In order to view "Roman Fever" through the lens of structuralism, I first ask students to bracket their idea of its theme (*la parole,* or what the text seems to be saying on the manifest level) so that they may examine its underlying structure (*la langue*). This exercise allows them to see how the structure of the story and the relationships between the particulars within the story create its meaning. I then ask the students

1. to mentally graph the story's elements along horizontal and vertical lines (i.e., when are characters or other particulars on the same plane? when is one character or particular above or below another?)

2. to locate all the relational words (i.e., the comparatives and superlatives) and movements (i.e., when does one character move ahead of or follow another? or when does the sun rise or set?)

3. to determine the binary oppositions (i.e., who and what are set up in opposition to each other? and how does this define who or what each is?)

4. to locate the mediation between the binary oppositions (i.e., what is the connecting bridge between the binary oppositions?) and how this relationship defines each particular

5. to reintroduce their earlier bracketed response to the story to determine how the structure of and the relationship within the text inform how they construct what the text means.

Students will immediately notice that, relative to everyone and everything else, Mrs. Ansley and Mrs. Slade occupy the same lofty vertical space. They are above everyone and everything, on a "lofty terrace" looking "down on the outspread glories" of Rome, speaking down to their daughters who have just left them for the court below (472). On the horizontal axis, Mrs. Ansley and Mrs. Slade appear to be equals. They move "across" the terrace together; they look "at each other, and then down" (472). They have lived "across the way" from each other for years (473) and have by chance "run across each other in Rome" (474). Now they "continued to sit side by side" (475).

"Yes, but" someone will note (having learned to read closely), "look at page 476. The 'glories' of Rome have suddenly become a 'great accumulated wreckage of passion and splendor' at Ansley's feet." "And," someone else might add, "It's not altogether clear if Ansley is viewing Rome or Slade when this observation is made." Usually, at this point someone else (thinking in terms of monuments to the past) will call attention to Mrs. Slade's recollection of Mrs. Ansley as a kind of wrecked beauty (473).

While Rome is initially situated beneath the two women in order that the women might be defined as above it—the victors who came, saw, and conquered; sightseers appropriating the other—now the boundaries between Slade/Ansley and Rome (and vice versa) are deliberately blurred. They become metonymically associated with, if not metaphors for, each other. It becomes obvious that Rome and the two women function structurally as parallel and overlapping systems. Mrs. Ansley and Mrs. Slade, at the top of this world, are also of this world. Like the women, Rome, once glorious, once the pinnacle of the world, is now both figuratively and literally falling down. The Forum and the Colosseum are empty, signifiers of past conquerors long rendered obsolete by a new world signified by Italian pilots. "Ah, yes," someone will recall, "The daughters have gone flying with Italian aviators" (473). Indeed. Although Barbara Ansley and Jenny Slade have descended, leaving their mothers to their "air-washed heights" (472), the two girls have descended only in order that they might literally fly. While Mrs. Ansley and Mrs. Slade view the once glorious but crumbling world of the past until it is too dark to see, their daughters soar above them in the new world's latest articulation in order "to fly . . . by moonlight" (473).

The significance of the relationship between day to night and the mothers to their daughters also becomes clear, for it too is a repetition of (what someone in the class will by now observe is) the ascendancy-descendancy structure of the story. At the beginning of the story it is long past noon, the sun is still bright, Rome is still glorious, and the two older women rule over both. But as the story progresses, the "golden light" begins to "pale" (475), there are "lengthening shadows" (476), the sky is "emptied of its gold" (479), and the moon rises along with the two women's daughters. Rome darkens and the women must descend from their pedestal. For all its brilliance, the old world and its generation will be supplanted by the new, just as the sun is supplanted by the moon. And indeed we learn the women no longer even try to "keep up" with their daughters (476); it would be as useless as the sun trying to remain at its apex or a gladiator waging war on a bomber pilot. Apparently, in this story only one particular can be at the top of the vertical axis at a time, and this ascendancy is predicated upon the descent, if not the destruction, of all others.

It is at this point that "Roman Fever" gets particularly interesting. While initially the two women can be seen as having risen and are now in the process of setting together (along with the sun), while they are on the same vertical plane, sitting "side-by-side" on the "lofty" terrace, we become aware that the ascendancy-descendancy structure is repeated once more in the struggle for ascendancy between the two. Like the sun to the moon, like aviators to gladiators, like mothers to daughters, they function in this story as (what should be obvious to everyone by now) binary oppositions. It is through their relationship with each other that they have meaning. Both women are reliant upon being not-the-other in order to give them self-definition. Because Mrs. Slade's point of view is represented in more detail than Mrs. Ansley's, we are made particularly aware that it is only in being not-Mrs. Horace Ansley that she is able to construct her identity. Thus, her whole life, it would seem, has been about one-upping Mrs. Ansley. Students will undoubtedly pick up on all the comparatives used in describing her: that Slade is "fuller, and higher in color" than Ansley (472); that Ansley is "smaller and paler" (472) and "much less articulate than her friend" (474). Furthermore, in marrying Delphin Slade, Mrs. Slade had the more socially and economically significant husband while Mrs. Ansley and her husband were, by comparison and in Slade's language, "nullities" (473). After all, the Ansleys and the Slades "had lived opposite each other—actually as well as figuratively—for years" (473). Mrs. Slade ultimately moves with her husband to upper Park, leaving the Ansleys behind and below (474). Yet, underlying her sense of superiority (which, of course, is an emotion only possible in terms of its relationship to that which is considered inferior), Mrs. Slade is incurably envious ("Would she never cure herself of envying" Mrs. Ansley, she moans [476]), which, of course, is also an emotion that is completely predicated upon relativity: just as one cannot feel superior unless someone else is perceived as inferior, one cannot be envious unless one perceives oneself as inferior to another. In short, if there were not a Mrs. Ansley for Mrs. Slade to be "fuller" than or "higher in color" than, better married than or fight her envy of, Mrs. Slade would cease to exist as Mrs. Slade. It is therefore hardly surprising that, if Mrs. Slade is going to be forced off her pedestal by the next generation, she is only going to do so after she has had the final triumph over Mrs. Ansley, for this last triumph will be a confirmation of her self-construction, a final articulation of who she perceives herself to be.

"But what about Mrs. Ansley?" someone will ask. "She seems sweetly oblivious to the fight for ascendancy which Slade is so invested in."

"In other words," someone else slyly adds, "She seems *above* Slade's fight for ascendancy."

And that is exactly it, isn't it. Mrs. Ansley is above the fracas, or, more particularly, she is above Mrs. Slade. Although she is "much less articulate than her friend," Mrs. Ansley is as implicated in the struggle for ascendancy as Mrs. Slade. It is simply that, in the knowledge that she had been Delphin's first choice and that she had Delphin's child, she is able to feel "sorry" for Slade from the condescending position of the magnanimous (475). Pity is, of course, another emotion that is only possible in terms of relativity: people pity those who are less fortunate than—or beneath—themselves. In other words, perhaps Mrs. Ansley is not initially interested in battling for ascendancy with Mrs. Slade because she perceives herself as having already won. But despite Mrs. Ansley's final triumph, there is one last battle to fight, one more blow she must deliver to maintain her position of ascendancy.

We can trace the struggle for ascendancy between the two women in how their movements parallel the underlying structure of the story as a whole. But first, it is worth looking more closely at the daughters who will supplant the women in the "air-washed heights," for it is in contemplating and fearing that the next generation will repeat her battle with Mrs. Ansley that Mrs. Slade is impelled to wage and win her final battle.

While always having felt herself to be "equal in social gifts" to her husband, on his death Mrs. Slade feels she has undergone "a big drop" (474). Now she must resign herself to living through her descendant's ascendance (474). And here, interestingly enough, we see Mrs. Slade applying what amounts to structuralist methodology to the Babs Ansley–Jenny Slade relationship. Just as she herself has done, Mrs. Slade wants her daughter to ascend in the social world through marriage, in this case to the young aviator who is a Marchese, but Mrs. Slade also realizes that her "Jenny has no chance beside" Babs Ansley: "I wonder if that's why Grace Ansley likes the two girls to go everywhere together? My poor Jenny as a foil—!"(476). While her Jenny has wings—for she is an "angel"—Babs has "rainbow" wings and can, therefore, fly more brilliantly (476). Babs, in Mrs. Slade's words, "was more effective—had more edge" (473). Exasperated and envious, refusing to allow

Mrs. Ansley this final triumph, Mrs. Slade stands up while the serene Mrs. Ansley continues to sit and knit (476). (At this point, we may hope that a student will note that the "afternoon and evening hang balanced in midheaven" [477]. Again we are made aware of the parallel and overlapping structures in the story.) This is a moment of truth: the moment of precarious balance between the two women as well as between day and night. It is the moment when Mrs. Slade determines that if she, like the sun, is to descend it will not be until she has crushed Mrs. Ansley beneath her feet. It is when Mrs. Slade, towering over Mrs. Ansley, who has dropped her knitting and is now looking up at Mrs. Slade, tells Mrs. Ansley she knows about the letter that her then-future husband Delphin Slade had supposedly written to Mrs. Ansley to beckon her to a dangerous and nonexisting tryst (478). Mrs. Ansley, roused from her easy complacency, responds by rising "unsteadily to her feet" (478); she "steadie[s]" herself, but, when Mrs. Slade reveals that she not only knows about the letter but had written it as well, Mrs. Ansley "drop[s]" back into her chair, seemingly defeated (478). As Mrs. Slade continues, towering above Mrs. Ansley, Mrs. Ansley's head droops and then "droop[s] again," and Mrs. Slade, looking down on her rival notes that Mrs. Ansley "seemed physically reduced by the blow" (479). Mrs. Slade, triumphant, now "leaning above her" rests in her victory (479); now it is her turn to offer the decidedly inferior and decidedly defeated rival words of patronizing and smugly condescending pity (479). But the battle is not over: Mrs. Ansley, seemingly down for the count, regains equivalency by turning slowly toward her companion and revealing that she had written back to Delphin and he had indeed met her. Mrs. Slade springs up (480), but it is the final leap of the mortally wounded. Mrs. Ansley, on the other hand, easily rises and then reveals that Babs is the product of her tryst with Delphin; she then, significantly, "move[s] ahead" of Mrs. Slade to the stairway (480). In this world, where only one particular can be at the apex, where only one particular can be at the forefront, Ansley is clearly the victor.

"So," someone will ask, "What is the mediator between the binary oppositions? Is it Rome? The Letter? Babs?"

The mediators are, of course, all these things, for they all function as the objects through which the two women are connected; it is through them that they wage war on each other in the never-ending struggle for power and ascendancy that defines them. Perhaps, however, the most obvious mediating bridge between the two women is Delphin Slade, for it is he who most clearly defines the parameters of Mrs. Slade and Mrs. Ansley's battle and therefore each woman's sense of self. Mrs. Slade has felt justified in casting herself as the superior woman in her relationship with Mrs. Ansley (even while she has also been incurably envious), because in the battle between the two over Delphin she had won him as a husband. However, in discovering that Delphin had not only met Mrs. Ansley on the fated night at the Colosseum but is also the father of Mrs. Ansley's child, Mrs. Slade undergoes another "drop." She is now literally as well as figuratively passed up by Mrs. Ansley. The forged letter, another object functioning as a mediating bridge between the two women, had been Mrs. Slade's attempt to get Mrs. Ansley permanently out of the way, leaving the prized Delphin Slade (and later his memory) to herself. But, of course, while Mrs. Slade marries Delphin, Babs— Delphin and Mrs. Ansley's rainbow-winged child, the child who easily out-flies Delphin and Mrs. Slade's—is the permanent signifier of Mrs. Ansley's relationship with Delphin—a bridge, a legacy, that signifies Ansley's permanent position at the apex of every overlapping triangular structure that defines the two women's relationship and their identities. Thus, even after Delphin dies, Mrs. Slade and Mrs. Ansley are locked in a relationship that continues to give each their definition. Unfortunately it continues to be one of rivalry and power and only one can come out of the battle victorious.

In returning to our initial, general discussion of structuralism, undoubtedly someone will ask whether in the world of the structuralist it is possible to be a self-contained, autonomous subject who does not rely upon others in order to give one self-definition. The answer is, of course, no. Wharton's story demands that we face this fact. It demands that we ask ourselves to what extent we rely on the defeat of others in order that we might have self-esteem. To what extent do we define ourselves in terms of the rich husband we snag or the beautiful woman on our arm? To what extent is our own sense empowerment predicated upon the disempowerment of others? Sometimes, the answers to such questions can be truly numbing.

Work Cited

Wharton, Edith. "Roman Fever." *Literature: An Introduction to Fiction, Poetry, and Drama.* Ed. X. J. Kennedy. 5th ed. New York: HarperCollins, 1991. 472–80.

Further Reading

Eagleton, Terry. *Literary Theory: An Introduction.* Minneapolis: U of Minnesota P, 1983.

Guerin, Wilfred L., et al. *A Handbook of Critical Approaches to Literature.* 3rd ed. New York: Oxford UP, 1992.

Levi-Strauss, Claude. "The Structural Study of Myth." Trans. Claire Jacobson. *European Literary Theory and Practice: From Existential Phenomenology to Structuralism.* Ed. Vernon W. Gras. New York: Dell, 1973. 289–316.

IV Encountering Other Perspectives

I am not sure that I have methods in composition. I do suppose I have—I suppose I must have—but they somehow refuse to take shape in my mind; their details refuse to separate and submit to classification and description; they remain a jumble—visible, like the fragments of glass when you look in at the wrong end of a kaleidoscope, but still a jumble. If I could turn the whole thing around and look in at the other end, why then the figures would flash into form out of the chaos and I shouldn't have any more trouble.

Mark Twain, "The Art of Authorship"

The teachers of this section demand increasing independence of students. No one, after all, benefits when teachers erect elaborate intellectual scaffoldings that students do not know how to construct by themselves. Whether students passively enjoy the construction or actively adopt the teacher's methods, the effort is wasted. Waste, for the teachers of this book, is a kind of pedagogical crime. For them, it is solipsistic as well as pedagogically backwards for teachers to assume that students must be prodded through the maze of the text. What is at stake here is the decanonization of the teacher's theoretical bias. Kathleen McCormick, in her book *The Culture of Reading and the Teaching of English*, suggests that behind teachers' reluctance to encourage their students' theoretical entrepreneurship lies the fear of lost authority. Writes McCormick, "the canonizing approach is the least threatening to the teacher because it discourages students from putting the teacher's authority into question" (189). In other words, at the heart of the decanonization is the question, "Who serves whom in the classroom?"

In using short stories, the teachers of this section turn the spotlight on their students. In that process, students, as well as teachers, must recognize that our interpretations are the products of our own biases, experiences, and theories—an insight that we largely owe to current literary theory. For their part, students discover both the uncertainty and the power behind theory, thereby freeing them to forge critical tools of their own. This kind of teaching objective, of course, changes the ways we teach, and that prospect is risky and likely to unsettle us. Regardless, the teachers here seek to de-objectify pat interpretations, to de-stabilize certainty, and to encourage students' confidence. As a result, they are all far more concerned with pedagogical strategies than with brilliant interpretations. While not uninterested in their own theories, they remain nonjudgmental toward those of their students—so long as students articulate their approaches and compare the results against other legitimate ones.

The classroom that builds on the generic issues presented in Part Three generates competent interpretation. Competence is not a matter of formulae or doctrines, and, in the essays that follow, multiple critical perspectives are offered. Critical theory is made provisional, a method promoted by Harvard psychology professor Ellen J. Langer as a necessary antecedent to mindful learning, learning that actually gets incorporated into a student's own value system. Russell Shipp, for instance, withholds his own interpretation of Rawlings's "Mother in Mannville" until after his middle school students have mastered using a rigorous method of identifying a story's theme; the process demands posing multiple interpretations and gauging them against the main elements of the story. Dennis Young asks his students to pose their own questions about Plato's "Myth of the Cave" and then to answer the questions of their fellow students. The exercise tempers student response to this allegorical story. Lawrence Pruyne arbitrarily assigns his students specific critical responses to "Cinderella" in order to demonstrate how various interpretive strategies illuminate one then another aspect of this seemingly simple tale. And, in the same spirit, Dianne Fallon refuses to allow her students to settle upon one facile interpretation of Gilman's "The Yellow Wallpaper." She enforces this condition by asking students to adopt the position of a character in the story and to examine several published interpretations of the story through that character's eyes.

Works Cited

Langer, Ellen J. *The Power of Mindful Learning.* Reading, MA: Addison-Wesley, 1997.

McCormick, Kathleen. *The Culture of Reading and the Teaching of English.* Manchester: Manchester UP, 1994.

Twain, Mark. "The Art of Authorship." 1890. *Selected Shorter Writings of Mark Twain.* Ed. Walter Blair. Boston: Houghton Mifflin, 1962. 225–26.

14 Creating Independent Analyzers of the Short Story with Rawlings's "A Mother in Mannville"

Russell Shipp
Iroquois Middle School, Niskayuna, New York

To put it bluntly: no conflict, no story.
    Robert Penn Warren, "Why Do We Read Fiction?"

My aim in teaching the short story is to give students a technique that they can use to probe a story on their own, without depending on a teacher or on the questions that anthology texts provide. The process is very systematic, with a built-in starting place regardless of the story. Readers progress through several basic steps that culminate in their framing fairly sophisticated questions and even tentative answers to those questions.

The short stories with which I have worked have all been those that even the practiced reader might misunderstand. My technique, in fact, is most successful in plumbing the depths of stories whose secrets lie well hidden, although it is equally applicable to stories that are less obscure. Here, though, I will focus on Marjorie Kinnan Rawlings's "A Mother in Mannville," a story that may be interpreted on different levels. First, the story is somewhat autobiographical. Before writing it, Rawlings had recently undergone an amicable divorce. On the surface, the story seems to be a curious portrayal of a boy who, in a sense, secures his integrity by lying. This is food enough for discussion, and perhaps for this reason readers have not been encouraged to probe further. However, it turns out that the boy represents another individual in the narrator's life, referred to ever so briefly when she says, while musing about the boy's integrity, "there's another whom I am almost sure . . ." (3). At the end of the story, the narrator learns through the boy that it is within the realm of a man with integrity to lie about how much he really needs her.

In approaching short stories, I assume that each story has a major problem or conflict between two forces, A and B. At some point at or near the end of the story, the outcome will determine which force proves to be the stronger. Thus, the last significant event should give the story closure. This effect is often created through an action, but it need not be. Sometimes, it is merely a revelation about the way things are, without focusing on a particular action. In order to get a rough idea of the likely forces involved in the conflict, we may, hypothetically, reverse the outcome. Because the stronger force determines the last significant event, it follows that, if the opposite force had been stronger, an opposite outcome would have ensued. These two forces, then, are stated as a tentative conflict, worded only roughly. If more than one possibility for the last significant event is possible, two or more hypothetical statements of conflict are needed.

With a rough definition of conflict or conflicts etched out, students should look at the title and generate as many possible meanings for it as can be imagined. Sometimes, an eye on the wording of the conflict will add some ideas. The next step should be a close analysis of the first one or two paragraphs—after all, authors of short stories often fashion beginnings that have a very relevant bearing on the nature of the conflict. Last, the most important, involved, and fascinating part of this method for short-story lovers is the process of questioning and brainstorming about peculiarities. Although some stories are certainly written more loosely than others, one can safely assume that authors purposely choose to include certain details and to word their stories to suit a particular objective. Questioning the purpose of unusual inclusions or unusual wordings often sparks fascinating insights. Once they probe such peculiarities, students, in many cases, will then be able to make more sense of the title, the beginning paragraphs, and the conflict. Sometimes their refined sense of the conflict varies considerably from their first attempt, a discrepancy that allows them not only to focus on theme but to consider the role emotions play in reading.

My eighth-grade students practiced with four or five stories throughout the year. As a final test, they were asked to apply their skills to "A Mother in Mannville." Below are two student test responses (with technical errors unchanged), followed by my own reaction to the story that I later gave as a model that might be useful to them in high school.

Student #1

The last significant event in the story A Mother in Mannville is when the narrator finds out that Jerry doesn't have a mother, and he doesn't have skates. The conflict of the story, in my opinion is the events leading up to the narrator discovering this towards [versus] the events leading up to the narrator not discovering this. Or the conflict could be the events having the narrator leave Jerry versus the events letting her leave him there not even knowing what happened to him on his trip.

In the first paragraph we learn how the orphanage boys hands are stiff in agony with numbness, Why? It also says that they take the milk to the baby cottage twice daily, why? Maybe the author is saying that these boys are workers and men and can handle this, but then when Jerry came she stated that he was not a man like she expected to get from the orphanage. Then when she saw him she said that she did not even think he was a boy. Maybe this has something to do with the title "A Mother in Mannville." Mannville, why Manville? Maybe this has something to do with the author, thinking Jerry is not a man. Or more probably it has something to do with Jerry wanting to be a Man because anyone whose mother was from Manville was a man. Getting back to his mother, not only was she supposed to be from a place called Mannville but she was also supposed to have large hands, which we learned when hearing of her glove size. Why also did he want to make her gloves? And why white ones? In the beginning of the story he also talked of white, this was when talking of the trees maybe Jerry considered mother nature to be his mother. But in the beginning it is very peculiar because the narrator says that she loves the mountains, and the very best things are the corn shocks and black-walnut trees. Why would she like the corn stalk with no corn instead of with corn, and why would the author make Jerry's hair the color of corn shocks?

Later in the story Jerry tells how he received skates from his mother. Maybe he is saying that he really wanted skates and has always dreamt for them. I think he is saying that he wishes he had a mother and lived in Mannville were he could skate, in the country he can't do this.

I think the theme of the story is that Jerry is getting the narrator to become his dream mother. After all, he got the puppy that he wished for, which was Pat, he even got a adult who cared deeply for him. He even got someone to give him presents. But in the very end the narrator says that this was a good orphanage which is contradicting her first statement in which the boys all are getting frost bitten hands. Also in the end the boy goes off to the white laurels, laurels were thought of as holy in Mediterranean times and you'd be crowned by a laurel wreath, maybe he is going off to find his mother, and will not return after finding out that the narrator who was his acting mother is leaving.

Student #2

The last significant event of the story is when Miss Clark, the woman at the orphanage, informs the narrator that Jerry has no mother, and there were no skates.

Now assuming this is the correct last significant event we can establish the outline of the conflict. It could be: circumstances that would further the narrator's notion that Jerry has a mother vs circumstances that would allow the narrator to learn Jerry has no mother.

Let us examine the title. A Mother in Mannville, why does the author choose to use a mother? Why not father? or uncle or grandmother? Maybe the author is referring to a similar experience of her own which involves a mother.

Usually the first paragraph yields a clue to the conflict. In this case the first paragraph talks of an orphanage in the Carolina mountains. Then it discusses that "sometimes in winter the snow drifts are so deep that the institution is cut off from the village below, from all the world." What does this mean? Why does the author include this? Possibly the institution would include Jerry and the other kids like him and the village, the people. Jerry and the other kids in the orphanage are isolated from all people, and from all the world.

Let us move to the peculiarities. In the next paragraph it talks about children's faces getting frostbit because they cannot protect them with their hands because they are busy. Why does the author use these examples? Could it symbolize something? Maybe that children in this world often are thrown out into the cold and are ignored, and they themselves cannot protect themselves.

Then it discusses how Jerry calls the rhododendron blooming in the mountains laurel. Why is this included? It is unimportant. Why can't he just call it rhododendron? Another meaning for laurel is to be honored, awed, or given special attention to. Jerry loves these laurels. Maybe this symbolizes the attention or love that he yearns for.

The narrator, in the beginning of the story refers that the mountains near the orphanage bring him back to his roots. Why is this included? Maybe the narrator can relate to Jerry? Looking at Jerry may remind him of his own childhood.

Then the narrator says Jerry has a brand of integrity that is special. He has never seen it as clearly on anybody else. Why is this included? Why wasn't a different quality mentioned? Could it be that Jerry, representing orphans, develop while they are isolated from the world a special integrity?

Clearly these examples do not show the polished language that students can create when they have time to revise their work. Note, however, the students' reasonably systematic approach and the quality of their questions and tentative responses. When they have had much more practice, they will have a good shot at analyzing stories that continue to baffle many teachers. The following is my own analysis of "A Mother in

Mannville," which I shared with my students after they had finished theirs.

* * * * *

The last line of the story reads, "'I don't understand,' she said. 'He has no mother. He has no skates.'" The conflict could be stated, the circumstance that would lead the narrator to discover that Jerry had no mother and no skates versus circumstances that would lead the narrator not to make the discovery or to learn he did have a mother and skates.

The title is very perplexing. Looking for the possible referents for *mother*, we have the following: the fictitious individual Jerry invented; the narrator in her relationship to Jerry; the narrator in her relationship to someone else; and Miss Clark, who has charge of the orphanage. What does *Mannville* suggest? Does it hint "a place for men"? Does the narrator learn something about men here? Does it imply that the narrator does not belong here? Is it an actual place? It's not listed in the Almanac. It was probably made up.

The first paragraph tells us that the orphanage is high in the Carolina mountains and that sometimes the winter snowdrifts "cut it off from the village below, from all the world. Fog hides the mountain peaks, the snow swirls down the valleys, and a wind blows so bitterly that the orphanage boys who take milk twice daily to the baby cottage reach the door with fingers stiff in an agony of numbness." The second paragraph goes on to talk of the cold and numbness. Look for figurative language here. What expressions might be interpreted in more than one way? How about the imagery of coldness? Is someone given a "cold treatment" in the story? How about being cut off, alone, isolated? Is either the boy or the narrator cut off and isolated? "Fog hides. . . ." Is something hidden in the story? Are mountain peaks goals or accomplishments or symbols of nobility or just mountain peaks? Why include the business of taking milk twice daily? Are the orphans being mothers? Should we interpret "numbness" as "unfeeling" or "callous" or "insensitive"? "Reach the door" could mean "get to a place where there is warmth," but it's hard to open because of the numbness? Could bitterly cold wind represent cruel things that are said? The important thing is not necessarily to find answers right away but to understand that the author sometimes talks directly to the reader in metaphorical language, and, if we are to pick up the message that could be there, we need to experiment with metaphorical possibilities.

Next, consider the peculiarities of the other paragraphs. Notice, in the third paragraph, the way the narrator talks about the rhododendron in the mountainside and, then in a separate sentence, says, "He called it laurel." This gives more emphasis to the word *laurel* than the author really needs if she is simply offering some background scenery. It would have been simpler to say "laurel" instead of rhododendron in the first place. Notice that the author has gone out of her way for some reason. *Rhododendron* and *laurel* refer pretty much to the same plant, but *laurel* has a meaning other than the plant. Laurel is a well-established symbol of victory or distinction. We would do well, then, to look for some kind of victory or distinction in one or more of the characters here.

Other peculiarities abound.

We understand that the narrator wanted isolation, that she had "to do some troublesome writing." Why "troublesome"? Wouldn't it be enough to justify her seeking isolation just to say she wanted to do some writing? Again, one needs to be suspicious when the author doesn't choose the simplest route. Do we need to find out what is troublesome? Do we need to know what was on the narrator's mind when she came to the mountains?

We learn that she is homesick from being in the subtropics and that the cabin she is renting reminds her of home. Is there something about her home that she has been thinking about and troubled by?

In reference to her dog, she calls it a "pointer dog." Did the author pick the word "pointer" for a particular reason? Does the dog point to something important?

At the orphanage she asked for a boy or a man to cut the wood. Why not just say "boy"? Is her asking for a man connected with the title?

Why does she compare his dropping wood to a consistent rain? Is it merely because of the rhythmic sound or does rain suggest something cleansing? When Jerry has cut wood the first time and the narrator first notices how much wood he had cut, she exclaims, "But you've done as much as a man." This is another reference to man. He shows a very adult-like responsibility. Is there any more to it than that? She is very impressed with his work and gives him twenty-five cents, a very substantial amount for a boy in 1936 when the story was written. As he is ready to leave, he tells her "I'll split kindling tomorrow.... You'll need kindling and medium wood and logs and backlogs." What is curious about this is that it's his idea, not hers, as though he were looking after her on his own.

When the narrator begins to talk about integrity, she says, "My father had it—there is another whom I am almost sure—but almost no man of my acquaintance possesses it with clarity, the purity, the simplicity of a mountain stream." Why do we need to know about her father and this mysterious other who had integrity like Jerry's? Is she pining for someone? Biographical data on the author will tell you that she was divorced three years before the story was written. Is that relevant here? Could she be thinking about some regrets? Also, why compare someone's integrity to a mountain stream? Recall, in the first paragraph, that the author talked about how "the snow swirls down the valleys." Is this not potentially a mountain stream?

Jerry's adult sense of responsibility is built in each successive paragraph. He waits for her to finish her typing. He knows not to interrupt and she, in her attention to her writing, forgets about him. It's as if he takes better care of her than she of him.

Why are the episodes with the dog necessary? They play hide and seek. The dog is a pointer and finds what? What is hidden that is embodied in Jerry?

The boy seems to seek her out as though he prizes her companionship, but, at one point, the narrator tells us, "The dog lay close to him, and found a comfort there that I did not have for him. And it seemed to me that being with my dog, and caring for him, had brought the boy and me, too, together, so that he felt that he belonged to me as well as to the animal." We gather the narrator is like a mother to him here.

The dog that brings them together is curious. Does the boy's relationship with the dog in any way parallel the relationship between the boy and the narrator? Do we see a loyalty in the dog as it stays with the boy that the boy has for the narrator? Can we justify the dog's existence in the story? Perhaps the author wants the boy to hang around in some capacity other than working for the narrator so that some kind of communion has a chance to develop. Perhaps the author doesn't want the reader to think that the narrator would be likely to encourage him to hang around for no other reason than to be with her. Having the dog there is sort of an excuse for having the boy hang around without her having the responsibility of entertaining him. The dog gives the boy an excuse to be near the narrator without having to admit it's the narrator he wants to be with.

What does it mean when the narrator says, "He was suddenly impelled to speak of things he had not spoken of before, nor had I cared to ask him." How do we take the words "nor had I cared"? Is she trying to keep him at arm's length because she knows she will have to leave soon?

Apparently Jerry invents a lie about his mother so that the narrator will not take pity on him. We see her full of deep resentment that his mother could leave him, could put him in an orphanage. Why is this resentment so necessary? We know from this that she has lots of heart, but, at the same time, the reader, and perhaps the boy as well, can see that her writing is her priority and she is reluctant to give too much of herself to anything outside her writing. Jerry does not want to be a nuisance, does not want to interfere with the narrator's peace of mind. The lie allows her the freedom to ignore him if she wishes. At least she won't give him attention simply because she feels sorry for him. Perhaps this is part of the integrity she noted earlier in regard to the ax handle. He wouldn't allow her to be inconvenienced on his account.

Jerry invents not only a mother but also items that his imaginary mother gave him or wanted to give him: a puppy, a suit, and skates. Why these items? Could he have brought up the issue of the dog so that she wouldn't feel bad about not wanting to give him her dog? Why, though, the suit and skates? Consistent with his not wanting to invite her pity, perhaps he wants her to think he has adequate clothing and things to do to entertain himself.

He says he is going to use the dollar his mother gave him to buy his mother gloves. Then they have a discussion about the size. Did the author have Jerry mention gloves in order to discuss size? He says he thinks she wears an 8 1/2 and she replies that she wears a size 6. Is the message from the author, perhaps, that the narrator is not "big" enough to be his mother? Or is this meant to be a man's size? "Mannville" seems to suggest a place for men and maybe she doesn't measure up.

The narrator's reaction to the dialogue is to hate the mother because Jerry is wanting to do things for his mother and the mother is returning so little, nothing but skates. If this is a parallel to Jerry and the narrator, is the author trying to tell us that the narrator is given much but returns little? Jerry gives a lot to keep the fires burning and looks after her path so that she doesn't trip along the way. Can this be generalized to mean he gives her warmth and protection and she gives him the dog to play with—skates, as it were—something to occupy him but not too much of herself.

The narrator states she will not leave the mountain without seeing Jerry's mother and learning why she can't be a real mother. If the narrator is the substitute mother, is the author saying to the reader that she will not leave the mountains before she understands herself a little better and why she had done whatever it was she did that may have something to do with the "troublesome writing"?

The narrator's next sentence is very strange indeed: "The human mind scatters its interests as though made of thistledown, and every wind stirs and moves it." Does this mean she has difficulty settling down with family life because there are too many things she wants to do? What else could it mean?

Why the reference to "Mexican material"? Is this some insight into the author's own private concerns that have to do with Mexico that we could not possibly know without considerable background on the author, or is it relevant to what is happening between Jerry and the narrator, or is it simply some place far, far away? The narrator mentions closing her Florida place. How is this pertinent to the story? Marjorie Rawlings really did have a place in Florida. Could this be a hint about the real underlying conflict in the story, a conflict well hidden? From Mexico she goes to Alaska to see her brother and after that she didn't know. She's a drifter. It could be she is giving us reason to understand why she couldn't possibly adopt Jerry, couldn't be his mother. But this doesn't answer all the references to "man."

Despite the anguish the narrator had shown earlier, she tells us she is relieved that he has a mother, however strange their relationship may be. Jerry's unique, manly integrity was apparently successful in not allowing her to feel too inconvenienced, too guilty for not being able to do much for him herself.

The narrator states she is ready to go after he has taken her "vermilion maple leaves" and "chestnut boughs of imperial yellow." The narrator sought the place in the mountains because the colors reminded her of home and she was homesick after being in the tropics, but now he brings her some of these colored leaves and she decides she is ready to go. Why? Also, why can't she simply notice these colors in the hills? Why does the author have Jerry bring the reminders of homesickness? Does Jerry remind her of someone that she is homesick for?

The narrator tells about her packing and making arrangements to leave. Included in all this is "arranging the bed over the seat, where the dog would ride." Why tell us about the dog? She can understand and deal with the comforts of her dog, perhaps, but not Jerry and/or the other man he may remind her of.

Why have Miss Clark tell the narrator that Jerry "was supposed to fire the boiler" that afternoon. Couldn't she simply say he took a walk? How is the boiler significant? It provides warmth, as did the wood he cut for the narrator. Are we to understand that he is too hurt by her going to want to provide any warmth?

The narrator doesn't get to see him and says she's relieved because she found it difficult to say good bye. But she has enough compassion to leave money so that Miss Clark can get him something for Christmas and his birthday. Jerry is doubtlessly pretty unhappy, but it would be difficult to be too hard on the narrator. She has not come across as a cold individual. She has been quite occupied with her work, but that's why she came to the mountains in the first place. We can't really blame her for not inviting Jerry to live with her. We're sorry that Jerry doesn't have a mother but that's not the narrator's fault.

Then the narrator learns that Jerry doesn't have a mother or skates. How would the narrator likely have behaved differently had she known he didn't have a mother? Would she feel differently toward him, toward herself, or about whatever reasons brought her there to begin with? It doesn't seem likely it would have changed much the contact she had with Jerry nor her decision to go, by herself, when she did. Indeed, what effect on the narrator are we to understand? She was fooled. So what? It's not likely the author simply set up the narrator to be disappointed in Jerry. What if, though, she suddenly realizes that a "man" of real integrity could fool her? He will not only look after her in the obvious ways and take responsibility for the mishaps, but will, also, go out of his way to make sure he has not invited pity or caused inconvenience. Perhaps the narrator will get in her car, after having talked with Miss Clark, and begin to realize fully that Jerry had indeed become dependent on her, wanted someone to look after him like a mother. Perhaps, then, this other man, to whom she barely made any reference, had also fooled her. Maybe he needed her a lot more than she realized, and he had too much integrity, like Jerry, to interfere with what he perceived she wanted. The author Rawlings had only recently been divorced when the story was written. Quite likely the author, like the narrator, is reconsidering what is a man of integrity. Perhaps her other man led her to believe he, too, had "skates," things he had that occupied him, when actually he was aching for motherly warmth and companionship.

The conflict stated so roughly at the outset may now be revisited. The detailed study of peculiarities indicates that the narrator is becoming aware of other ways that a "man" could manifest integrity ("manville"), and that a form of deception might not be incongruent with integrity. The theme would then be something like this: In the milieu of a man with real integrity is a pride that will tend to veil the depth of emotional dependence, a selflessness intended to minimize the inconveniences of the loved one.

Again, although I'm convinced this interpretation has substance, my aim is to provide only an example of the kind of thoughtfulness that students must bring to any story that they encounter.

Work Cited

Rawlings, Marjorie Kinnan. "A Mother in Mannville." *Twenty Grand: Great American Short Stories*. Ed. Ernestine Taggard. New York: Bantam, 1976. 1–8.

15 Plato's "Myth of the Cave" and the Pursuit of Knowledge

Dennis Young
George Mason University

If a writer of prose knows enough about what he is writing about he may omit things that he knows and the reader, if the writer is writing truly enough, will have a feeling of those things as strongly as though the writer had stated them. The dignity of movement of an ice-berg is due to only one-eighth of it being above water.

Ernest Hemingway, *Death in the Afternoon*

Plato's banishment of the poets from his ideal political state may be one of the greatest of literary ironies. The often anthologized "Myth [or Allegory] of the Cave," from Book VII of *The Republic,* displays Plato's genius for poetically representing his ideas in lively and unforgettable dialogues. In particular, the "Myth of the Cave" (hereafter, "Myth") furnishes a wonderfully succinct introduction to Plato's doctrine of Ideas or Forms, his notion of the good and the beautiful, his belief in the soul and virtue, and his view of education and the attainment of knowledge. Amazingly, Plato does it all in about five pages. That students stand to gain by knowing Plato's ideas can hardly be debated. Indeed, Alfred North Whitehead once wrote that all Western philosophy could be read as a "series of footnotes to Plato" (39). Beyond giving an accessible entry to Plato's world, the "Myth" is an excellent springboard for students to write about their own philosophy of education.

From Darkness to Light

Plato's "Myth" defies literary classification: it is at once story, dialogue, allegory, myth, riddle, exposition, philosophical debate, and poetic figure. Part of its appeal is the drama, the story developing in the heat of engaged discussion. Socrates typically investigates ideas and reality by letting the other person ask and eventually answer his questions, thus leading his students to a real and immediate understanding of truth. The Socratic method, also called the "midwifery" of Socrates, strives to

[margin notes: good + beautiful / soul + virtue / education + the attainment of knowledge / Plato's beliefs]

extract truth from Socrates' counterparts in dialogue, with the ultimate aim of giving birth to ideas and truth.

The opening line of "Myth" announces its concern about how human nature is "enlightened or unenlightened" (205). The metaphorical "enlighten" calls for interpretation, immediately suggesting illumination, flashing, shining, and light—all images of the understanding psyche. More accurately, though, the original Greek word, *Paideia* (and *apaideusia*), means at once enlightenment, education, civilization, culture, knowledge of the good. More encompassing and richer than the English translation, *Paideia* thus implies that the enlightened individual constitutes the life blood of a culture. Throughout *The Republic*, Plato insists that the primary role of the state is the education and enlightenment of its citizens, for without enlightened citizens the body politic rapidly degenerates.

In the "Myth," Plato illustrates the difference between authentic (enlightened) and illusory (unenlightened) knowledge with a striking image: prisoners, who "have been there since childhood" (205), are chained to the wall of an underground cave where they can never turn around to see the light of a fire that is higher up and at a distance behind them. The prisoners mistake for real the shadows of marionettes (puppets and wooden animals) that pass in front of the light. When one of the prisoners escapes, he leaves the cave by way of a steep ascent, entering the world outside and glimpsing reality. The prisoner gradually adapts to the sun's dazzling brightness and understands the world as it is. However, when he returns to the cave's world of shadows, the man faces the ridicule of those who still see only shadows.

The great task facing the prisoner-philosopher (that is, all of us) is to emerge from the cave of ephemeral shadows and bring the darkened mind back into light, the true source of being. Light, truth, and goodness are continuously linked. The idea of the Good is to the intelligible realm what the sun is to the visible realm: in the same way that the sun allows growth and visibility, so does the Good grant to all objects of reason their existence and their intelligibility. Knowledge thus brings harmony between the human soul and the cosmic order, an order governed and illumined by the supreme idea of the Good.

The Cave and the Classroom

I have found that students enjoy reading the "Myth," for its allegorical form demands "translating" into language that makes sense to each reader. Perhaps because of its riddle-like quality and its fantastic mythic world, students find it imaginatively and intellectually appealing. Plato's story leads to a world that we all somehow know. Because most students have felt the bite of oppression and the desire for liberation and understanding, they quickly recognize the cave as the world of illusion and distorted thought. The image of chains binding prisoners (reminiscent of Blake's "mind-forg'd manacles" in his poem "London") strengthens the idea of restricted thought. Removing these chains requires "conversion" of thought through education. Curiously, the word "conversion" means, literally, "leading out" (Latin: *ex* = "out"; *ducere* = "lead").

To help students get a handle on Plato's image, I first ask them to work together in groups to draw a picture of the scene. This picture should include the prisoners in the cave, the figurines or marionettes, the fire, the parapet, and the steep rugged ascent out of the cave. The last image to draw is the sun outside the cave. (The exercise, I imagine, brings back memories of third-grade picture-drawing sessions.) Almost invariably, one student or another reveals his or her artistic talents, impressing the class with a vivid, amazingly detailed picture. We discuss the pictures, pointing to inconsistencies and possible omissions while, of course, applauding excellences. In all, the drawing session (at least partially) demystifies Plato's complex ideas, establishing a basis for our discussion and an image to interpret.

What does this unusual imagistic story mean? How can we make sense of it? I ask students to write out at least three questions they have about the "Myth." The class discussion turns on several of these student questions, some of which follow:

> If the animal figures or marionettes represent the illusion of reality, what do the shadows represent?
>
> Who are the people carrying the animal figurines or marionettes?
>
> What might the "steep and rugged ascent" out of the cave represent; why is it "steep and rugged"?
>
> What does Socrates mean when he says that the soul enacts a conversion?
>
> In what way is the sun an appropriate image of reality, authentic knowledge, and truth?
>
> Is everyone capable of achieving authentic truth or are only the choice philosophers privileged?
>
> What makes the soul different from the self?

Student questions like these, frequently sophisticated and complex, initiate engaged and lively discussion. Plato's notion of soul is particularly vexing, for today we tend to think of humans as having a body and a mind. Soul for Plato, however, is central to education and knowledge:

he writes, "the power and capacity of learning exists in the soul already" (209). As such, learning may be imagined as a recovery of the pristine state of the soul and all its original knowledge; those "professors of education are wrong," Plato says, who think that "they can put knowledge into the soul which was not there before, like sight into blind eyes" (209). The learner enacts a "conversion" from the state of mystified and darkened knowledge to remember the light of day, "the true day of being." One student succinctly and perceptively summed up our discussion: "The soul and the mind do not have the same memory."

Through true *seeing*, the soul gains access to the truth of both world and soul. Given this idea, the discussion may turn to the metaphorical implications of "light" and "seeing" as we recall ways that these words are used to indicate intellectual awareness: "Can you shed *light* on this matter?"; "Can you *see* my point?"; "Do you *see* what I mean?"; and "I *saw* the *light*." The familiar idea that "the eyes are the windows to the soul" hits home, for to see something is to appropriate its essence without bodily contact. "Sight is the beginning of knowledge; without it, wisdom can be only rudimentary. Metaphors of education as conversion and ascent are linked by the metaphors of light and seeing. For example, such expressions as "Let me illustrate an idea" (Latin *in* = "in," *lustrare* = "to make bright") reveal that seeing, light, and learning are mutually reinforcing.

Writing, Dialogue, and Discovery

To increase the personal meaning of Plato's "Myth" for students, I use two assignments. The first asks them to work collaboratively, articulating and answering questions they have about the text; the second prompts them to apply Plato's ideas to their own lives. Because of its collaborative nature, the first assignment is especially useful before and during class discussions of the "Myth." Students are requested to reflect on their reading and then write a 200- to 300-word note (about a page) to a classmate in which they describe some aspect of the text that they are having trouble understanding—a specific area they are having difficulty interpreting or fully comprehending. I tell them in the assignment, "You should make distinctions where you can—that is, describe what you do understand and what you don't. You should refer to one or more particular passages in the book where you are experiencing difficulty. Provide a context for what you don't understand—so your reader can see your difficulties and thereby give you some assistance."

With this exercise, I intend to help students clarify their thinking about the text as well as describe particular problems to a classmate that they really want to know more about.

The second part of the same assignment asks students to take the notes classmates have given them and consider them carefully, review "Myth" and our class discussions about it, and then respond to their classmates with thoughtful notes of explanation and exploration. I ask that students explain what they can, and where they are not sure of particular aspects themselves to explore reasonable possibilities. Again, my hope from this assignment is that students will not only help each other understand and gain a better critical appreciation of Plato's "Myth" but that, in constructing their responses, they will learn more about the text. By writing to another classmate, students collaboratively interpret the text at the same time that they engage in the activity of dialogue so highly prized by Plato and Socrates.

My second writing assignment calls for students to (re)consider Plato's "Myth" in terms of their own experiences as "truth-seekers." The "Myth" is about seeking truth, discovering what is real. As Socrates says, the prisoners are "like us" (206), implying that we all have to break the chains of illusion to find what is real, even if it defies conventional wisdom. For this assignment, I ask students to reflect on their own lives and consider how they pursue truth. I go on to say, "If you wish, make reference to 'Myth' in your paper and consider your own views of truth and learning in relation to Plato's. Show through examples your way of truth-seeking." This essay can elicit engaged and meaningful applications of Plato's worldview to student lives, and it offers an alternative way to approach textual understanding.

Even though Plato's "Myth" may initially seem daunting, students can understand and appreciate it if teachers provide careful guidance and hands-on activities. Some students are particularly drawn to Plato's ideas once they conceptualize the world he creates, and after understanding the "Myth" they are much more prepared to grapple with other works by Plato. They could find worse company.

Works Cited

Plato. *The Republic and Other Works.* Trans. Benjamin Jowett. New York: Doubleday, 1989.

Whitehead, Alfred N. *Process and Reality: An Essay in Cosmology.* Corrected ed. Ed. David Ray Griffin and Donald W. Sherburne. New York: Free Press, 1978.

16 Through Cinderella: Four Tools and the Critique of High Culture

Lawrence Pruyne
Western New England College

Never trust the artist. Trust the tale. The proper function of a critic is to save the tale from the artist who created it.

D. H. Lawrence, *Studies in Classic American Literature*

Few stories are as widely known as Cinderella. Most students will know the basic story, many in some detail. This makes it the perfect text with which to demonstrate various schools of criticism as well as the differences between "high" and "low" cultures. Toward these ends—exposing first-year college students to several critical tools and a critique of cultural norms—I usually begin with traditional, high, and popular tellings of Cinderella, followed by examinations of the story through the lenses of materialist, psychoanalytic, feminist, and transpersonal critiques.

To begin, I send my students home with mythic and poetic versions of the Cinderella story. The myth acquaints them with the unsavory details of the original: the death of Cinderella's mother is foregrounded, her father's "incestuous" urges remain apparent; the prince pursues her with an ax, chopping open the bird house in which she is hiding; and the evil stepsisters get their eyes pecked out by birds. I also give them Anne Sexton's poem "Cinderella" (which appears in *Transformations*, a collection she published in 1971). An example of canonized high culture, Sexton's poem is not a pasteurized version for mass consumption; instead, it indicts the fairy tale as false and dangerous.

I ask my students to recount the events of the Cinderella myth before delving into Sexton's poem. A widely published version, documented from German folk culture by the brothers Grimm, can be found in Alan Dundes's compendium, *Cinderella: A Folklore Casebook*. Many students will be acquainted with *Grimm's Fairy Tales*, which strikes a familiar note before they move to Sexton, whose poem is notably less accepting of the tale. Although Sexton's depressive personality may be at work, highlighting Sexton's condition, or her condemnation of the tale, is not the goal. Rather, the point is that "high" culture treasures idiosyncrasy. The canon tends to promote individualism and the deeply personal interpretation. Sexton's interpretation is highly critical, taking the Cinderella fairy tale as just that, a fairy tale that never happens. In contrast, Walt Disney's animated feature *Cinderella* presents the binary opposite of Sexton's version in its upbeat pop iconography. The majority of Americans come to know Cinderella by seeing this cartoon in a theater or on video, and that familiarity works to dissipate the unease Sexton may have generated. It's not necessary to watch the whole film in class; just show key scenes, bracketing them with the introduction and finale.

Rather than commenting on the legitimacy of high or low cultures, my intention is simply to identify them as such. In the ideological relationship between text and audience, which version do we consider the standard? Which treatment is touted as artistic? What does that say about art? The key, then, is that the presentation styles of high and low culture are graphically demonstrated in the contrast between Sexton's contempt for, and Disney's homogenization of, the original version of the myth. For Sexton, the story never happens, while in the cartoon there's no blood, lust, or violence.

Breaking classes into smaller groups both promotes individual reading and initiates students into particular critical points of view. After the class has been divided, I ask that each group focus on various critical stances, including materialism, feminism, psychoanalysis, or transpersonal views. During specified class dates, each group offers an introduction to their critical view and uses it to analyze Cinderella. A basic reading is assigned to the entire class, and group members, to build or enrich their presentations and arguments, also dig in the library for further examples of their critical tool.

For the materialism group, I usually assign the last half of Raymond Williams's article "Base and Superstructure in Marxist Cultural Theory" as an initial reading. Allow plenty of time for a complete and thorough materialist-oriented analysis, including questions and discussion. Materialist critique has evolved into an examination of the structures of society that disseminate its personality, asking whether those structures are strictly economic or used to generate and distill cultural values by wielding other forms of influence. Most budding Marxists will stick to economics. They will probably cite Cinderella's poverty and the prince's wealth, saying, "The controlling power of wealth is shown because the people all flock to the king's ball."

The venturesome will also begin to critique the myth as a vehicle of social programming, which may lead to a discussion of the social roles of literature and art.

When brought to bear on Cinderella, a materialist critique has limitations, as do all critical stances. Turn to the TV/VCR and view the Disney scene in which the mice turn into horses, the pumpkin into a carriage, and Cinderella's rags into a splendid gown. Ask students, "Where did this wealth come from?" Lift your eyebrows. "Was there a source within society? How can a materialist philosophy help us understand this text, at this point?" Quickly, it will be obvious that classic materialist critique cannot satisfactorily explain the magical appearance of wealth and social standing. If you pull the rug out from under your students, however, give them something else to stand on: "Materialist analysis is only one of many critical tools," I console. "Would the group offering psychoanalytic analysis come up front please."

Students may be acquainted with Freudian theory, including such major concepts as the id/ego/superego model of the psyche, the Oedipal and Electra complexes of child development within the family, and Eros and Thanatos, the instincts for self-preservation and death. Reminded of these concepts, they may rehearse (in their fashion) the most popular Freudian commentary on Cinderella, which posits that Cinderella's father wanted to have an incestuous affair with her. Radical Freudian readings, however, are usually challenged energetically: "Gimme a break. Freud was a nut case." On we press.

A gender-oriented reading immediately redeems criticism because Cinderella is explicitly about gender roles. The students who choose membership in the group are usually feminists before they reach my class, and so they are already handy with its key ideas. For those new to feminist theory, I assign an article by Elaine Showalter, "Feminism and Literature." As with the other critical approaches, allot plenty of time for a thorough discussion. Students will note that Cinderella's father dominates the household, that the prince is a vortex of male domination around whom the story spins, and that a kingship indicates patrilineage—a social system based on male exploitation of the female.

Again, turn to the TV/VCR. Show Disney's version of the kitchen scene—historically, a setting of feminine creativity and power—where Cinderella is assigned the impossible task of picking up all the seeds, seeds being a symbol of the masculine in nature. "So what," a student will say, "if the birds help her out a little? The masculine is still the focus. It's still seen as more important than anything else." In response, I mention that at the beginning of the myth an amulet is planted by birds in Cinderella's hair. It is the amulet that gives her the ability to summon supranatural assistance. In the kitchen scene, it is the birds that separate or gather all the seeds for Cinderella, thereby enabling her to attend the ball; I refer them to the place in the myth where birds mete out punishment by pecking out the eyes of the evil step-sisters, and ask the students to compare that with the cartoon version where the birds are benevolent companions. As an added hint at the nature of gender roles, I show the scene where the prince fits the glass slipper on Cinderella's foot. He is on his knees, a clear posture of subservience, and the link between them is the glass slipper created by the fairy godmother.

Despite the power of feminist critique, the activity of the birds in accomplishing their superhuman task defies its analytical range. Understanding the magical elements of the fairy tale, and magical fiction in general, requires yet another critical approach. Jungian (also called archetypal or "transpersonal") interpretation of the text is very useful because Cinderella, a myth, enacts the shifting of energies too large to be encompassed by socially based critiques. As an introduction, I assign an article in Dundes's case book, Maria Louise von Franz's "The Beautiful Wassilissa." Another useful anthology for this issue is *Cinderella: 345 Variants of Cinderella, Catskin and Cap o' Rushes*, a trendsetting work of mythological anthropology compiled by Marian Roalfe Cox in 1893. The gist of von Franz's article is that Cinderella documents the shifting of feminine energies from one generation to the next. Salient elements are the death of Cinderella's mother, which initiates the shift of feminine power to her; the bestowal of the amulet; the pursuit of Cinderella by both the prince and her father, indicating a struggle of subtle energies toward a new equanimity; the magical elements that enable her marriage to the prince, demonstrating that the shift of feminine power to Cinderella is, in fact, a fait accompli; and the blinding of the evil stepsisters, who have worked at cross purposes to the balancing of energies achieved by the marriage of the prince and Cinderella. My purpose here is not to promote transpersonal analysis above the others. Rather, the purpose of this exercise—and this should be plainly stated— is to show that, by highlighting different aspects of a text, different critical tools create equally valid yet quite different readings.

It's important to stress that learning to practice various critical methods is more effective than becoming wedded to a single stance. A particular critique may not open a text for fruitful analysis, which means that other analytical tools should be used. That, in fact, is what this exercise with Cinderella accomplishes. Students are exposed to different schools in the critical arena, each with strengths and limitations, and they discover how each tool functions to explain a text. Most important, they learn that critical theory should serve a text, not a text a theory. Indeed, when we impose theory, we rob ourselves of literature's capacity to *surprise* us.

Works Cited

Cox, Marian Roalfe. *Cinderella: 345 Variants of Cinderella, Catskin and Cap o' Rushes*. London: The Folklore Society, 1893.

Dundes, Alan, ed. *Cinderella: A Folklore Casebook*. New York: Garland, 1982.

Further Reading

Rubenstein, Ben. "The Meaning of the Cinderella Story in the Development of a Little Girl." *Cinderella: A Folklore Casebook*. Ed. Alan Dundes. New York: Garland, 1982. 219–28.

Sexton, Anne. "Cinderella." *Transformations*. Boston: Houghton Mifflin, 1971. 53–57.

Showalter, Elaine. "Feminism and Literature." *Literary Theory Today*. Ed. Peter Collier and Helga Geyre-Ryan. Ithaca: Cornell UP, 1990. 179–202.

Williams, Raymond. "Base and Superstructure in Marxist Cultural Theory." *Contemporary Literary Criticism: Literary and Cultural Studies*. 2nd ed. Ed. Robert Con Davis and Ronald Schleifer. New York: Longman, 1989. 386–90.

17 Getting behind Gilman's "The Yellow Wallpaper"

Dianne Fallon
York County Technical College, Wells, Maine

I have a three-by-five [card] . . . with this fragment of a sentence from a story by Chekhov: "and suddenly everything became clear to him." I find these words filled with wonder and possibility. I love their simple clarity, and hint of revelation that's implied. There is mystery, too. What has been unclear before? Why is it just now becoming clear? What's happened? Most of all—what now? There are consequences as a result of such sudden awakenings. I feel a sharp sense of relief—and anticipation.

Raymond Carver, "On Writing"

When stories are contained within a story, how can we uncover them, and what might they mean? These are the questions I ask myself and my students. Because I teach at a two-year college where the majority of students are juggling work and family responsibilities, "Introduction to Literature" is the first and only college literature class they may ever take. Thus, getting students to make personally meaningful connections to stories is vital. By the semester's end, I want students to be able to get "inside" these texts, to play around with the interpretative possibilities, and in doing so make connections between short fiction and their own lives. A related goal is to get students thinking about how their "subject position"—their cultural backgrounds, gender, race, class, age, and life experiences—can both open up and limit the possibilities for response and interpretation. In sharing the varied interpretations generated by the class, we begin to see, hear, and learn in ways that differ from those we experience as isolated, individual readers.

Of course, making connections and creating dialogue is neither an automatic nor consistent process, and it is one that some students may resist. "It's just a story," one student said repeatedly in a class this past semester. "The writer just wanted to tell a story and that's all it is." We were "reading" too much into the text, he insisted. Trying to figure out what the story "meant" was to detract from what he saw as the main goal of literature—amusement and escape, maybe mixed in with a little food for the brain, but not too much.

I'm sure some others silently agreed with this position. It is for these students that I like teaching Charlotte Perkins Gilman's "The Yellow Wallpaper"; the story is a puzzle that resists resistance to interpretation. First published in 1892, "The Yellow Wallpaper" was based on Gilman's own experience of depression and treatment, of which she said, "I had been as far as one could go and get back" (*The Living* 121). Her doctor, the noted neurologist S. Weir Mitchell, insisted that, to get well, his patient must "live as domestic a life as possible" (*The Living* 95). But after several months, Gilman realized that her domestic life was causing her depression, and she fled to California with her baby. There she became a writer and feminist activist; three years later, she wrote "The Yellow Wallpaper."

"The Yellow Wallpaper" is a series of entries in a secret journal kept by a woman confined in a country estate. Her physician husband John has brought her there to rest and relax in order to recover from "nervous depression"; however, she becomes increasingly obsessed with the yellow wallpaper in her room and comes to believe that beneath its swirls and patterns lies a trapped woman who can be liberated if the narrator can rip down the wallpaper. As the story ends, the narrator apparently has gone mad; her husband faints when he opens the door to the sight of her creeping around the room on her hands and knees. She, at least, is convinced that she has succeeded in freeing the woman imprisoned behind the wallpaper.

The obvious symbolism of the wallpaper itself, upon which the narrator dwells obsessively, and the fact that the story is loaded with ambiguities invite a series of questions for writing or discussion. Is the narrator mentally ill, or is her husband driving her insane with his medical treatment? Is she confined at a peaceful country estate, in a haunted house, or in an institution for the mentally ill? What is signified by her description of her bedroom as a child's nursery, or by the bars on her windows, the fact that her bed is nailed to the floor and the gate closed at the top of the stairs? Most important, why is this woman so obsessed with the patterns on the yellow wallpaper, and how or why is that wallpaper significant? Feminist literary critics have examined these questions and others at length. Here, I shall summarize how three critics address the symbolism of "The Yellow Wallpaper" and how their ideas can be used in a class like the one I recently taught.

Allow me to say that I am uncomfortable with the idea of "teaching" "The Yellow Wallpaper," or any short story for that matter. While sometimes I may present relevant background information or ideas I have about a story, my focus is on having students articulate responses and interpretations to texts; they teach themselves and one another as they read and discuss stories. Throughout a semester, I use a variety of prompts and exercises to help students get "inside" texts, including informal journal responses, in-class freewriting on direct questions (e.g., is "The Yellow Wallpaper" a Gothic ghost tale, a story about one woman's nervous breakdown, or a feminist protest against patriarchy, and why?), and dramatized role playing. At times, I assign a follow-up writing activity to explore one or two issues more fully. Thus, while I provide critical summaries here as a resource for teachers, I would seldom, if ever, present either these readings or my own to initiate class discussion, though I might later call upon them to help sharpen student response.

In 1973, the Feminist Press rescued "The Yellow Wallpaper" from literary obscurity by republishing it. Elaine Hedges's Afterword for that edition is very useful to the general reader. In addition to providing a great deal of background information on both Gilman's life and her composition of the story, Hedges discusses the story's symbolism. In Hedges's view, the swirling pattern on the wallpaper symbolizes the situation of the wife: like the narrator, the pattern remains "mysteriously, hauntingly undefined and only vaguely visible" (Hedges 51). As the narrator searches for meaning in the pattern's "lame uncertain curves," the paper "slaps [her] in the face, knocks [her] down, tramples upon [her]" (25). Thus, the pattern serves as a metaphor for the confined lives of nineteenth-century women who must struggle for self-definition while trying to break free of patterns defined and designed by men.

For Paula Treichler, the wallpaper represents female language. In the story, the narrator's stereotypical "female" voice—hesitant, marked by questions and uncertainty—contrasts with that of her husband John, who speaks the rational language of diagnosis and medical science. Significantly, the narrator is a writer who is not permitted to write. But, as the figure behind the wallpaper becomes more clear, the narrator's language becomes bolder and more direct. "The right to author or originate sentences," Treichler writes, "is at the heart of the story and what the yellow wallpaper represents: a figure for women's discourse, it seeks to escape the 'sentence' passed by medicine and patriarchy" (71). In this case, the "sentence" is the medical diagnosis that confines the woman writer to a room, efficiently and effectively preventing her voice from being heard.

A third critic, Susan Lanser, wonders if "The Yellow Wallpaper" reflects not only a feminist critique of patriarchy but also an unconscious expression of Gilman's anxiety about racial issues. The color yellow, Lanser notes, carried with it negative associations of disease, cowardice, and uncleanliness that may have been related to various ethnic groups from Eastern and Southern Europe and Asia (e.g., the "Yellow Peril" of Chinese immigration). Although Gilman actively participated in various progressive reform movements and frequently condemned America's racist history, she also belonged for a time to eugenics organizations and opposed unlimited open immigration; in her books and articles on social change, she often took nativist and racist positions, advocating open immigration for certain groups of "better" stock and limits for others, and proposing the compulsory enlistment of African Americans in a militaristic industrial corps. For Lanser, then, "The Yellow Wallpaper" can be understood as "a pastiche of disturbed and conflicting discourses": she writes, "the wallpaper's chaos represents what the narrator (and we ourselves) must refuse in order to construct the singular figure of the woman behind the bars: the foreign and alien images that threaten to 'knock [her] down, and trample upon [her],' images that as a white middle-class woman of limited consciousness she may neither want nor know how to read" (425). Contained within Lanser's reading is a critique of contemporary feminism and its tendency to represent middle-class white women's experience as universal. "If the wallpaper is at once the text of patriarchy and the woman's text," Lanser says, "then perhaps the narrator is both resisting and embracing the woman of color who is self and not self, a woman who might need to be rescued from the text of patriarchy but cannot yet be allowed to go free" (429).

I provide these three readings to illustrate the wide range issues for discussion of "The Yellow Wallpaper." Working individually or in small groups, students can write their own interpretations about what the wallpaper means, afterward comparing their readings against perspectives offered by their classmates, me, or critics like Hedges, Treichler, or Lanser. Which readings (including those offered by the class) are most convincing? Asking class members to explain why they find a particular reading compelling can serve to highlight the issue of how the reader's background contributes to making meaning.

In addition to identifying the central symbol of the wallpaper itself, the three readings summarized here provide a springboard to questions that are more general but no less important. The readings of Hedges and Treichler both propose that the individual woman's psychopathology is caused by general patriarchal oppression. Is "The Yellow Wallpaper" a story about one woman's descent into madness? Or is it a metaphor about what happens (or can happen) to all women?

If so, does the metaphor hold true today? Why would Gilman choose to write one story versus the other? And in a more general sense, to what extent are people's problems individual—the result of their own actions and choices—and to what extent is individual suffering the result of societal or institutional oppression (e.g., sexism and racism)?

Treichler's focus on discourse and language leads to broader questions about women and language in the nineteenth century and today. In the nineteenth century, what did it mean for women to be prohibited from writing and speaking? Are there any parallel prohibitions today? Is language a neutral carrier of reality, or does it create reality? Does it make a difference if we use gender-neutral language? Is there such a phenomenon as "women's language," and, if so, how does it differ from "male" language? And finally, which language carries with it more power?

In some ways, Lanser's reading seems the most remote from my students, for her intended audience is middle-class feminist academics who have made "The Yellow Wallpaper" an emblem of their cause without necessarily examining the story's limits in representing the diverse range of women's lives. Treichler's article raises interesting questions about race and social class. What is the narrator's social and economic position? Is her neurasthenia limited to the middle class? If we are to read the story as a metaphor for women's oppression, which women are we talking about? What kind of women were in a position to receive the "rest cure"? Is it likely that servants, factory girls, and slaves suffered from such depression, and, if so, what did they do about it? How might their problems be different from the narrator's? What about today? Are there differences in the way women from varied backgrounds perceive and receive the message of feminism? An interesting exercise is to ask the class to define feminism and then ask all students, male and female, where they stand on feminist principles—i.e., do they consider themselves "feminists"? Why or why not?

Finally, the ending of "The Yellow Wallpaper" always merits discussion in class. The narrator has become the woman behind the yellow wallpaper: "I've got out at last," she cries, "You can't put me back!" (36). She claims liberation, but she is reduced to crawling around the room—hardly a gesture of freedom. What does this disturbing image suggest about the possibility for getting out from beneath the wallpaper? Were other endings then possible, and what might they have been? What endings might be possible now? (In the recent film *Thelma and Louise*, why did the two heroines end their quest for freedom by driving off a cliff?) As a follow-up activity, students might rewrite the ending, choosing either a nineteenth-century or modern setting.

When I teach "The Yellow Wallpaper," there is never enough time to address all that the story suggests. In a recent class, I chose to begin discussion by asking class members to write for ten minutes, inhabiting the perspective of a character other than the narrator (e.g., the husband John, his sister, the housekeeper, or even the woman behind the wallpaper). This was the first time I'd tried this particular exercise, and I was curious to see what students would make of the other voices in the story. Here is one student's response:

> I'm really busy with my doctoring sick people around the city and when I come home I have to deal with my sick wife that does not want me to comemite [sic] her. . . . I really think I should. She's getting wose [sic] everyday. My poor little boy is being raised by my sister and I sure don't want him seeing his mother like this. . . . It would scar him for life. What should I do? Maybe she'd making me crazy. I need a vacation . . . without her. . . . Sometimes I wonder if she even knows I'm there. . . . She's in her own little world . . . and I can't break into it. When is the last time . . . when was she well. . . . How did this happen. . . . I am a man I need. . . . Well you know. . . . Ummmmmm. How should I say let my fustration [sic] out. . . . It's been a long long time. . . . Well how old is my son? God Help us!!

This journal entry was written by a shy young woman—I'll call her Nan—who viewed herself as an unsophisticated reader and rarely spoke in class. "I don't see it," she would say anxiously when class members discussed their interpretations of various stories or poetry. "I don't see how they got that." Yet in becoming "John," Nan cut to the essence of "The Yellow Wallpaper," suggesting that the narrator's husband wants to be rid of his sick intellectual wife because she has become a burden who might damage himself or their son, an abnormal woman who refuses to fulfill her marital duty of providing him with regular opportunities for sex. After the student read her freewriting aloud, the class discussed it at length. Was "John's" reaction natural or normal? Why or why not? Was he exacerbating his wife's illness, or was his patience being stretched to the limit? What were some of the fears, issues, and resentments lying beneath his response? In unpacking this student text, classmates further probed Gilman's.

The last paragraph in Nan's text led to a discussion of sex and marriage in the nineteenth century. What were the usual consequences for women, I asked, when they engaged in sexual intercourse? What choices did they have for limiting pregnancies? How did this situation relate to the narrator's position as a writer? Do these same questions have relevance for women today? If so, how?

"John's" response also sparked a discussion about women and medical treatment. In "The Yellow Wallpaper," the narrator refers to Dr. Mitchell, the nineteenth-century neurologist who invented the "rest cure," which the narrator points to as the source of her problem—the dictum not to work. I told the class a story about how during graduate school I'd gone to see a doctor for some breathing trouble. Without having undergone any sort of minimal physical examination, I was told that my problem was probably related to stress and was handed a prescription for the tranquilizer Xanax.

A quick class poll revealed that almost all students perceived that doctors today are quicker to prescribe tranquilizers for women than for men. Is there a relationship, I asked, between the "rest cure" of the nineteenth century and treatments for "female anxiety" today? If so, why are women given prescriptions for "rest" or "tranquilization"? Are their lives inherently more stressful than men's, or do tranquilizers and other depressants serve to silence women in ways similar to the "rest cure"? More generally, what are the benefits, today, in the widespread use of drugs to control mental illness, and what are the drawbacks?

In the end, for many students, reading short fiction opens other worlds and values; for others, it is a confrontation to be avoided. In most classes, a blurry combination of the two groups is a likely result. Such confusion, I think, is a good sign that students have resisted the imposition of a universal meaning; no longer can they claim that a story is simply a set of words that depicts events or puts forth one message apparent to all. My aim, then, in getting behind "The Yellow Wallpaper" is that students leave class as puzzled (or maybe more so) than when they first entered. While the "lesson" generated by the swirl of contradictory ideas and possibilities may not be neat or obvious, I smile that "The Yellow Wallpaper" has prepared students for life outside my classroom.

Works Cited

Gilman, Charlotte Perkins. *"The Yellow Wallpaper."* New York: Feminist Press, 1973.

———. *The Living of Charlotte Perkins Gilman: An Autobiography.* New York: Appleton-Century, 1935.

Hedges, Elaine R. Afterword. *"The Yellow Wallpaper."* By Charlotte Perkins Gilman. New York: Feminist Press, 1973. 37–63.

Lanser, Susan S. "Feminist Criticism, 'The Yellow Wallpaper,' and the Politics of Color in America." *Feminist Studies* 15 (Fall 1989): 415–41.

Treichler, Paula A. "Escaping the Sentence: Diagnosis and Discourse in 'The Yellow Wallpaper.'" *Feminist Issues in Literary Scholarship.* Ed. Shari Benstock. Bloomington: Indiana UP, 1987. 62–78.

V Discerning the Story's Cultural Perspective

Why Short Stories?

At its highest level [the short story] meets the challenge laid down by Kay Boyle: "to invest a brief sequence of events with reverberating human significance by means of style, selection, and ordering of detail, and—most important of all—to present the whole action in such a way that it is at once a parable and a slice of life, at once symbolic and real, both a valid picture of some phase of experience, and a sudden illumination of one of the perennial moral and psychological paradoxes which lie at the heart of la condition humaine."

Clifton Fadiman, *The World of the Short Story*

As readers begin to understand what underpins their responses to literature and to ask good questions, they also begin to widen their sense of where literature can take them. They begin, in other words, to consider how literature is relevant to society. Sometimes, they see themselves as participants in that bigger picture; sometimes, they experience a moment of cosmic irony in which they suddenly realize that the picture does not revolve around themselves. Either way, they grow as citizens.

Citizenship is an issue that has concerned writers and readers since antiquity. How we behave as citizens depends upon how we read and react to the texts of our lives as well as the texts of others' lives— how we appraise ourselves and our needs against other citizens and their needs. Stories expand the range of life experiences readers may consider, thus widening their empathetic range. The problem is that, as each new text freezes into print a moment in time, our reading context, as well as the social implications of our reactions, continues to change. Thus, to understand the diversity represented in stories, readers must be proficient at reading the cultural cues presented there.

A written story can never perfectly capture an actual moment of life. A thousand words, in a sense, cannot equal the picture. The words themselves are static forms that rely on—are at the mercy of—readers to bring it life. Without readers, Hamlet says, books are just "words, words, words." This disparity between life and words so troubled Socrates that he eschewed writing altogether, leaving to others the transcription of his discourses. Plato transcribed his words, but added his own Platonic twist, imbuing the discourses with his own perspective. Short story writers, like Plato, give readers a glimpse of the world, but it is a glimpse through the writer's eye, with added refraction designed to heighten the reader's experience. Raymond Carver, in his essay "On Writing," emphasizes that "The short story writer's task is to invest the glimpse with all that is in his power" (18). In doing so, the writer urges readers to attend to the values in the story, sometimes to ratify or reject them, sometimes simply to accept that they exist. We allow literature to offer its commentary on where we stand.

Determining where one stands is no small thing. American readers have been knocked off balance by all sorts of issues, including those attendant to diverse sexual and ethnic populations. Shattered in the fray is the myth of a single American dream. Short stories give perspective and insight to a variety of worlds we cannot experience firsthand. In "Expanding the Margins in American Literature Using Armistead Maupin's *More Tales of the City*," Barbara Kaplan Bass presents her students with a voice from the sexually diverse Castro district of 1970s San Francisco. Bass focuses on Maupin's character Michael Tolliver, who at one point in *More Tales of the City* corresponds with his mother about his gay lifestyle. In having students adopt Tolliver's epistolary mode, Bass expands how students see both the technical and substantive range of the short story. Bass is asking her students to widen their social context. In that same vein, E. Shelley Reid uses Toni Morrison's "Recitatif" to reveal to her students their own cultural presumptions and stereotypes: indeed, Reid centers on the "general, unspoken understanding in my classes and those of my colleagues that *talking about race* is the same as (or will soon be identified with) *racist talk*." As usual with teachers represented in this book, the result is that "all readers get to be both dealer and players, shuffling and re-reading their perspectives. . . ."

This section concludes with two essays that directly link inferences about social context to what students have already gathered about the nature of their response to literature. Jennifer Seibel Trainor uses Toni Cade Bambara's "The Lesson" to show how an author may "challenge the mainstream understanding of capitalism and meritocracy . . . ." In order to show how Bambara issues this challenge, she has her students track their reading assumptions and how Bambara subverts them. Bambara works to remold their cultural perspectives. These concerns are precisely those of Susan Berry Brill de Ramirez, who uses Sherman Alexie's "Witnesses, Secret or Not" to show how Native American literature involves a cooperation between storyteller and reader. When they themselves cooperate, students not only expand their experience but are led away from narrow bookishness toward informed discrimination of literary merit.

Work Cited

Carver, Raymond. "On Writing." *Fires: Poems, Stories, Essays.* New York: Vintage Books, 1989. 13–18.

18 Expanding the Margins in American Literature Using Armistead Maupin's *More Tales of the City*

Barbara Kaplan Bass
Towson State University, Towson, Maryland

All stories, as we have said, are based on conflict; and the resolution of the fictional conflict is, in its implications, a judgment too, a judgment of values. In the end some shift of values has taken place. Some new awareness has dawned, some new possibility of attitude has been envisioned. . . .

Robert Penn Warren, "Why Do We Read Fiction?"

In trying to create a salad bowl version of American literature, many new anthologies include texts representing a variety of cultural groups. For teachers, these new texts often provide a different viewpoint of the American experience and a forum for discussing social and ethical issues about the way all sorts of people think and act. As readers of these texts, students learn the tolerance, appreciation, and sympathy for *difference* that is basic to an educated citizenry.

Although we can identify representatives from almost all minorities in our new anthologies, I must emphasize *almost* all: the gay and lesbian voice is still largely muted. Indeed, it is easier for us to ignore that voice and instead stick with the "safe" writers and "safe" subjects; but, if we truly believe in the principle of tolerance, then we must not flinch when we meet intolerance. One way to stand firm is by exposing our students to the best literature from *all* segments of American life. Whether gay or straight, we have much to gain by sharing this literature.

A good place to begin this process is the work of Armistead Maupin. Maupin grew up in the conservative South. Settling in San Francisco when he returned from serving in Vietnam, Maupin learned to accept himself as gay in the open and warm atmosphere of that city. When he began writing his column, "Tales of the City," for the San Francisco *Chronicle*, he filled it with likable characters of every sexual orientation and immediately won the hearts of San Franciscans, who eagerly awaited each new episode. When the "Tales" were later published in novel format by HarperCollins, the book was at first categorized under regional literature or cult fiction, and Maupin was designated as more of a chronicler of pop culture than as a serious writer. Recently, however, he has earned more critical acclaim both here and abroad. The six-hour film version of the first book in the series, *Tales of the City*, which was produced by Channel Four in Great Britain, received a warm reception when shown in the United States on public television in 1994, and Showtime recently aired the movie version of the second book in the series, *More Tales of the City*, in June 1998.

If I were presenting this information at the high school rather than the college level, I might pair *More Tales of the City* with the fine young-adult novel by Bette Greene, *The Drowning of Stephan Jones*, which explores homophobic behavior among a group of teens in a small town in the Ozarks. My first-year college students, however, are not that much older than high school seniors, and, like their high school counterparts, have begun to see homosexuality "normalized" on television shows such as *Melrose Place*, whose gay character, Matt, is treated sympathetically, and in the movies, where stars such as Tom Hanks and Kevin Kline have portrayed gays in mainstream life. Many have had AIDS touch their families and are glad to have a forum to analyze their confusion and distress. In my composition classes we explore the theme of social justice—environmentalism, sexism, racism, gay rights—and the various ways people interpret what "social justice" means. Everyone reads the same basic text (*More Tales*, for example, for gay rights) but the students divide into groups to discuss one issue in more depth, reading articles, both pro and con, on the topic of their choice. They then present their findings to the rest of the class in some creative way. At the high school level, I can envision an interdisciplinary approach: science classes exploring the biological basis of behavior or the impact of AIDS; social studies exploring the constitutionality of homophobia (i.e., the treatment of gays in the military seems to sanction this type of discrimination), Anita Bryant and the orange juice boycott, or Stonewall and gay liberation; sociology examining the gay culture, perhaps reading Frances FitzGerald's *Cities on a Hill,* in which Maupin himself takes FitzGerald on a tour of the Castro district in San Francisco; and English classes reading *More Tales of the City.*

At the heart of the *Tales* series is sweet, vulnerable Michael Tolliver, one of the five main characters who make up the "family" that lives at 28 Barbary Lane. Although Michael is gay, his experiences are not exclusive to homosexuals. To ease your students into this world, you may want to begin with just three chapters in *More Tales of the City,* the second novel in the series, in which Michael receives a letter from his mother and sends her his reply. In these chapters, titled "Thinking Out Loud," "Save the Children," and "Letter to Mama," Michael's mother, unaware of her son's homosexuality, has written to tell him that she has joined Anita Bryant's anti-homosexual Save Our Children campaign. Michael then replies to her, revealing his secret. Most of my students are so taken with Michael and his friends in these three short chapters that they choose to read the rest of the novel and often buy the rest of the series to read on their own. Still, I would suggest that you read the entire book before you assign it and, in case there are objecting parents, offer your high school students another option. In my experience, though, no one has refused to read it.

Here is Michael's "Letter to Mama":

Dear Mama,
   I'm sorry it's taken me so long to write. Every time I try to write to you and Papa, I realize I'm not saying the things that are in my heart. That would be OK if I loved you any less than I do, but you are still my parents and I am still your child.
   I have friends who think I'm foolish to write this letter. I hope they're wrong. I hope their doubts are based on parents who loved and trusted them less than mine do. I hope especially that you'll see this as an act of love on my part, a sign of my continuing need to share my life with you.

I wouldn't have written, I guess, if you hadn't told me about your involvement in the Save Our Children campaign. That, more than anything made it clear that my responsibility was to tell you the truth, that your own child is homosexual, and that I never needed saving from anything except the cruel and ignorant piety of people like Anita Bryant.

I'm sorry, Mama. Not for what I am, but for how you must feel at this moment. I know what that feeling is, for I felt it most of my life. Revulsion, shame, disbelief—rejection through fear of something I knew, even as a child, was as basic to my nature as the color of my eyes.

No, Mama, I wasn't "recruited." No seasoned homosexual ever served as my mentor. But you know what? I wish someone had. I wish someone older than me and wiser than the people in Orlando had taken me aside and said, "You're all right, kid. You can grow up to be a doctor or a teacher just like anyone else. You're not crazy or sick or evil. You can succeed and be happy and find peace with friends—all kinds of friends—who don't give a damn who you go to bed with. Most of all, though, you can love and be loved, without hating yourself for it." But no one ever said that to me, Mama. I had to find it out on my own, with the help of the city that has become my home. I know this may be hard for you to believe, but San Francisco is full of men and women, both straight and gay, who don't consider sexuality in measuring the worth of another human being.

These aren't radicals or weirdos, Mama. They are shop clerks and bankers and little old ladies and people who nod and smile to you when you meet them on the bus. Their attitude is neither patronizing nor pitying. And their message is so simple: Yes, you are a person. Yes, I like you. Yes, it is alright for you to like me too.

I know what you must be thinking now. You're asking yourself: What did we do wrong? How did we let this happen? Which one of us made him that way? I can't answer that, Mama. In the long run, I guess I really don't care. All I know is this: If you and Papa are responsible for the way I am, then I thank you with all my heart, for it's the light and the joy of my life.

I know I can't tell you what it is to be gay. But I can tell you what it's not. It's not hiding behind words, Mama. Like family and decency, and Christianity. It's not fearing your body, or the pleasures that God made for it. It's not judging your neighbor, except when he's crass or unkind. Being gay has taught me tolerance, compassion, and humility. It has shown me the limitless possibilities of living. It has given me people whose passion and kindness and sensitivity have provided a constant source of strength. It has brought me into the family of man, Mama, and I like it here. I like it.

There's not much else I can say, except that I'm the same Michael you've always known. You just know me better now. I

have never consciously done anything to hurt you. I never will.
Please don't feel you have to answer this right away. It's enough
for me to know that I no longer have to lie to the people who
taught me to value the truth.
    Mary Ann sends her love.
    Everything is fine at 28 Barbary Lane,
Your loving son,
Michael   (221–23)

A good way to launch into these chapters is to ask the students to write their own letters, either to you, to Maupin, to a character in the book, or to someone they know, reacting to what they have read. Students tend to focus on what they have in common with Michael—distance from their parents, a need for unconditional acceptance, the pain of keeping a secret. Begin the class with students' volunteering to read their letters, using them as a springboard for discussion. If students are reluctant to volunteer, have them get into groups of three or four to read their letters to each other. Afterward, ask them to summarize their ideas for the rest of the class. This approach alleviates some of the anxiety associated with the subject, putting emphasis on what they *wrote* rather than on what they *think*. You might also ask them to read over their own letters and first underline something they have learned and something they have a question about to use as a basis for discussion.

    Another approach that has proven successful in promoting discussion is to bring into class a grab bag of items—clean out your junk drawer at home for objects to use in this lesson. Ask the students to select an item. Once they have their choice in hand, ask them to write a paragraph connecting it in some way to the book. You'll be surprised at the creative connections they will make: a strip of film negative becomes a paragraph on the negative attitude toward homosexuals in our culture; a small box of Lucky Charms cereal relates to the variety of people in society coming together to create something good; a snow globe becomes a symbol of isolation.

    If you would like to take a more prescriptive approach toward these chapters, you might ask the students to respond to some specific questions in reader-response journals before they come to class. Why does Michael decide to write this letter to his parents? Should he have written to them? Why or why not? What does he want from them? Will his parents change their minds about homosexuals after they read his letter? Michael writes his letter while in the hospital suffering from a temporary paralysis; why would Maupin put him in this situation? How else is he paralyzed (other than physically)? These questions have spurred discussion of other issues, such as whether it is possible to be both Christian and homosexual, why anti-homosexual prejudice exists, whether gay life and family life are mutually exclusive, why the government insists on a "don't ask/don't tell" policy for gays in the military, whether it is possible to accept homosexuals and reject homosexuality, and, last, how we should determine an individual's worth.

You may also spend time examining more closely Michael's mother's letter in which she voices some common myths about homosexuality. Ask the students to pair up and to locate some of these myths, for example, that homosexuals can be "recruited." Ask the pairs to write on the board what they have found and discuss why these are, in fact, myths. I try to cover the following myths: (1) I don't know any gays or lesbians; (2) appearance makes homosexuals obvious; (3) homosexuality is a disease and homosexuals ought to be cured; (4) gays dislike women and lesbians dislike men; (5) homosexuals shouldn't be allowed to raise or work with children because they sexually abuse them; (6) homosexuals recruit straight people and make the children they raise into homosexuals; (7) homosexuals have sex on their minds most of the time; and, (8) if I avoid gays and bisexuals, I will be safe from AIDS. You may be able to obtain brochures from local gay groups or book stores that list these myths and explain the facts behind these issues. Other discussion that arises from these chapters includes whether AIDS is God's way of punishing gays, whether what we perceive about gays is sexual or cultural—and what we mean by culture, whether gays will ever be assimilated into the larger culture, and how homophobia compares against racism, sexism, and anti-Semitism. We end by focusing on our similarities rather than our differences. The lesson is that we all need acceptance and connection to society.

Each semester my students' journal responses strengthen my resolve to keep Maupin in my syllabus. Students have responded in a variety of ways to the question, "What did you learn from reading these chapters?" One young man wrote, "I have to admit that when I read this I had already made up my mind that I didn't like it because it was about homosexuality. But I learned that having an open mind changes a lot of one's views. I know my views were changed about this story. I enjoyed it more when my mind was clear and open to suggestions." Another wrote, "This was really the first time I was able to hear the side of a gay person. I never knew the pain they have to go through. By reading Michael's letter to his parents, I was able to realize some false beliefs I had about homosexuals. After I read this story, I could accept Michael as a human being who has the right to live his life the way he wants." And finally, "Reading this story made me think about how gay people pretty much want the same things as heterosexuals: love, friendship, and acceptance."

There are additional approaches to dealing with these chapters in class. On a literary level, you might discuss the similarity between the work of Charles Dickens and that of Maupin, whose intricate plots and surprise twists and connections are quite Dickensian. You might also note the similarity between the titles *A Tale of Two Cities* and *Tales of the City,* or discuss serial fiction written for magazines, another point of comparison between Dickens and Maupin. Each book, too, is a sociological portrait of the era in which it was written. On the level of how literature reflects society, Maupin's books become darker and less playful as the specter of AIDS arises. In fact, in the fourth novel in this series, *Babycakes,* Maupin mentions AIDS, the first author to do so in a work of fiction.

There are other themes in Maupin's work that are worth exploring, especially in the conflict between appearance and reality. It isn't simply the distinction between gay and straight that Maupin proves to be superficial; he demonstrates that our humanity goes beyond our external differences. In order to foster this understanding, it is important to offer students articles that present both sides of the issue so that they can find themselves somewhere in the reading; otherwise, those who are firm in their negative beliefs will become even more unlikely to open up to new ways of thinking. Stress that it is possible to accept new ideas without discarding old ones, which, of course, is part of the process of education. It is important for you to remain neutral, pointing out fallacious arguments on either side. Be sure to provide some articles that argue against equal rights for homosexuals, and spend some time discussing these points of view. Divide the students into groups, with each group responsible for presenting one article to the class. The groups share their findings and help each other answer the questions they have raised. One variation of this technique is to ask each group just to write the questions they have about the issues on a big piece of newsprint. Then each group passes its questions to the next group, which attempts to answer them.

However you present Maupin, your students will be able to find themselves somewhere, no matter what their own sexual orientation. Through the work of this contemporary writer, we can begin to move our students beyond often knee-jerk reactions to difference, beyond even tolerance, and toward new levels of sympathy and appreciation.

Works Cited

Anderson, Terry. Telephone interview. 24 September 1991.

Bender, David, and Bruno Leone, eds. *Opposing Viewpoints*. San Diego: Greenhaven, 1995.

FitzGerald, Frances. *Cities on a Hill: A Journey through Contemporary American Cultures*, New York: Simon & Schuster, 1986.

Greene, Bette. *The Drowning of Stephan Jones*. New York: Bantam, 1991.

Maupin, Armistead. *More Tales of the City*. New York: HarperPerennial, 1980.

Nelson, Emmanuel, ed. *Contemporary Gay American Novelists: A Bio-bibliographical Critical Sourcebook*. Westport, CT: Greenwood, 1993.

Further Reading

Singer, Bennett, ed. *Growing Up Gay: A Literary Anthology*. New York: The New Press, 1993.

Works by Armistead Maupin, all published by HarperCollins:
The Tales Series:
Tales of the City, 1978
Further Tales of the City, 1982
Babycakes, 1984
Significant Others, 1987
Sure of You, 1989
Maybe the Moon, 1993

19 Shuffling the Race Cards: Toni Morrison's "Recitatif"

E. Shelley Reid
Austin College, Sherman, Texas

When you can state the theme of a story, when you can separate it from the story itself, then you can be sure the story is not a very good one. The meaning of the story has to be embodied in it, has to be made concrete in it. A story is a way to say something that can't be said any other way, and it takes every word in the story to say what the meaning is. You tell a story because a statement would be inadequate. When anybody asks what a story is about, the only proper thing is to tell him to read the story.

Flannery O'Connor, *Mystery and Manners: Occasional Prose*

Toni Morrison's "Recitatif," according to answers my students gave on a short survey recently, is a story that is "mostly about" the friendship between two girls, with some attention to the topics of growing up, memory, innocence, and "society." Morrison's only published short story is indeed about the friendship between Twyla and Roberta, two girls who meet in a New York orphanage as children (circa 1950), and how their friendship develops (or suffers) as a result of four subsequent meetings over the next three decades: in a Howard Johnson's restaurant, in a pricey supermarket, at a school-integration protest picket, and in a coffee shop on Christmas Eve. What these student responses very carefully left out, however, is the small fact that one of the girls is white and one black. Moreover, Morrison, by bringing her considerable talents to bear on the problem of "remov[ing] all racial codes from a narrative about two characters of different races for whom racial identity is crucial" (*Dark* xi), provides no definitive clue as to which girl belongs to which race. In class, then, the story gives students an unusual opportunity to investigate and discuss with others the ways in which

A version of this article was presented at the Other Voices: American Women Writers of Color Conference in Ocean City, Maryland, in October 1995.

individuals, groups, and the larger culture construct racial identities, without being asked to make a definitive judgment on either of the main characters, or being able to label one conclusion "right" and another "wrong." Despite—or perhaps because of—student or instructor concerns about talking frankly about race, "Recitatif" can be a tremendous teaching tool.

A short glance at Morrison's text should help illustrate the task facing each reader. The existence of racial difference, along with the first of the non-clues about the girls' racial identities, comes to light in the opening scene. Here Twyla, at age 8, describes her first meeting with Roberta:

> The minute I walked in and [the matron] introduced us, I got sick to my stomach. It was one thing to be taken out of your own bed early in the morning—it was something else to be stuck in a strange place with a girl from a whole other race. And Mary, that's my mother, she was right. Every now and then she would stop dancing long enough to tell me something important and one of the things she said was that they never washed their hair and they smelled funny. Roberta sure did. (438)

Each of the subsequent interludes demonstrates that race is a central issue for the two women, all the while providing signs that leave the identity question open. Which is the white girl's mother, the loud one with the tight green pants that make her rear end stick out, or the one "bigger than any man" (441) with the huge Bible in her hand? Which is the black teenager, the one with the big hair and huge earrings who is on her way to see Jimi Hendrix, or the exhausted waitress who hasn't heard of Hendrix? Who marries the fireman and who the IBM manager? Frilly pink socks, asparagus, political cynicism, mental illness, extended families, and diamond rings all have vivid connotations when joined to specific racial backgrounds, but they do not themselves mark racial boundaries. And to complicate the racial issue, Morrison adds very clear markers of class: the difference between Twyla's working-class life and Roberta's upper-middle-class life is itself almost enough to explain the conflicts between them.

As a result of this deft maneuvering, "Recitatif"—perhaps even more than Morrison's shape-shifting novels—proves to be a very different story for each reader. Without clear direction from Morrison, readers who draw conclusions about a character's race do so based on their own assumptions about and attitudes toward issues of race, class, and gender. (A male student of mine who had based his judgment of Roberta's whiteness on her large, cross-wearing, Bible-toting mother explained that he'd just never known any black people who were like that.) In a larger class setting, therefore, it is inevitable that students will have different, often opposite, answers to the obvious opening ques-tion—"Do you think Twyla is black or white? What led you to think this?"—and will immediately have things to say to one another. (One respondent to the student above explained that such women were common in the Hispanic community in which she grew up, so she had guessed that Roberta was Hispanic.) These multiple readings can be the foundation of a vibrant class discussion. Indeed, because the reactions of students are most powerful if derived entirely from their own reading experiences, I would not recommend "preparing" students to read "Recitatif," even by suggesting generally that the class discussion will focus on issues of race and social class, or implying that there is a "trick" or difficulty in reading the story. Instead, I have successfully started discussion periods by having students write down some of their initial responses and assumptions (one survey I have used is reprinted at the end of this chapter). Written responses validate everyone's perspective; they can allow class-wide, low-risk participation through a show of hands ("How many of you answered that ___?") to start the discussion. Written responses can also allow students to view their own reactions from a distance ("Well, I first wrote down that ___, but now I can see how it might be different.").

I treat the early part of class discussion as an information-gathering project; unless students' conclusions are directly offensive or factually incorrect, they should be included as viable possibilities based on the individual and societal backgrounds from which each student is reading. Some students may be quick to see that they are reacting based on unfounded yet powerful stereotypes, or on images from their childhoods or from media productions. Students who are not yet ready to identify the sources of their assumptions—"I just think of 'Twyla' as a 'black name'"—may close down or lash out if pressed to do so at the start. Instead, because of the nice balance of Morrison's story, it is often just as effective simply to ask if anyone else came to a different conclusion based on the same "clue"—several of my students have identified "Twyla" clearly as a "white name," especially considering the character's working-class background. While one pedagogical goal may indeed be to change or expand students' perceptions about race, making judgments and assigning responsibility early in the class may polarize or even shut down discussion (what one of my colleagues, in the wake of the Simpson murder trial, has called "the O. J. syndrome"). Morrison's story allows almost unlimited room to explore our society's most serious issues, and readers should be encouraged to take advantage of that opportunity without declaring winners and losers.

By focusing on the story's inconclusiveness, teachers can help avoid or mitigate particularly offensive or hurtful statements. In classrooms or communities in which racial tensions are particularly high, instructors may need to set some additional ground rules before beginning class discussion. In many classrooms, however—mine included—instructors will face a quite different set of obstacles to discussion. Conditioned by what they perceive as a punitive "PC" climate, or raised in families who pride themselves on their "color-blindness," some students will be reluctant to engage the issue of race at all, particularly within a classroom setting where their behavior should be exemplary. One of my students, for instance, found it a "relief" that Morrison was "willing to transcend the racial backgrounds which often confine our view of things"; he was thus happily able to read the story from "a non-racist point of view." His response echoes a more general, unspoken understanding in my classes and those of my colleagues that *talking about race* is the same as (or will soon be identified with) *racist talk*. Other students had similar reactions. "I was not interested very much in the racial conflicts. I just read it without bias," wrote one; "The race seems only a Red Herring when it comes to the relationship of the women," commented another; and a third expanded her comments with a familiar "liberal" party line: "I think that rather than focusing on the color of the two girls' skin, the issues that surrounded the different ways of life each led and [the] way they were regarded by society, and one another, is more important."

Yet Morrison's own comment that for these characters "racial identity is crucial" disallows the "transcendence" with which some students would be more comfortable. Focusing the discussion on abstract yet clearly racial issues—how media images create stereotypes, how racism has been and continues to thrive in U.S. institutions such as schools and corporations—may allow them to join back in the discussion without feeling that their personal integrity is being challenged.

Another discussion stopper is guilt. As students realize that they have succumbed to a very human need to categorize (a response that Morrison evokes strongly) and have done so based on "evidence" that disappears under close examination, their comfort level with their own reading plummets. "I felt like a bigot . . . like the stereotype queen," wrote one student, while another saw her assumptions as evidence of a personal moral failure: "I really was mad because I did not grow up in a house that condoned such prejudices." One of my students explained further, suggesting that this reaction itself probably falls along racial lines:

> I had a great conversation with one of my friends. . . . [S]he doesn't like to describe people using their race. She added that being white almost forces her to think this way because using racial terms would denote her as a racist. . . . Being of another race . . . frees me from this social restraint . . . to describe me by noting my race is totally acceptable and fitting.

While guilt can initially be a productive reaction, prompting response and change, in our current culture it can also be a rationalization for *not* taking action or participating in further discussion. Students who perceive issues at this level of complexity are often key players in class discussion; they are the students instructors would hate to lose. One approach is to help them see their personal "failure" as connected to the larger problems of a society that is awash in stereotypes and is thus often unable to discuss complex issues like race with honesty and clarity of thought—to show how they have been shaped by, and now have the opportunity to help shape, the world. They and their peers may also find it useful at this point to go back to the text, to delve more deeply into the paradox of Morrison's story, in which racial identity is critical but impossible to ascertain. Again, written responses from students, in journals or short response papers, can be useful: assigned after the initial discussion, they allow students to comment on or alter their initial responses, providing instructors with a space to respond to individual students' concerns.

There are, to be sure, other topics for discussion. "Recitatif" is highly allusive, with references from Jimi Hendrix to school busing. As my students have been quick to point out, Morrison also raises questions about class, about growing up and forming friendships, about resolving family relationships (particularly concerning the girls' mothers), about peer and societal pressures, and about the reliability and importance of memories. Finally, as the two characters work to uncover the truth (or truths) surrounding a brutal attack on one of the orphanage's kitchen workers, Maggie, we see that they—like the story's readers—must grapple with their own prejudices, fears, and personal failings. But because it matters deeply that the characters are of different races, and it matters which character is which race (a black girl snubbing a white girl is a very different story from a white girl snubbing a black girl—whether or not it *should* be, which is yet another story), teaching "Recitatif" without first acknowledging the elephant in the room would be a farce.

Acknowledging Morrison's particular elephant, and giving students permission and tools to acknowledge it, can lay the groundwork for further discussions of race. Certainly, the personal dimension of readers' answers, and the variable levels of acceptance that different groups have for frank talk about race, may make discussion risky for some students (and for their instructors). Yet Morrison's story opens up the least threatening space for such discussion—without sacrificing equanimity, complexity, or intensity—that I have encountered in contemporary short fiction. There is no single "winning hand"; all readers get to be both dealer and player, shuffling and maneuvering their perspectives on race and culture. The only losers are those who won't come to the table and ante up. In an era of hyperbole and accusations, "Recitatif" is a thoughtful dialogue waiting to happen, an enlightening experience for instructors and students alike.

Works Cited

Morrison, Toni. "Recitatif." *Calling the Wind: Twentieth-Century African-American Short Stories.* Ed. Clarence Major. New York: HarperCollins, 1993. 438–53.

———. *Playing in the Dark: Whiteness and the Literary Imagination.* Cambridge: Harvard UP, 1992.

Appendix: Survey about "Recitatif"

In reading "Recitatif," I (check all that apply)
_____ concluded that Twyla was white.
_____ concluded that Twyla was black.
_____ changed my mind about the characters' races while reading.
_____ tried to decide which character was which race but couldn't.
_____ didn't try to decide one way or the other.
_____ was more interested in other issues.
For each line you checked, write a brief explanation, based on examples from the text, of the evidence that was/is important to you.

I think "Recitatif" is mostly about _____.
I did/didn't enjoy reading the story because _____.

Other comments about "Recitatif":

20 Readers, Cultures, and "Revolutionary" Literature: Teaching Toni Cade Bambara's "The Lesson"

Jennifer Seibel Trainor
University of California at Berkeley

So when one is telling a story, and one is using words to tell the story, each word that one is speaking has a story of its own too. Often the speakers or tellers go into the stories of the words they are using to tell one story so that you get stories within stories, so to speak . . . I think what is essential is this sense of story, and story within story, and the idea that one story is only the beginning of many stories, and the sense that stories never end.

Leslie Marmon Silko, "Language and Literature
from a Pueblo Indian Perspective"

The teacher's edition of the anthology I use in my first-year literature course describes Toni Cade Bambara's short story "The Lesson" as a revolutionary critique of the inequitable distribution of wealth in America (Barnet, Berman, Burto, and Stubbs 239). With that advance warning, we find a story that follows several African American children from Harlem who travel to downtown Manhattan in the company of an adult mentor, Miss Moore. Once there, they visit F. A. O. Schwartz, the famous, fantastically expensive toy store. The children, including Sylvia, the narrator of the story, are awed by what they see, especially by a toy sailboat costing $1,000.00.

At Miss Moore's prompting, the children discuss what it would mean to have that kind of money. "Imagine," Miss Moore says, "what

Reprinted by permission of *The Leaflet*, the journal of the New England Association of Teachers of English.

kind of society it is in which some people can spend on a toy what it would cost to feed a family of six or seven for a year." Beyond one or two comments like this one from Miss Moore, the lesson of the story's title is not spelled out for the children, who are left to interpret the day's events on their own. "White folks crazy," one of them decides. "Equal chance at happiness means an equal crack at the dough," says another. "Ain't nobody going to beat me at nothin'," concludes Sylvia at the day's end (998).

My students' response to the story tends toward a predictable middle-class naiveté, heavily peppered with reliance on stereotypes and a subtle but determined resistance to the text's more radical implications. Writes Laura, a first-year student from California:

> The lesson Miss Moore is trying to teach is really aimed more at the parents than at the children. She is trying to show the parents that they need to teach their children, instead of just letting them run wild all day. They need to instill the values of hard work and discipline. Showing their kids all the things they can have if they follow these values will help instill them.

From Brian, another first-year student:

> The lesson Miss Moore teaches the narrator is simple: she shows her that wasting time and money will lead to a dead end, where you will never be able to buy the nice things the children saw on Fifth Avenue.

And from Kevin:

> The story shows that one of the reasons people can't get out of the ghetto is that they never get a chance to see all the nice things that hard work and staying in school will get you. Miss Moore is trying to show them what the world has to offer if they'd just work hard enough to get it.

Several features of these responses deserve comment. As they have read, the students have substituted their own values in place of those apparent in this "revolutionary" text. In fact, their values stand in sharp contrast to those that a more experienced reader would impute to the author of the story.

Although my students have misread, they have done so in an (implicit) attempt to resist ideas that challenge the mainstream understanding of capitalism and meritocracy they share. Ironically, the very ideology the story seeks to expose is precisely the one my students assume in their attempts to make sense of the text. The challenge of teaching "The Lesson," then, is the necessity of somehow questioning our students' assumptions about a system in which they are immersed, a system that, as my students' responses imply, shapes the choices they make and provides a familiar structure, or narrative, that affirms those choices. To teach "The Lesson" successfully requires more: it requires helping students see the connections between ideology and literature—how, in short, the stories we tell do or do not help us to understand ourselves.

Interestingly, the problems of teaching "The Lesson" are those that practitioners of critical pedagogy face in their attempts to critique elements of the dominant culture in the classroom. As these teachers have made clear, teaching that challenges the stories we tell—stories, for example, about fundamental tenets of American capitalism, or gender and racial ideologies—meets heavy resistance from students. Unfortunately, however, in discussing the problem of student resistance to their teaching, critical pedagogues themselves rely on a familiar teaching narrative: assuming an enlightened, or to use a more current version of the term, empowered, status, critical teachers often see their teaching as a process of enlightening, or empowering, others. But this process echoes one of our oldest narratives of teaching and learning, Plato's "Allegory of the Cave," as the students become analogous to those who are set free and "dragged" up the slope of the cave. When students resist, in other words, it is all too easy to assume their resistance is an inevitable part of growth. Rather than understanding the sources and implications of student resistance, our job as critical teachers, according to this narrative, is simply to overcome that resistance and to drag the students out of darkness.

We can see this narrative at work in C. H. Knoblauch's 1991 essay on teaching "The Lesson." Attributing his students' resistance to their privileged middle-class status, Knoblauch concludes that white, middle-class students have nothing to gain by discovering a critical consciousness that challenges the dominant culture. Their resistance, he maintains, is an attempt to cling to the ideologies that support and maintain their interests and privilege. Only by somehow transcending such privilege (leaving the cave) can critical learning take place, but his students, comfortable in their caves, refuse to leave. By attributing his students' resistance to their economic backgrounds and class interests, however, Knoblauch risks reducing the complexities of critical teaching and learning to a simple equation between competing socioeconomic classes. More tellingly, he fails to examine his own reliance on a Platonic narrative of teaching that, like his students' reliance on the myths of middle-class existence, limits his ability to see possible shadows.

Nancy Armstrong's analysis of domestic literature in eighteenth- and nineteenth-century England helps to answer Knoblauch by explaining how the rhetorical features of stories themselves invite conservative readings of even radical texts. Noting that domesticity focuses on marital alliances between different genders and classes, Armstrong argues that middle-class readers are able to formulate from their reading of novels a cultural identity based on myths of economic upward mobility and homogenous class interests. Narrative structure (in this case, the familiar marriage plot of domestic fiction), not any overt conservative move on the part of the writer or reader, reinforces these myths. These structures depend on shared assumptions about causality, unity, origin, and resolution that are characteristic of Western thought. Consequently, readers may miss the point of any text that disrupts or challenges middle-class hegemony—so much so that we impose even on those texts that seek to undermine them a traditional conception of beginnings and endings, goals and results, and lessons and morals—much as my students want to do with "The Lesson."

At the center of sound critical teaching, then, is an awareness of how texts elide certain issues. What kinds of class discussion and learning do they circumvent? I would like to suggest that, by applying some fundamental literary and rhetorical principles to these stories—those we tell ourselves, those our students tell, and those we teach—we can render the "problem" of student resistance a rich site of learning and growth, rather than an obstacle to be overcome. Indeed, the ways in which my students resist "The Lesson" invite the reader-response technique of analyzing their responses alongside the texts that produced them. In this way, student resistance provides teachers a context for examining with students the rhetorical and political dimensions of reading. If we understand student resistance as stemming not from students' class interests, as Knoblauch does, but from reading strategies practiced by middle-class readers on texts created by and contingent upon those readers, then we may see why students have trouble interpreting "The Lesson." It is not only, as Knoblauch argues, because they have an interest in seeing the middle-class values challenged in the text prevail; rather, it is also because a conservative evaluation of the text resides in the text's very narrative. Any successful teaching of the story, then, must make students aware of both dimensions.

In order to get my students to see the complexity of Bambara's story, I begin the term with a unit on money and work that includes Lorraine Hansberry's *A Raisin in the Sun*, a text that shares several important features with "The Lesson." Although this play challenges the middle-class myth of upward mobility, it is often read by students, as well as by general audiences, as a triumph of the American Dream. A typical response comes from my student Mia:

> The play shows how each person's dream can come true after all: everyone stuck to their dream, didn't give up and kept working toward it and in the end they got what they wanted.

Another student comments on the Youngers' triumph over racism:

> I was really glad Walter didn't give in to Mr. Lindner. It shows that even though things used to be pretty bad, if you stand up for what you believe in, like Walter did, issues like racism don't have to be a problem. You can still get what you want. The ending made me think how far we have come since those days thanks to people like Walter.

In approaching Hansberry's play, I ask how it depicts, as she herself said in an interview, the tragic failure of the American Dream for blacks. I pose this question early in the discussion, then focusing students on more traditional issues concerning narrative structure. To do this, I give the students the following quotation, taken from a general textbook in a chapter on plot: "Plots move toward resolving conflict. They do this by granting desire." I then ask the students both to examine the action of the play through this lens and to consider which character they would designate as the most important. After working in groups, students report back to the whole class. What emerges from the discussion is that Walter, who most see as a central character, cannot achieve his dream; the play does not grant his desire. The question for the students then is how does the play achieve the resolution and closure they all felt the ending provided?

One answer is that, although Walter's dreams of radical upward mobility do not and cannot come true (and this impossibility is how the play attempts to subvert the Horatio Alger myth of American economic reward), this narrative assertion is eclipsed by the conventions at work in the rest of the play. Readers (or viewers) are thus allowed to ignore the essential message Hansberry sends through the character of Walter by focusing instead on Ruth and Mama, whose dreams, much more modest in nature, do come true. That audiences derive enough satisfaction from the granting of two relatively minor characters' dreams to read the ending as happy, and that they can as a result of this satisfaction essentially ignore the fates of Walter and Beneatha, is a telling indication of the force of our need for resolution and closure.

To help students understand how strong is our need for conventional narrative structure, I ask them, as a prereading exercise, to scan the opening descriptions of the Youngers' home and then, based on those descriptions, to write a brief prediction of what the play might be about. When they are finished, I ask for volunteers to summarize from their writing and I jot various narrative structures on the board as they talk. Their narratives appear on the surface to be original and creative. Some students predict a triumph over racism, others a death in the family, others still a struggle with the ghetto conditions the opening scene sets up. Running through these apparently different ideas, however, are shared elements: all the plots rely on adversity and triumph over it, or, to use more traditional literary terminology, conflict and resolution. I point this out and then ask students to jot down plot ideas that don't conform to these elements. The students are surprised at how difficult this question proves, and we segue into a discussion of our need for certain kinds of narratives and how we resist stories that don't meet these needs.

After we have read the play, I tell the students about the discrepancy between audience response and Hansberry's intentions, and we discuss why Hansberry might have seen the ending as tragic rather than happy. Again in small groups, the students collaborate to write different endings to the play or to find places earlier in the text where the play might have ended on a more obviously tragic note. This exercise quickly makes apparent a set of reading strategies that repeats Hansberry's initial gesture of textual closure. To "close" the play at all, my students discover, they must resolve the play's dramatic action. But resolution to a play that takes on American racism and economic inequities would require a plot about radical revolution or, conversely, an equally radical homogenizing of differences. Unwilling to depict revolution, my students inevitably settle for the latter, allowing audiences to come away from the play with their own values intact, despite the play's attempt to deconstruct them. Regardless, discussion makes students aware of their choice and, perhaps, uneasy about it.

These activities set up our discussion of "The Lesson." Radical though it may appear, the story contains several rhetorical and thematic elements that provoke predictable responses from the reader. For example, the title of Bambara's story initiates middle-class interpretive gestures by signaling the presence of a Sunday-school-like moral that "good" readers derive from the text. Those students who have been trained only to see literature as containing universal themes and Hollywood-style closure where good overcomes evil are left at a loss. On the surface, the ghetto setting and language of the narrator cue conventional assumptions about race and poverty in capitalist America—

namely, that luxuries and wealth reward the industrious, poverty punishes the weak. If, however, students are prepared to read not only the text but their responses to it, then they will come to see both "texts" as performing certain cultural functions.

Before the students read "The Lesson," I tell them that the story involves poor African American children from Harlem on a trip to Fifth Avenue, where they encounter, for the first time, the luxuries money buys. I ask the students to predict the lesson of the story's title. The students offer lessons very similar to the postreading responses quoted earlier. Then I initiate a discussion focused on those features in the text, encompassed in the brief outline of the story's plot that I gave earlier, that either specifically question or rely on these assumptions. We brainstorm the purposes behind reading literature and discover that most of the class believes literature to be about "universal themes" or "learning" about life. I then connect their answers to the story's title and ask the students to consider the implications of this connection. We move on to setting, brainstorming and discussing assumptions about New York ghettos and Fifth Avenue. Again I suggest connections between the setting, our assumptions about it, and our readings of the story, inviting students to consider the implications of the connections. Finally, we brainstorm assumptions about poverty and wealth. Given these conventional assumptions, and given the narrative movement toward closure that we noticed in *A Raisin in the Sun,* I ask, what kind of lesson might this story narrate?

At the next class meeting, after students have read the story, I ask them to freewrite about the story's title and to consider what might be the lesson of the story. We investigate the responses from the point of view of narrative structure. With responses like Mia's, Brian's, and Kevin's, I ask the students to examine textual features and reader's assumptions in light of how they circumscribe interpretation, making "work hard/get ahead" seem a probable interpretation in a story that distinctly defies such bourgeois simplification. I then ask students to find places in the text where Bambara subverts these assumptions.

My strategy thus uses, rather than avoids or transcends, student resistance. Resistance is part of the text that teaches students about the power of both cultural and textual conventions. By identifying the conservative elements of the text, students are able to question those elements from a perspective that is not threatening because it is not personal. Often implicitly critiquing their own values, they are explicitly engaged in an examination of narrative and rhetorical conventions and the way Bambara uses—and subverts—them. At the same time, they gain an awareness of the way narratives shape—even make possible—how we understand our lives. The result is a less resistant student readership. As teachers, our pedagogy is more deeply rooted, as should be all classroom literature discussions, in rhetoric itself, in engaging students in an examination of the ideological implications of the production and consumption of texts.

Works Cited

Armstrong, Nancy. *Desire and Domestic Fiction: A Political History of the Novel.* New York: Oxford UP, 1987.

Bambara, Toni Cade. "The Lesson." *Literature for Composition: Essays, Fiction, Poetry, and Drama.* Ed. Sylvan Barnet, Morton Berman, William Burto, and Marcia Stubbs. New York: HarperCollins College, 1996. 993–98.

Barnet, Sylvan, Morton Berman, William Burto, and Marcia Stubbs, eds. *Literature for Composition: Essays, Fiction, Poetry, and Drama: Instructor's Handbook.* New York: HarperCollins College, 1996.

Knoblauch, C. H. "Critical Teaching and Dominant Culture." *Composition and Resistance.* Ed. C. Mark Hurlbert and Michael Blitz. Portsmouth, NH: Boynton/Cook, 1991. 12–21.

Silko, Leslie Marmon. "Language and Literature from a Pueblo Indian Perspective." *English Literature: Opening Up the Canon.* Ed. Leslie A. Fiedler and Houston A. Baker Jr. Baltimore: Johns Hopkins University Press, 1981. 54–72.

Further Reading

hooks, bell. *Teaching to Transgress: Education as the Practice of Freedom.* New York: Routledge, 1994.

Luke, Carmon, and Jennifer Gore. *Feminism and Critical Pedagogy.* New York: Routledge, 1992.

21 Learning to Listen to Stories: Sherman Alexie's "Witnesses, Secret and Not"

Susan Berry Brill de Ramirez
Bradley University

Story has its own life, its very own, and we are the voice carried with it.

Simon J. Ortiz, *After and before the Lightning*

For several years, I have struggled with the difficulty of teaching literary worlds that are in many ways foreign to my students' experiences (both literary and lived). Teaching American Indian literatures is a case in point. As a non-Native professor working at Bradley University, a school in Peoria, Illinois, with few, if any, Native students, I rely heavily upon secondary sources authored by Indian writers to provide the explanatory material my students need. Such material can help students make the textual connections necessary to their comprehension and appreciation of the readings. American Indian literatures, strongly informed by their oral storytelling roots, invite their readers to participate in their story worlds in ways that diverge substantially from Western literary critical reading strategies. The job of literature teachers is to guide students in/to these story worlds through a reliance on the strategies of the oral traditions themselves—I say "in/to" to convey the conjunctive process of approaching the story worlds ("to"), entering them as listener-readers ("into"), and becoming active participants in those stories ("in").

One of my recent classes focused on Southwest Indian writers. For this class, I was able to bring the students out to Indian country for over two weeks. The students lived and worked on the Navajo reservation, doing volunteer work for the tribe (such as photography for the tourism bureau or helping with the babies and children at one of the larger day care facilities). They learned about the culture and the traditions from local oral historians, met Indian writers and listened to readings of their work, and, most important, became a part of that world for a period of time. As a result of inhabiting that world, the students read American Indian novels, stories, and poetry with far greater ease than had my other students back at Bradley. Moreover, they stopped seeing the Indian worlds of the stories as, to use the terminology of colonialist discourse, "other" from their own worlds as they learned to read themselves (as co-creative listener-readers) into the worlds of the stories.

The connections my students were able to make by visiting the Navajo reservation are those that I would like for all of my students to make. The dilemma for me is how to bring my students in Peoria into the Indian worlds of the stories without leaving Peoria. I have been convinced that this is possible, but it means stepping outside the bounds of common pedagogy and Western literary critical practice and exploring new ways of reading and teaching—new pathways, as it were. In particular, it means turning to American Indian oral storytelling traditions and discerning their underlying structures and language games.

My strategy for reading and teaching American Indian literatures centers on a discussion of their *conversive* literary structures and reading techniques (with *conversive* combining both senses of *conversion* and *conversation*). Here, I apply these techniques to Sherman Alexie's short story "Witnesses, Secret and Not," although the methods are applicable to the broader collection of American Indian literatures, as well as to other world literatures that are closely tied to their respective oral traditions. One key to this process lies in the very nature of storytelling, which requires the interactive presence of its listeners or, in the case of written stories, readers. As Leslie Marmon Silko explains, "the storytelling always includes the audience and the listeners, and, in fact, a great deal of the story is believed to be inside the listener, and the storyteller's role is to draw the story out of the listeners" ("Language and Literature" 57). In other words, the storyteller and the listeners actually co-create the story through their interactions with each other. To do so, storytellers use a range of linguistic, paralinguistic, and kinesic strategies (such as repetition, voice shifts to a second-person voice speaking directly to the listeners, facial expressions and bodily movements, familiar phrases, and intentional periods of silence), all of which involve the listeners as direct parts of the telling event and, thereby, as participants within the told story itself. Listeners are expected to respond thoughtfully and behaviorally, perhaps with knowing nods or vocal responses. As Silko explains about Laguna storytelling, "The Laguna people always begin their stories with 'humma-hah': that means 'long ago.' And the ones who are listening say 'aaaa-eh'" (*Storyteller* 38).

We can see the conventions of storytelling in Alexie's "A Drug Called Tradition," a story in which several young men struggle to find their selves and their visions at the bottom of bottles of alcohol. One of the young men, the storyteller Thomas Builds-the-Fire, leaves the others after telling them a story. Alexie writes,

> Before he left for good, though, he turned back to Junior and me and yelled at us. I couldn't really understand what he was saying, but Junior swore he told us not to slow dance with our skeletons.
> "What the hell does that mean?" I asked.
> "I don't know," Junior said. (21)

This passage is followed by several lines of blank spacing on the page—room for his readers to respond, time to think about Thomas's advice, and space to help delineate a shift in voice. Alexie then turns to his listener-readers and writes, "There are things you should learn" (21). With this voice shift, Alexie very clearly intertwines his readers with the young Indian men, Junior and Victor. Junior and Victor do not understand Thomas's story and his parting advice, and we might not either. But Alexie steps in and tells us that understanding is important. He then helps everyone, including us, to understand Thomas's advice. In this one voice shift and empty spacing, then, Alexie incorporates strategies from oral storytelling into his written story so that his readers take on actual roles *within* the story.

Because students are accustomed to having an outside role as readers, teaching Alexie's stories—and also other works by Indian writers—means that classroom time allotments for the readings need to be increased. Students more familiar with traditional British and American literatures expect novels and short stories to arrive complete, with no requirements that they co-create and complete the stories. American Indian literatures, however, demand that students take on active roles as listener-readers. Their relational interactions will lead to insights that can come only from reading and reading again, finding themselves within the story and interacting with the storyteller/author and with the other persons in the story (both the written characters and other listener-readers). In fact, without our spending the extra time needed to process these orally informed works, the stories will either frustrate students or, worse, appear to them as shallow, undeveloped, and simplistic.

In my first-year American literature course, I have taught Alexie's collection of short stories *The Lone Ranger and Tonto Fistfight in Heaven*. With this book and the other assigned works of American Indian literatures, I slow the pace of the class by dividing the students into groups, with each group focusing on just a few of the stories. I also explain to the class that these stories, like poetry and other more orally informed writing, require more time, more reader interaction, and an intimacy between the listener-reader and the story behind the text (analogous to the relationship between a listener and a storyteller). And, as in the case of poetry, I encourage the students to read the works aloud.

The groups have two specific charges. One is for all group members to select one story that they will learn and retell orally to the group. These retellings are to be done in the students' own words even though specific lines may be repeated verbatim. Students may speak with their own voice, or, as storytellers, they may step into the first-person voice of one of the characters, perhaps even Alexie himself; alternatively, students may create an entirely new voice from which to tell the story. These storytellings are told within each group because there is insufficient time for all students to tell their stories to the entire class. This strategy also helps those students who are not comfortable performing in front of a class but who may be outstanding storytellers within their small groups. Then, each group shares one of their storytellings with the class as a whole. Through this exercise, students learn the interactive reality of storytelling both as storytellers and as storylisteners. And, perhaps most important, students, in order to learn a story well enough to tell it effectively, become participants in the story as fully as are its ostensibly fictional characters.

Storytelling is not drama in the sense of working from a script. Like a jazz performance, storytelling is improvisational, with the story evolving through the interaction between the teller and listeners. While there are basic elements of specific stories that appear in each telling, how these elements are played out will necessarily shift from telling to telling and from teller to teller. In fact, when Alexie performs his work in public, he often changes the words and even sometimes the actual events of the stories. Alexie, like a number of other Indian writers, is courageously pushing the boundaries between the literary and the oral. His public "readings" are storytellings, and the conversively interactive forms of his stories move us light years away from the critical strategies of modern and postmodern *literary* theories. Having students retell his stories—the "heresy of paraphrase" of the New Critics—enables them to cross the literary divide into Indian America.

In order to prepare students for their further interactions with Alexie's stories, I discuss a range of conversive literary strategies. In the process, I emphasize how reader responsibility decreases as texts become more discursively "objective" (a continuum might be drawn from speeches and letters, which presume an interactive audience, to textbooks, in which the reader is largely absented through the objective and distancing third-person voice). Although there is not space to discuss each of these at length, I do want to identify the range of conversive literary structures that appear in American Indian literatures, including voice shifts to a second-person voice (speaking directly and personally to the reader), voice shifts to a first-person plural voice of inclusion, repetition and deliberate explanations (both to help the reader's understanding of the underlying issues and significances within the story), formulaic introductions and endings (e.g., "A long time ago . . ."), archaic words, mythic time, mythic events, song, ritual, prayer, stories and storytelling within stories, "carrying it hither" (situating the story in the listener-reader's world and time), intersubjectivity and an emphasis on relationships and connections (e.g., the self as having meaning, not individually, but in relation to other selves), objects taking on subjective status (e.g., animals, vegetation, rocks presented as persons with their own subjectivity), conjunction of the imaginary and the real, personalities and emotions evoked rather than described (minimalism), stories and conversations that extend beyond the boundaries of the written text, moral and ethical lessons, the interactive and interrelational role of readers as listener-readers, and the transformative capacity of the stories to effect real change in the perceptions and lives of their listener-readers. Of course, writers like Alexie may not use all of these strategies, but, by being alert to them, we may identify the extent to which oral traditions shape meaning and our responsibilities in that process.

The short stories in Alexie's *The Lone Ranger and Tonto Fistfight in Heaven* offer good examples of how orally informed literatures demand alternative reading strategies if readers are to *enter* the stories as listener-readers. In "Witnesses, Secret and Not," Alexie tells the story of a thirteen-year-old reservation boy's trip into Spokane with his father. The story is very simple. They drive into Spokane, see drunken Indians, including one whom they know from the reservation, stop at a fast-food restaurant for lunch, go to the police station where the father is questioned about the murder of a friend of his, and then return home. The entire story takes place in less than one day. And yet, within a very few pages and with the spare pen strokes of a conversive literary structure, Alexie conveys volumes about reservation life, racism, the judicial system, diet, the human condition, men's issues, family relations, and a boy's coming of age.

"Witnesses, Secret and Not" is told in the first-person voice of the boy, who speaks directly to the reader in a comfortable manner that creates the intimacy of the storytelling event. Alexie's listener-readers are brought directly into the story, at times being the boy's confidant, at other times being present and sharing the events with him as they occur. The story moves back and forth between the present-tense events of the story and the boy's added commentary offered to his listener-readers. As listener-readers of the story, we both watch the boy's father walk uncomfortably into the police station and hear the boy's impressions of the event. The boy tells us, "I watched my father walk toward the police station. Wearing old jeans and a red T-shirt, he looked very obvious next to the police uniforms and three-piece suits. He looked as Indian as you can get" (219). In these few lines, Alexie communicates the weight of five hundred years of racist objectification that defines non-whites as different, other, and thereby inferior. The oppositionality of such a perspective is so pervasive that, off the reservation, an Indian boy will slip into the mindset of the dominant culture and perceive even his own father in such terms. Reflecting on his perceptions, the boy explains,

> I could spend my whole life on the reservation and never once would I see a friend of mine and think how Indian he looked. But as soon as I get off the reservation, among all the white people, every Indian gets exaggerated. My father's braids looked three miles long and black and shiny as a police-issue revolver. He turned back and waved to me just before he disappeared into the station. (219)

In this brief passage Alexie demonstrates the transformative power of storytelling and, within a literary framework, of conversive literary structures. As Paul V. Kroskrity explains, storytellers situate their stories in their listeners' worlds, a strategy he calls "carrying it hither" (197). However, because storytelling is not only the creation of the teller, but requires effort on the part of both teller and listener, storytellers must make it possible for their listeners to become part of the story world. The teller has the responsibility to bring the story close to the listeners who, in turn, have the responsibility of becoming active participants in the telling event and story. Knowing that his audience extends beyond the bounds of the Spokane Indian reservation, Alexie provides the necessary explanatory information to give his non-Indian readers the familiarity they need to become intimate and interactive listener-readers of his stories. After noting how the boy's father looked walking into the police station, Alexie then explains the perception more clearly to make sure that his listener-readers understand the changing perceptions Indian people experience in relation to the institutionalized racism in the United States. Alexie ends the quoted passage with the boy telling us, "He turned back and waved to me just before he disappeared into the station" (219). In the father's gesture, we see the very real pathos underlying the connection between father and son. We don't read that the boy waved back, an absence that shows the perceptual distance that has begun to separate father and son as the boy begins to look at his father through the objectifying eyes of the dominant culture's racism.

Throughout the story, the metaphor of disappearance is used to represent the extent to which Indian people are marginalized and erased within the values, expectations, and realities of the dominant culture. As Alexie writes, "Sometimes it seems like all Indians can do is talk about the disappeared" (222). The father's own disappearance in the station is further evidenced in his interactions with the police detective, who never speaks *with* but rather *at* or *down to* him. After rejoining his father, the boy explains that he and his father "walked out of the police station, feeling guilty. I kept wondering if they knew. . . . I stole my cousin's bike and wrecked it on purpose. Kept wrecking it until it was useless" (222). In the boy's behavior, we see five hundred years of frustration and anger misdirected onto his cousin's bicycle.

In the brief penultimate paragraph, Alexie writes, "My father got completely out of control once because he lost the car keys. Explain that to a sociologist" (223). The boy's father, Alexie's father, the storyteller's father, here the imaginary and the real converge and overlap as an intimate detail in the father's life is shared with the listener-reader in a manner that assumes a familiarity and understanding beyond that of an outside and objectively distanced sociologist. Alexie expects the listener-readers of his story to understand. And, in the separation of those two sentences as a separate paragraph, Alexie emphasizes their importance through the spacing that gives the listener-reader the extra time in which to reflect and respond.

Alexie then brings us into the family home: "When we got home everybody was there, everybody" (223). The family was all together waiting for their return, understanding the significance of the trip off the reservation, into the city, and to the police station. "My father sat at the table and nearly cried into his food. Then, of course, he did cry into his food and we all watched him. All of us"—family and Alexie's invited listener-readers, too (223). And we are expected not merely to observe his father cry as distanced outsiders but as intimate, caring friends welcomed into the world of a reservation family. Through our real and storied relationships with the father, his son, and family, we watch those tears understanding the historicity behind generations of Indian men emasculated, marginalized, and disappeared.

Through the conversive literary structures in the text and conversively relational reading strategies, listener-readers participate in the story with an intimacy that connects the readers more closely to the story world. When I have approached these literatures in the classroom with traditional Western critical methods, there are usually some students who complain that "all these Indian writers do is white-bash." Without close (if any) contact with Indian country, they approach these works as outside readers, feeling that the writers are blaming them and all other white people for the difficulties experienced by Indian peoples living in our country. While it is true that those of us with white color privilege reap the color advantages within a racist country, this does not mean that we cannot step across the various boundaries that separate us from Native America and begin to knit together the fragmented fabric of humankind. Indian people understand that all things in our world are interrelated. As Peggy Beck, Anna Lee Walters, and Nia Francisco explain, "Through this interdependency and aware-ness of relationships, the universe is balanced" (13). Indian writers like Sherman Alexie welcome their readers, Indian and non-Indian alike, into the worlds of their stories.

Even when Alexie shares his rage at five hundred years of horrific atrocities perpetrated against the indigenous peoples of the Americas, he is not yelling *at* us in a distancing manner. He is venting his anger and frustration *to* us, just as might a friend or family member simply needing the release and wanting us to understand as only close and caring listeners can. To read and to teach Alexie's writing, and the writings by many other Indian writers, we need to honor our side of the storytelling compact. This means not only reading these stories, but listening to them, and listening to them with the open minds and understanding hearts expected of listener-readers. In this way, we are involved much more deeply than is possible through the more superficial level of a distanced mental engagement, for here under-standing comes from the interwoven actions of mind and heart, with the mind being the transmitter and organizer of information and thoughts, and the heart, ultimately, being the actual seat of conversive knowing. This process is truly encompassing, a fact that explains why storytelling and conversive reading are transforming activities for their listeners and listener-readers.

Works Cited

Alexie, Sherman. *The Lone Ranger and Tonto Fistfight in Heaven*. New York: HarperPerennial, 1994.

Beck, Peggy, Anna Lee Walters, and Nia Francisco. *The Sacred: Ways of Knowledge, Sources of Life*. Tsaile and Flagstaff, AZ: Navajo Community College P and Northland, 1990.

Kroskrity, Paul V. "Growing with Stories: Line, Verse, and Genre in an Arizona Tewa Text." *Journal of Anthropological Research* 41.2 (1985): 183–99.

Silko, Leslie Marmon. "Language and Literature from a Pueblo Indian Perspective." *English Literature: Opening Up the Canon*. Ed. Leslie A. Fiedler and Houston A. Baker Jr. Baltimore: Johns Hopkins UP, 1981. 54–72.

———. *Storyteller*. New York: Arcade, 1981.

Further Reading

Alexie, Sherman. *Indian Killer* and interview with the author. Audiocassettes. Read by Sherman Alexie. San Bruno, CA: Audio Literature, 1996.

———. *Smoke Signals: A Screenplay*. New York: Hyperion, 1998.

Bauman, Richard. "Verbal Art as Performance." *American Anthropologist* 77.2 (June 1975): 290–311.

Brill, Susan B. "Discovering the Order and Structure of Things: A Conversive Approach to Contemporary Navajo Poetry." *Studies in American Indian Literatures* 7.3 (Fall 1995): 51–70.

Frey, Rodney. "Re-telling One's Own: Storytelling Among the Apsáalooke (Crow Indians)." *Plains Anthropologist* 28 (May 1983): 129–35.

McIntosh, Peggy. "White Privilege: Unpacking the Invisible Knapsack." *Peace and Freedom* July/August 1989: 10–12.

Tannen, Deborah. *Talking Voices: Repetition, Dialogue and Imagery in Conversational Discourse*. Cambridge: Cambridge UP, 1989.

VI Refining Taste

We have forgotten, I think, how unnatural writing is. . . . Writers—easy and natural writers—have always been, first of all, readers. Just as the spoken language is absorbed by the ear, so written language has to be learned from the pages of writers. . . .

Helen Vendler, "What We Have Loved, Others Will Love"

Like it or not, much of what we do in educating students involves taste. Taste, at its best, allows us to separate the vacuous and conventional from the intriguing and original. We become, in the best sense, epicureans, seeking not pleasure alone but the refinement of it. As epicureans of the short story, our attention turns to style. Style must be suitable to the topic, or else the topic will be undermined or satirized: it is part of the organic wholeness of the short story. Robert Penn Warren attests to this in saying that, for instance, the ornate and gentle style of Henry James would not work in describing the action of cold-blooded murder in Hemingway's "The Killers":

> As an example of the relation of words, of style, to the expressive whole which is fiction, let us take Hemingway. We readily see how the stripped, laconic, monosyllabic style relates to the tight-lipped, stoical ethic, the cult of self-discipline, the physicality and the anti-intellectualism and the other such elements that enter into his characteristic view of the world. Imagine Henry James writing Hemingway's story "The Killers." The complicated sentence structure of James, the deliberate and subtle rhythms, the careful parentheses—all these things express the delicate intellectual, social, and aesthetic discriminations with which James concerned himself. But what in the Lord's name would they have to do with the shocking blankness of the moment when the gangsters enter the lunchroom, in their tight-buttoned identical blue overcoats, with gloves on their hands so as not to leave fingerprints when they kill the Swede? (65)

Warren recognized, with Wallace Stevens, that "A change of style is a change of subject."

Subject is not the only issue with style, of course. Raymond Queneau demonstrates the semiotic range of style in his classic *Exercises in Style* (1947), where he retells the same simple plot in one hundred hilariously different ways. Style is the author's fingerprint: idiosyncratic choice and sequence of words, the length and cadence of sentences, and hand-picked images—the stylistic fingerprint that makes it possible, even hundreds of years after an author's death, to authenticate authorship through diction, vocabulary, and rhythm. To imagine one author's works written in the style of another is to imagine a completely different work of art, with a different spin on its meaning, because a different sculptor has cast it into words.

Style in writing, like style in clothing, is a function of the times. The nuances and modes of language are inextricably bound up with the ideas being bandied about in a particular era. A writer reaches to new patterns of writing to express new patterns of thought. Modernist fiction, for example, often uses highly idiosyncratic style in conveying the opposing ideas of social alienation and egotism. To such writers, the objective narrative voice of earlier periods was inadequate to communicate what it meant to be part of a "lost generation." Hemingway measured his world with laconic words; Gertrude Stein reacted to hers with vexing repetitions. In the postmodern era, narrative experimentation was pushed again. For instance, in the labyrinthine musings of John Barth's "Lost in the Funhouse" and the deconstructed plots of Donald Barthelme's "The Balloon," the process of fiction-making all but eclipses content. Style jars us awake, and that's the point.

Style that is consistent with a particular literary movement identifies it as part of that movement. But style that is "out of synch" with the times or with prevailing opinions of what constitutes literature often gets dismissed as "bad." Bad style is style that somehow betrays the meaning. Style that is overly sentimental might be deemed "bad" unless it exaggerates sentimentality to the point of self-mockery; then it is clever. Conversely, highly sophisticated writing can appear erudite and masterful, until it loses all realism; then it is pompous. Styles come into and go out of fashion, as they reflect or oppose prevailing cultural values. One generation's flowery excesses leads to the next generation's sparse, laconic prose, as the styles of the older generation are replaced, along with its values. Style contributes to what is accepted as "good" literature and serves as a marker for each era's literary elite, the cultural savants who define good literature and thus shape the course of literary history through their selections.

In this section, two essays discuss ways to involve students in assessing what constitutes literary merit. Peter Kratzke's students deconstruct the canon as a natural outgrowth of discovering the syrupy excesses of Dreiser's "Typhoon," and Tom Hansen's students consider the mercenary goals of the short fiction producer as they assess fictional flaws—perhaps the product of hasty writing—that they find in Connell's "The Most Dangerous Game." Another aspect of style lies in affinities and allusions between texts. The allusions made by an author may be conscious or unconscious mimicking or homage to works and events that influenced and shaped the writer's style and interests. Foucault says that authors are mere conduits of the cultural conscience, yet it is the individual artist's affinities to his or her culture that give rise to that individual's genius and contribution back to society. Here two essays address ways to recognize intertextual allusions and influences in stories. Pat Onion has her students examine the traditional American Indian story that underlies Erdrich's story "American Horse" as a way to teach them the skill of mediating between cultures, and Richard Mezo traces visual and historical allusions in Joyce Carol Oates's story "Where Are You Going, Where Have You Been?" that she fused into her unique and compelling story of lost innocence, breathing new life into an old motif.

Like every other form of art, literature is no more but nothing less than a matter of life and death. The only question worth asking about a story—or a poem, or a piece of sculpture, or a new concert hall—is, "Is it dead or alive?"

Works Cited

Barth, John. "Lost in the Funhouse." *Fiction 100*. 5th ed. James H. Pickering, ed. New York: Macmillan, 1988. 88–103.

Barthelme, Donald. "The Balloon." *Sixty Stories*. New York: Putnam, 1981. 53–58.

Ellis, John. *Literature Lost: Social Agendas and the Corruption of the Humanities*. New Haven, CT: Yale UP, 1997.

Queneau, Raymond. *Exercises in Style*. 1947. New York: New Directions, 1981.

Warren, Robert Penn. "Why Do We Read Fiction?" *New and Selected Essays*. New York: Random House, 1989. 55–66.

22 "Sometimes, Bad Is Bad": Teaching Theodore Dreiser's "Typhoon" and the American Literary Canon

Peter Kratzke
Michigan State University

In literature, as in art, manner is everything and matter nothing; I mean that Matter, however important, has nothing to do with the art *of literature; that is a thing apart. In literature it makes very little difference what you say, but a great deal how you say it.*

Ambrose Bierce, "The Matter of Manner"

In survey classes that establish a sweep of literary history, four principal issues of textual evaluation arise: meaning, method, genre, and canon (Posner 220). The first three issues are usually encompassed by the intrinsic consideration of theme. However, the last issue, canon, is more difficult because it looks to the extrinsic relationship between a text and its readers. In survey classes, this relationship is one-sided: the text is allotted a stamp of canonicity simply because it is in the anthology at hand, and its readers lack critical authority simply because they are first-year students and sophomores. Teaching Theodore Dreiser's "Typhoon" (1926), I have found, is an ideal occasion to uncover the nature of the canon. Students generally like the story—it is vivid and melodramatic—but, once they begin reading it aloud, once they begin examining their assumptions of its "literariness," they also feel empowered to conclude, in the words of the singer Huey Lewis, "sometimes, bad is bad."

The plot of "Typhoon" bears review here. Ida Zobel, a daughter of German immigrants, lives a repressed life, overseen by the severe hand of her widower father William and taught in a private school by "an aged German spinster of the name of Elizabeth Hohstauffer . . ." (1222).

Awakening to the rush of adolescence in the midst of the Jazz Age, Ida meets Edward Haptfuhrer, a self-styled "Lothario" (1234) who makes sport of conquering the naive Ida. Ida becomes pregnant, and Edward forsakes her. Ida is desperate, procures a gun, and, "as much to her astonishment as to his . . ." (1240), shoots Edward after he pushes her. Before he dies, Edward admits "he had wronged [Ida]" (1241). The press sensationalizes Ida's plight, and a rich woman, Mrs. Chandler, befriends her. A sympathetic jury acquits Ida, and Mrs. Chandler provides her a safe retreat. After Ida delivers her child, Eric, she is still tormented by guilt, and she drowns herself.

"Typhoon" is included in the *Heath Anthology of American Literature,* a widely used text that is noteworthy for its attempt to expand the canon by including underrepresented authors and cultures. In the *Instructor's Guide* to the *Heath,* contributing editors James M. Hutchisson and James L. W. West III advise that the response of Dreiser's audience might be different from our own. They write, "It's a good idea to show students how thoroughly trapped and damned Ida Zobel is by an illicit pregnancy. Children of the 1990s will likely try to foist their own standards back onto her time and place" (489). Hutchisson and West admit, in other words, that the story's plot does not directly connect with contemporary audiences. If that is so, one may ask why it is canonical and, indeed, worth reading *as* literature.

The canon of American literature represented by the *Heath Anthology* raises a number of questions: Who determines the canon? Why do certain works represent their authors? What should be done with authors who while no longer culturally relevant are nonetheless important to literary history—when their work, in other words, passes from the living stuff of literature to the cultural artifact of history? And, what position should be held by authors who have good ideas but are bad writers? With "Typhoon," students often ask such questions: after all, if the story is not only disconnected from contemporary culture but, as Hutchisson and West also admit, marked by "verbal clumsiness" (489), why call it literature? Why should not the text simply die as so much bad fiction? Students who find Dreiser's style distasteful are in good company: Donald Pizer, a noted author on Dreiser, suggests that much of Dreiser's fiction "is marred by an inept prose style in which journalistic cliché, rank sentimentality and clumsy syntax compete for attention" (150–51). Philip Gerber, in his 1992 Twayne study, notes that Dreiser had been dubbed "the world's worst greatest writer" (113).

In "Typhoon," Dreiser's language is almost comical. This aspect of the story gives students a good laugh, often inspiring them to talk in

Dreiser-ese for several days. An example chosen almost at random will suffice here. In his confrontation with Ida about her pregnancy, Edward physically threatens her and says that he is probably not even the father. Ida, confronted with Edward's "threatening and savage look" (1237), thinks,

> The fierceness of his face—The horror of it! The disgrace! The shame! . . . That charge he had made! His rage! His hate even, and at the end of all this—her father! Her stepmother! If he, she— they—should come to know! And when they did! But no—something else must happen before even that should be allowed to happen. She must leave—or—or—better yet maybe drown herself—make away with herself in some way—or—or—. (1237)

Such exclamatory phrasing, perhaps effective at first, quickly grows tiresome. Hutchisson and West apologize for it by noting that "Typhoon" is a good example of "Dreiser's late style, a fragmented, free-association that attempts to accomplish many of the same things that stream-of-consciousness writers like James Joyce and William Faulkner were trying to do during the 1920s" (491). The canon is paved with similar attempts, however, and the reader squirms when near the story's end Ida contemplates her future years and the possibility of new lovers: "But no—no—not that. Never. She did not want that—could not—would not endure it" (1245).

In addition to histrionic language, Dreiser uses imagery in "Typhoon" with the subtlety of the proverbial brick through a jeweler's window. Notably, he describes Edward's interest in Ida as so much sport. In Edward's initial approach of Ida, "The thing to do was to outwit her father" (1226). For Edward, there is "No doubt as to his victory at any point" (1226), and he is "no longer hopefully interested by the possibility of defeat" (1227). Rather, he focuses on "the pride of showing to all the others how easy this conquest had been" (1228). Soon, his friends note that "He's got her on the run now" (1232). Once he conquers Ida, Edward feels "satisfied—his restless and overweening ego comforted by another victory—no danger of loss or defeat here . . ." (1232). Indeed, "The whole thing from the beginning had been so brazenly and even showily executed. If anything it was his masterpiece in brazen adventures thus far" (1234). Because Dreiser's imagery is so dogged, students find "Typhoon" an easy text from which to marshall evidence of hackneyed language and imagery. In a sort of contrary pedagogical effect, then, it trains them for their meeting with better literature.

If Dreiser's use of language and imagery raises suspicion about the canonicity of "Typhoon," his characterization does not help the case. Once again, reading the story has the effect of showing students why psychological depth, and not just ostensible change, is so important to literature. Dreiser's characters are all demonstrably "flat." William is self-serving: after Ida shoots Edward, William laments, "All his and his wife's care! And now the neighbors! His business! . . . This is terrible. And myself an honest man!" (1241). Edward, whose repentance is only noted in the newspapers, is never more than a shallow member of the nouveau riche; at one point he assesses his situation, "Gee—these skirts! It does beat hell!" (1234). Only Ida might achieve some depth, but it is not to be: the story's first line reads, "Into a singularly restricted and indifferent environment Ida Zobel was born" (1221), and, by the story's end, her suicide too clearly shows that she has not transcended those restrictions. Dreiser's apologists—critics no less than the likes of Alfred Kazin and Charles Walcutt—have consistently deflected attacks on Dreiser's artistry by citing his probing view of human tragedy. They say, as a sort of rallying cry, that Dreiser's matter transcends his manner. Their deflection is no doubt effective and true in regard to Dreiser's novels. (*Sister Carrie* and *An American Tragedy* are undoubtedly significant books.) However, Dreiser cannot overcome his narrative deficiencies in a short story like "Typhoon." Rather, his thesis of naturalistic tragedy eclipses his narrative, with his authorial intrusions fairly shouting his sense of determinism. For instance, near the story's beginning, Dreiser explains at length that William's "dictatorship" only yields "repression—and even fear at him which in the course of years took on the aspect of careful courtesy supplemented by accurate obedience" (1223). Ida's "accurate obedience" hides her sexual awakening, and, soon enough, she naively confuses lust for love: "There was a kind of madness, an ache in it all. Oh, for pleasure—pleasure!" (1225). In case his thesis is not patently clear by the story's end, Dreiser intrudes, this time in a fragment: "Yet in the main, and because her [Ida's] mood and health seemed to require it, left to contemplate the inexplicable chain of events which her primary desire for love had brought about" (1242). Whereas the author of classic literature approaches themes with the stealth of a cat burglar, in "Typhoon" Dreiser drives a steamroller.

Finally, indicting "Typhoon" as simply bad might best be called shooting fish in a barrel. However, in survey classes, considering Dreiser's story as non-literary can be a useful, even satisfying, experience. Students, in beginning to define for themselves what constitutes literature, dare to disagree with respected literary critics on the canon—and they have a case. In their appraisal of a given author, they come to realize that not everything written by that author is great. And, last, they realize that canonized authors are not gods of composition who exist beyond the realm of their own aspirations and abilities. Rather, students take heart in Dreiser's weaknesses, and they reappraise their own writing as not that—just—well—Oh, dear!—bad.

Works Cited

Dreiser, Theodore. "Typhoon." 1926. *The Heath Anthology of American Literature*. 2nd ed. Vol. 2. Ed. Paul Lauter et al. Lexington, MA: Heath, 1994. 1221–45.

Gerber, Philip. *Theodore Dreiser Revisited*. New York: Twayne, 1992.

Hutchisson, James M., and James L. W. West III. "Theodore Dreiser (1871–1945)." *Instructor's Guide for the Heath Anthology of American Literature*. Ed. Paul Lauter et al. Lexington, MA: Heath, 1994. 489–91.

Pizer, Donald. "Theodore Dreiser." *Dictionary of Literary Biography*. Vol. 12. Detroit: Gale, 1982.

Posner, Richard A. *Law and Literature: A Misunderstood Relation*. Cambridge, MA: Harvard UP, 1988.

23 Teaching Flawed Fiction: "The Most Dangerous Game"

Tom Hansen
Northern State University, Aberdeen, South Dakota

It was [John Gardner's] conviction that if the words in the story were blurred because of the author's insensitivity, carelessness, or sentimentality, then the story suffered from a tremendous handicap. But there was something even worse and something that must be avoided at all costs: if the words and the sentiments were dishonest, the author was faking it, writing about things he didn't care about or believe in, then nobody could ever care anything about it.

Raymond Carver, Foreword to *On Becoming a Novelist* by John Gardner

For many of us, the short story is the most rewarding literary genre to teach, not only because a number of our students read fiction on their own but also because television and movies have given them a comfortable familiarity with realistic narrative. They feel so at home with it that they don't question—don't, much of the time, even perceive—its conventions. They tend to think of stories as being somehow natural, as opposed to poems, which they think of as artificial. Because the artifice of poetry is so obvious to them, they view a poem as a made object—subject, as all made objects are, to manufacturing flaws. Stories are like life itself: real. The notion that a story ought to be "picked apart" to reveal not only its inner working but also, sometimes, its flaws, strikes many of them as unfair. It "ruins" the story. It obliges them to discriminate.

Students use *good* and *bad* as subjective terms. A thing is good if they like it, bad if they don't. If they hear their English teacher use these terms in a way that seems to be as objective as it is authoritative—not as if *good* and *bad* were matters of opinion but as if they were matters of

---

This essay previously appeared in the *Ohio Journal of the English Language Arts* 31.2 (Fall/Winter 1990): 20–22. Copyright ©1990 by Tom Hansen.

fact—they feel insecure. And why shouldn't they? We seem to be telling them not to trust their own subjective reactions. Sometimes they ask, "How can you tell if a story is good or bad?" If we say, "It's a complex process," and don't offer any explanation, they feel we are keeping something from them. If we tell them that the process requires a degree of maturity and judgment which results from having read a lot of fiction and having lived a lot of life, they feel we are disqualifying them from participation in the process. If we can afford the time, it would be better to spend a week explaining and demonstrating some of the considerations that this complex process involves.

Better yet, we should let them see for themselves, preferably in a story they have already studied in class. My favorite is Richard Connell's "The Most Dangerous Game," a frequently anthologized old chestnut. Because it is a fast-paced, struggle-to-the-death adventure story, students like it. Most of them get caught up in the suspense and read it fairly rapidly to find out how it ends. They find themselves liking it just as much after they spend class time examining it for plot, character, setting, point of view, and other elements of fiction. They begin to have faith in this analytical approach to short stories; by showing them how the story works, it helps them understand why they like what they like.

Now our trap is set. But we have to spring it subtly, ideally by allowing students to spring it on themselves. This requires that we not approach the story as if it were a shining example of failure. After all, they have just discovered that it succeeds in a number of ways. A more fruitful approach is to let them in on something they don't know but will be intrigued by: the hidden story behind many well-known stories, the one that explains where stories come from—how freelance fiction writers practice their trade and what market conditions they labor under. Once students are aware of these two things, they realize that a story, far from being natural, is a product made by a lone human being working under far-from-ideal circumstances.

Freelance Writers of Fiction

Freelancers take their name from the medieval knights-errant, whose allegiance was bound to no king or cause, and who were, therefore, free—which is to say, for hire, usually to the highest bidder. Freelance knights were essentially mercenaries who fought for pay and, often enough, for the love of fighting, just as their modern literary counterparts, freelance writers, write for pay and the love of writing. Unlike salaried writers, who work on the staff of newspapers or magazines, freelancers are self-employed. They make their own work assignments, force themselves to complete them, and then try to find paying markets for their finished work. No one gives them deadlines and no one issues them paychecks at the end of every month. They get paid if and when they sell work. A month with no sales is a month with no income. So unless they have inherited or married money, freelancers are constantly under pressure to produce and to find an immediate buyer for their work.

The ideal buyer for fiction freelancers is any well-known, high-paying magazine—one of those monthlies which regularly publish quality fiction. *Redbook* pays $1,000 and up for short stories (Holm 793). *Good Housekeeping* pays $1,000 minimum for a writer's first appearance in its pages (Holm 789). *The Atlantic* pays $2,500 for stories from 2,000 to 6,000 words (Holm 472). *Harper's* pays from $.50 to $1.00 per word (Holm 475). Obviously, there is money to be made in writing fiction. If a freelancer sells a story a month to one of these magazines, he or she can make as little as $1,000 or as much as $2,500 or more. But there are thousands of freelancers writing fiction today, and these commercial magazines publish very few stories per issue, frequently no more than two. Most new fiction today first appears in literary journals, but few of these journals pay more than $500 per story, and many of the most prestigious of them pay only $10 to $20 per printed page (Holm). Obviously, a freelancer must sell as much and as often as he or she can.

To maximize the chances of making a sale, a freelancer tailors each story to the magazine he or she plans on submitting it to. The writer will get perhaps a year's worth of back issues of a particular magazine, study the stories in it carefully, looking for clues that reveal the editor's preferences as they appear in recurring patterns of similarity from story to story, such as the age or gender or occupation or domestic situation of the protagonists, the kinds of crises they encounter, the various types and levels of conflict they become embroiled in. Freelancers do not purposely imitate stories already published in such magazines, but they can't afford to depart far from the pattern those published stories reveal.

They want to write the best stories they can, but they are realists—often with families to feed. They know how transient is any given issue of a magazine: one month on the newsstand, then consigned to oblivion. They know how seldom people look at back issues, except in doctors' waiting rooms. More than that, they know that people tend to read magazines, even their favorite magazines, the same way they read newspapers: as fast and as effortlessly as they can. Freelancers realize that few people, except for English teachers and their students, read fiction in a careful, attentive way. In short, they know that their stories will get a quick read—a fairly rapid once-over.

Needing to make that sale in order to pay their bills, aware that the particular issue in which their story appears has a shelf life of one month only, and knowing full well that their story will get a quick read—laboring under these market conditions, freelancers are all too often tempted to give a story the best quick write they can. Finished with it, they submit it to a magazine and take the rest of the day off. The next day, they start work on a new story. They will make it as perfect as they can under the circumstances. Sometimes, for good reasons or bad, they fall more than just a little short of that hoped-for perfection. Sometimes a slow, careful read reveals just how fast and careless a freelancer's writing can be.

"The Most Dangerous Game"

Richard Connell's "The Most Dangerous Game" may not have been written under quite such pressing circumstances, but it does show evidence of having been written too quickly. Students seem to find this evidence most compelling when they, rather than the teacher, are the ones to uncover it. They are quite willing to do this if told that they should consider the story not judgmentally, as a bad story filled with flaws, but neutrally, as a series of writer's strategies, some successful and some perhaps not so successful. They need to be reminded that writers, like murderers, have to plan everything in advance, even down to the smallest detail—cold-bloodedly plotting in order to determine precisely how they will gradually entangle their protagonist in a web of complications and how, by the story's end, they will extricate the protagonist from these entanglements.

Among those strategies Connell employs, the following usually intrigue students and generate lively discussion:

1. The Use of Setting to Establish Atmosphere. The moonless night, the mysterious reference to Ship-Trap Island, which even experienced sailors superstitiously dread, and where not even cannibals would live. . . . As an attempt to create atmosphere, this is a variation on "It was a dark and stormy night." Yet it is not always night. Once students begin reading and discussing this story in the broad daylight of common sense, the eerie atmosphere melts away. For example, the marine lighting system that lures ships onto submerged rocks seems very

modern in a story first published in 1924, and yet it is "old charts" that give this island its fearful name. It is said to be so menacing that even experienced sailors fear it; yet, as we shall soon see, a number of ships must regularly stop there to make deliveries. Finally, Whitney's comment about cannibals is worth having students explore. Would a tribe of cannibals, perfectly adapted to such a jungle environment, really be afraid of anything they might encounter on this island? How does Whitney come by this information? What is Connell's purpose in having him tell this to Rainsford?

2. The Initial Complication. Somehow Connell has to get the self-possessed, no-nonsense Rainsford off the ship and onto the island. Most students don't pay close attention to exactly how this happens. A way to remedy this is to have one student slowly read the falling-overboard scene while another simultaneously acts it out in mime, slowly, detail by detail. It soon becomes evident that Rainsford's exit is implausible and badly contrived (by Connell). The absurdity of his leaping upon the deck rail to better increase his chances of peering through the darkness—which he has just told Whitney he cannot see four yards into—is embarrassingly obvious. And his lunging to retrieve his pipe after one of the ship's ropes knocks it out of his mouth is an action which all his instincts as a professional hunter should warn him against. This scene utterly backfires on Connell. Instead of creating a moment of high drama, it illustrates, comically and quite inadvertently, yet one more way in which smoking can be dangerous to one's health.

3. The Physical Appearance of the Antagonists. Careful attention to the physical appearance of Ivan and Zaroff reveals how far Connell is willing to go in order to tip off even the most imperceptive of readers that these two are, from the outset, the villains of the piece. Students immediately recognize Ivan as a stock figure from horror stories and monster movies—the intellectually challenged assistant to a brilliant yet quite mad scientist—but they usually do not visualize Zaroff until asked to give a precise description of him, including his remarkably red lips, his mouthful of pointed teeth, and his symbolically black moustache, eyebrows, and eyes. A consideration of why these details are so frightening leads directly to a discussion of plausibility and author's intention: Why did Connell make Zaroff's lips so red and his teeth sharp? This is the point at which many students begin to see that Connell goes too far; that he is asking too much if he expects us to believe that Zaroff—or anyone else this side of Transylvania—really looks like this.

4. The Use of Setting to Characterize Zaroff. One of the things Connell has done to make readers dislike Zaroff is to present him as a wealthy, lone-wolf hedonist whose life is devoted to the pursuit of sophisticated pleasures. This is revealed through the details of his clothing, the linen, crystal, and silver with which his table is set, and the particular foods and wines he serves during Rainsford's brief stay with him before they hunt. Those students who remember that Zaroff and Ivan are supposed to be alone on this unknown island soon begin to see the obvious—that Zaroff could not possibly maintain his luxurious lifestyle without the frequent services of a milkman, an egg man, a wine merchant, a cook, a dish washer, a housekeeper, a tailor, and a dry cleaner. Far from being mysterious and unknown, this deserted island must be a regular package-drop point on the Federal Express or UPS delivery route.

5. Miscellaneous Details. As students get into the spirit of seeing this story as a series of tactical decisions made by its author, they judge a number of them to be fairly ineffective. For example, Connell obviously had his reasons for weighting the balance of power heavily in favor of Zaroff at the outset, but in order for Rainsford to win in the end, he must begin to even the odds against him. Students appreciate the exotic yet apparently plausible traps Rainsford sets in hopes of killing or disabling Zaroff. One of those traps, the Burmese tiger pit, merits close attention: when the reader stops to consider its approximate dimensions, the tool Rainsford digs it with, the probable time it takes him to dig and then outfit it with pointed stakes at the bottom and then disguise it, the large pile of dirt that must have been left over afterward and the way (unspecified by Connell) he disposes of it so Zaroff will not see it, he or she has to conclude that Connell has disregarded the principles of physics.

The Last Laugh

As we discuss the story in class, I often suggest that the story itself is as deceptive as Zaroff's island. Just as Zaroff has his well-concealed strategies for luring unsuspecting sailors onto the rocks and holding them prisoner, so Connell has his well-concealed strategies for luring unsuspecting readers into his story and holding them there. Ironically, those of the fictional villain are better concealed than are those of his real-life author. Perhaps Zaroff simply chose his with more care. Perhaps he is better at man hunting than Connell is at story writing. But Zaroff, a master at taking unfair advantage of others, has an advantage over his creator. On Ship-Trap Island, Zaroff has world enough and time—thanks to his apparently limitless wealth. But Richard Connell, like the rest of us, has to contend with the demands of the real world—and does the best he can, we assume, under the press of circumstances. That literary compromises have been made should now be obvious. Yet few stories in recent decades have been more anthologized in high school and college literature textbooks than "The Most Dangerous Game." If there is a last laugh here, perhaps Connell has it—a thought that students find comforting, probably because it makes them feel better about a story they still like even though they now begin to see that some of its authorial strategies are not particularly successful.

Works Cited

Connell, Richard. "The Most Dangerous Game." *Literature, Structure, Sound, and Sense*. 6th ed. Ed. Laurence Perrine and Thomas R. Arp. San Diego: Harcourt Brace College, 1993. 8–23.

Holm, Kirsten C. *Writer's Market 1998*. Cincinnati: Writer's Digest Books, 1997.

24 Reading Louise Erdrich's "American Horse"

Pat Onion
Colby College

American Indian literature is becoming a very important, recognizably important, part of American literature as a whole. And we are just now rethinking the boundaries of American literature, and we are obliged, I think, to include oral tradition, elements of oral tradition, that we did not even think of including twenty-five years ago.

N. Scott Momaday, *Winged Words: American Indian Writers Speak*

American Horse" (1983), one of Louise Erdrich's earliest pieces of fiction, shows two signature marks of the novels that rapidly succeeded it: indelibly vivid, wit-sharpened characters and an underlying passion for justice. A member of the Turtle Mountain Band of the Anishinabe (Chippewa) people, as well as of German American descent, Erdrich once told Joseph Bruchac that she came into her power when she gave her Chippewa voice full rein (77). At the same time, she yields to no one in her mastery of Western literary techniques, such as the dramatic monologue, stream of consciousness, and the extended trope (also a traditional technique). Her deep roots in Anishinabe tradition, combined with her facility with the conventions of Western genres and her mixed heritage, make her a prime subject for "media-tion" analysis. By her successful mediation between two cultures, she fulfills her stated mission of "protecting and celebrating the cores of cultures left in the wake of catastrophe" (qtd. in Ruppert 131).

Mediation theory, as described by critic James Ruppert and others, offers a way of looking at Native literature that avoids shaping the work as a dialogue between oppressor and oppressed, in this case necessarily casting the Indian in the role of victim. Rather, the mediation theoretical approach encourages readers to notice how a writer such as Erdrich negotiates between two cultures, dramatizing cultural exchanges that are constantly in motion, in constant living flux. The writer becomes a kind of "fancydancer," to borrow writer Sherman Alexie's trope, sure-footed in her ability to enter two worlds.

This way of moving through the text, while pleasingly aesthetic, also carries, especially in Erdrich, a highly serious mission. Not only is Erdrich "protecting and celebrating the cores of cultures left in the wake of catastrophe," but she is also realigning the reader's perceptions, helping the reader to dance a multicultural dance. In "American Horse," for instance, we have a character, Vicki Koob, a social worker whose apparent task it is to assess the American Horse home. With her "trained and cataloguing gaze" (56), she calibrates the space between door and threshold and notes the refrigerator stock of turkey necks, recording in her "perfect-bound notebook" (55) this damning evidence of inadequacy. The scene she records as she walks through the American Horse "shoebox-style house" (52), however, invites the reader to draw different conclusions. She may not get it, but the reader does: this shoebox is a home. Evidence is in the frugality and care expressed in the quilts made by Albertine's mother, the neat disposition of the furniture, and the whimsical décor (this is what someone likes) of bubble glass lamp and three-dimensional picture of Jesus. In this important description of the American Horse home, Erdrich does something remarkable: she makes the reader see that white Vicki Koob's gaze is culture-bound, and she simultaneously invites the reader to look through a different lens, to see things differently by reading over Koob's head. Erdrich leads the reader to use bicultural vision.

To immerse students in the bicultural experience, I begin with row readings—that is, I ask students to take turns reading paragraphs or sentences from the story. Reading aloud allows them to hear Erdrich's rhythms, and students have to hear her to understand how her printed words mediate an essentially oral text. Good opening readings are the description of the American Horse home (55–56) or the description of the Harmony/Albertine conflict (58–60). The first reading can lead to discussion of a large issue: What is "home"? What is Vicki Koob's apparent idea of "home"? What is ours? Where will Buddy be better off, with the social welfare system or with Albertine and Uncle Lawrence?

Erdrich has, of course, complicated these issues. On the one hand is the extreme poverty, and the description of Buddy's mother Albertine as a "tall strong woman who took two big men to subdue when she didn't want to go in the drunk tank" (57). On the other hand is the abundant evidence of a circle of love, in the "home" discussed above, in Uncle Lawrence's fierce defense of the homestead, and in the opening passages delineating the primal relationship between mother and son. At some point in the discussion, I ask the students to look closely at these opening passages, told from Buddy's point of view, to ponder what Erdrich suggests about the price of severing this mother-son bond. My experience is that some students initially argue that poverty is so corrosive, especially when combined with alcohol, that Buddy needs saving. Others argue that the "home" and maternal love that Buddy is being "saved" from, can never, ever be replaced. The final paragraph of blood, ripping body, and screams suggests to me an abortion, confirming the darker reading.

I use this as an opportunity to teach about tropes, which I explain are not just recurring images, but images that retain important content from previous incarnations—images that trail history. Central to the story is the repeated trope of conflict between machines and technology (in Buddy's nightmare, Harmony's gun, or Vicki's notebook) and vision and tradition (Albertine's memory of butterfly "grace," Uncle Lawrence's trickster maneuvers). The recurring opposition between technology and vision, machine power and dream power, trails behind it a long history of conflict between indigenous peoples and the two most destructive Western technologies, the gun and the written word. Vicki Koob's name is, of course, "book" in reverse; the closer one reads the text of the story, the more clearly she is implicated as a destroyer.

When I talk about Erdrich's story with students, I point out images to them, asking them to reflect on the implications. Note how all the color and life are with the American Horse family: Uncle Lawrence's face is a "fierce little cake" (53); Albertine's feet are "two trout" (49). Even when unconscious she connects to the earth, for in the end she seems to be "running full tilt into the ground" (61). In contrast the team of three child-stealers arrives in a "husk of metal . . . emblazoned with the North Dakota State Highway Patrol emblem which is the glowing profile of the Sioux policeman, Red Tomahawk, the one who killed Sitting Bull" (51). The driver is Officer Harmony, the tribal police officer who, like Red Tomahawk, uses his inside knowledge against his own people. Vicki Koob, with her failed antiperspirant, tries unsuccessfully to thwart nature, and Brackett is one who fails to "win the hearts of women" (55). By opposing the American Horse family with its natural affiliations to these misfits of nature, Erdrich engages our sympathy for the family. The child stealers are going against what is right and natural. In effect, she realigns our perceptions.

Anyone who doubts how actively Erdrich is involved in manipulating reader sympathies should look at her reworking of the story in

Chapters 15 and 16 of *The Bingo Palace* (1994). Here the waters are considerably muddied, for the boy's adoptive grandmother, Zelda, whom he loves, is a member of the team coming to get him, and the "shoebox" house, so lovingly described in the original, now is a disaster of neglect and disorder, with "tattered quilts and cheap, pilled dime-store blankets," "scored" chairs, and a "yellowed oilcloth" (175). With these subtle changes, Erdrich removes the powerful double vision of the original story, leaving no doubt here that the boy needs to be removed from this dysfunctional home.

Erdrich works from deeply unconscious sources; witness her surprise, on finishing *Love Medicine*, at the similarity between her character Gerry Nanapush and the Anishinabe trickster Nanabush. Often she mediates a traditional story by contemporizing it, playing with it, transforming it into modern terms. The similarity between "American Horse" and the traditional story "Oshkikwe's Baby" points to just such a transformation. Erdrich mediates the old story, transforming a witch into the Federal Welfare system as it existed prior to the 1978 Child Welfare Act (an Act that provides funds for tribes to administer their own child welfare programs). I divide students into small groups and ask them to compare the two stories, to become mediators themselves. Sometimes I use the example of how "Cinderella" lurks under the film *Pretty Woman* to get them to see how cultural trails work. I ask them to choose a note-taker and a reporter, and to consider questions such as How are the two stories similar? What does the "source" story tell us about the contemporary story? Students love to do this, partly because the enigmas of the traditional story fascinate them.

"Oshkikwe's Baby," as narrated by Delia Oshogay and interpreted by Maggie Lamorie, tells how a witch steals Oshkikwe's baby to make it her servant. Ignoring her sister's dream that warned her of danger, Oshkikwe leaves her baby unattended to collect firewood and returns to find the baby gone; when she frantically searches the area she finds nothing but the hindquarters of the witch and a little piece of the baby's cradleboard. Because of the witch's power, the baby grows rapidly to manhood and fails to recognize Oshkikwe when she finds him and tries to convince him that she is his mother. Finally she shows him her breasts, which he has so recently nursed, the piece of his cradleboard, and the hindquarters of the witch. Of these, his mother's breasts are the most convincing. Students notice the parallels between Oshkikwe and American Horse (both "real mothers" are characterized by nurturing breasts), between Vicki Koob and the witch (both associated with disgusting body excretions), as well as the parallel motifs of prophetic dreams and child stealing. However, in the traditional story the baby eventually effects a return home by tricking the witch.

The ambiguous ending of Erdrich's story suggests the difficulty of the contemporary Native American situation. The traditional story underscores cultural alienation as an evil (the child cannot recognize his own mother) and suggests what might have to happen to Buddy: he will have to get himself back home by playing a trick. He will have to learn to mediate between two cultures more successfully than she did. The first step, to see past the dominant view of his culture, would lead him to recognize and accept his own mother, his roots.

Those roots are treated with respect and earnestness in "American Horse," a story that teaches the reader, especially the non-Indian reader, the full dangers of failing "to read the face of the other" ("American Horse" 59). By mediating two cultures and placing the reader in the center, Erdrich strips Western readers of our cultural blinders—her way of "protecting and celebrating the cores of cultures left in the wake of catastrophe."

Works Cited

Bruchac, Joseph. *Survival This Way: Interviews with American Indian Poets.* Tucson: U of Arizona P, 1987. 73–86.

Erdrich, Louise. "American Horse." *Spider Woman's Granddaughters: Traditional Tales and Contemporary Writing by Native American Women.* Ed. Paula Gunn Allen. New York: Fawcett Columbine, 1989. 42–52.

Oshogay, Delia. "Oshkikwe's Baby." *Spider Woman's Granddaughters: Traditional Tales and Contemporary Writing by Native American Women.* Ed. Paula Gunn Allen. New York: Fawcett Columbine, 1989. 37–40.

Ruppert, James. *Mediation in Contemporary Native American Fiction.* Norman: U of Oklahoma P, 1995.

Further Reading

Barnouw, Victor. *Wisconsin Chippewa Myths and Tales and Their Relation to Chippewa Life.* Madison: U of Wisconsin P, 1977.

Erdrich, Louise. *The Bingo Palace.* New York: HarperCollins, 1994.

Moore, David L. "Decolonizing Criticism: Reading Dialectics and Dialogics in Native American Literatures." *SAIL* 6.4 (Winter 1994): 7–35.

Sarris, Greg. "Reading Louise Erdrich." *Keeping Slug Woman Alive: A Holistic Approach to American Indian Texts.* Berkeley: U of California P, 1993. 115–46.

Wong, Hertha D. "Adoptive Mothers and Thrown-Away Children in the
    Novels of Louise Erdrich." *Narrating Mothers: Theorizing Maternal
    Subjectivities.* Ed. Brenda O. Daly and Maureen T. Reddy. Knoxville: U
    of Tennessee P, 1991. 174–92.

25 Opening the Door to Understanding Joyce Carol Oates's "Where Are You Going, Where Have You Been?"

Richard E. Mezo
University of Guam

If I didn't know the ending of a story, I wouldn't begin. I always write my last lines, my last paragraph, my last page first, and then I go back and work towards it. I know where I'm going. I know what my goal is.

Katherine Anne Porter, "Interview with Barbara Thompson"

Readers may remember *Smooth Talk*, a 1985 film based upon "Where Are You Going, Where Have You Been?" (WAYG, WHYB?; see Figure 1). In comments made about the film, Joyce Carol Oates speaks of the origins of her story, a real-life tragedy concerning a psychopath ("The Pied Piper of Tucson") who raped and murdered teenaged girls in the early or mid 1960s (67). However, the transformation of a raw story into the art of fiction in this instance has produced an entirely different experience—there is, for example, no suggestion of rape or murder in the short story. Oates says that an early draft "had the rather too explicit title 'Death and the Maiden'" (68). In the early stages of writing the story, Oates was thinking about an old theme that was once popular in early German art—perhaps best represented by Hans Baldung Grien (see Figure 2). But the title changed over the course of developing the short story to become the present "Where Are You Going, Where Have You Been?" This new title is borrowed from another painting—from Gauguin's 1897 masterpiece titled *D'où venons-nous? Que sommes-nous? Où allons-nous?* (Where have we come from? What are we? Where are we going?) (see Figure 3). Although Oates's title is close to Gauguin's original, there are significant variations: the first and the last clauses have been switched around—the first is last and the

Figure 1. Laura Dern plays Connie in the film *Smooth Talk* (1985). The Museum of Modern Art, New York; Films Stills Archive.

Figure 2. Hans Baldung Grien, *Die drei Lebensalter und der Tod* (c.1510). Kunsthistorisches Museum, Vienna.

Figure 3. Paul Gauguin, *D'où venons-nous? Que sommes-nous? Où allons-nous?* (1897). The Museum of Fine Arts, Boston. Arthur Gordon Tomkins Residuary Fund.

last first. In addition, the middle clause is left out altogether. And, finally, the *nous* becomes *vous* (*we* becomes *you*) in Oates's title.

The significance of these changes may easily be addressed in a classroom discussion, but perhaps students should first examine copies of the two works of art. The *Death and the Maiden* painting is a graphic depiction of tragedy, suggesting that all earthly beauty and innocence will finally be overcome by death, and that such is the way of the world. The not-so-subtle message for viewers is that we must look higher for beauty or for justice—toward those things not found in this world. On the other hand, Gauguin's canvas celebrates earthly beauty as well as ritual and human community. One astute observer remarks, "here Gauguin—as André Breton recently put it—has 'reeled off the human predicament' and pictured life in all its precarious balance between birth, love and death . . . [with the statue in the painting representing] the primitive tradition of 'nature's wholeness'" (Estienne 98).

The key of art (plastic art) then, opens a door onto the broad vistas of understanding, not only for the short story WAYG, WHYB? but also for a valuable realization about the process of creation in all works of art. But there are still two other keys to the story that the reader must use. One concerns the story's structure, in which there is a clear dividing point. Students may be informed that the story is a two-part narrative that has no outward dividing mark and then be asked to divide the story at its most logical point. Most will make that division at about the time that Arnold Friend (An Old Friend) comes to visit. And indeed that is the point at which the narrator stops showing the reader Connie and her family and friends and concentrates upon Connie and her relationship with Arnold Friend and Ellie Oscar. Just before Arnold arrives, the narrator tells the reader that "Connie sat with her eyes closed in the sun, dreaming and dazed . . . and when she opened her eyes she hardly knew where she was. . . . She shook her head as if to get awake" (30).

Arnold does not come for Connie until after she is in a condition of dazed and dreamy half-consciousness. Certainly her condition explains much that would otherwise be literally impossible in any "realistic" story. There is no way, for example, that the best detective in the world (or the most determined stalker) could know the things about Connie and her family that Arnold knows. Strangely, Arnold knows that Connie's family is at Aunt Tillie's barbecue and that Mrs. Hornsby had joined them. It is even stranger that he also knows about the "old woman down the road, the one with the chickens and stuff," because, as Connie says, the old woman is dead. All these very deliberate and repeated suggestions that Arnold has supernatural powers lacking in ordinary mortals lead to one inescapable conclusion—that this second part of the story is not realistic, but fantastic. It is a dream. Given some time and a few suggestions, students will come to this same conclusion.

Another key is to be found in the character Arnold Friend. Of course he is Connie's antagonist (she is the protagonist; her sister June is a very traditional foil). Arnold has been misidentified by some critics as a devil or a satanic figure. But this old friend, although frightening, is not "evil"; his function is to lead Connie from the world of a child, the world of innocence, into the world of experience—the sometimes terrifying world into which Connie moves at the end of the story—from the "safe" doorway of her protecting house "into the sunlight," into the "vast sunlit reaches of the land," and into Arnold's waiting arms. Connie is not coerced into her decision to go; Arnold has never entered her house or physically touched her at all. In fact, he cannot force her into experience; Connie must make up her own mind and come with him voluntarily. In accepting Arnold and his world, Connie is entering the world of adulthood and experience—she is accepting her own sexual identity. Her only alternative is to remain a child—like her sister June—living in the house of her parents.

The true identity of Arnold Friend, the man who "had come from nowhere . . . and belonged nowhere," may be suggested to students by reading and discussing one of e. e. cummings's poems, "in Just—" (The first line of the poem suggests an "injust[ice]" or the unjust demands made by experience.) In the poem's Edenic setting, "mud-luscious . . . [and] puddle-wonderful," in the spring of the year, innocent children are at play. But biding his time in Eden is the "little lame balloonman" ("queer . . . goat-footed") who, in the long run, will not be denied. He whistles seductively on his pipes, threatening innocence; yet despite his seemingly undesirable qualities, his function is a necessary one. As the students are led to discover Pan and his pipes in cummings's poem (along with the Pan-ic generated by this god) and begin to associate the poem with WAYG, WHYB?, many elements of the story start to make sense: Arnold's physical appearance (his age, his face or mask, the trouble he has standing or walking in boots, the hair that looks like a wig); the popular music and its seductive role in blue-collar society; the simulated sexual act as Connie attempts to call the police while Arnold waits passively outside; the expansive, sunlit world of nature that Arnold brings with him as counterpoint to the limited world of working-class asbestos ranch houses and "fly-infested" restaurants that are typical of Connie's environment. Pan, the somewhat frightening god of the woods, appears to Connie at the time of her first sexual encounter with Eddie, foreshadowing later events in the dream sequence. At the end of the story, Connie apparently accepts her sexuality and moves on into the world of adulthood and experience. Connie's necessary journey through life (a journey all must undertake) is reflected in the title "Where Are You Going, Where Have You Been?"

Works Cited

cummings, e. e. "chanson innocente." *The Norton Introduction to Poetry.* 2nd ed. J. Paul Hunter, ed. New York: Norton, 1981.

Estienne, Charles. *Gauguin.* Trans. James Emmons. Geneva: Skira, 1953.

Oates, Joyce Carol. *"Where Are You Going, Where Have You Been?"* Women Writers: Texts and Contexts Series. Ed. Elaine Showalter. New Brunswick: Rutgers UP, 1994. 23–48.

———. "'Where Are You Going, Where Have You Been?' and *Smooth Talk*: Short Story into Film." *"Where Are You Going, Where Have You Been?"* Women Writers: Texts and Contexts Series. Ed. Elaine Showalter. New Brunswick, NJ: Rutgers UP, 1994. 67–72.

Afterword: Writing by the Flash of the Firefly

In his foreword to *Hugging the Shore*, a compilation of his literary essays, John Updike comments, "Literary criticism is to writing fiction and poetry as hugging the shore is to sailing in the open sea" (xv). Somehow, in Updike's estimation, creative and critical writing do not share equal risks. (Perhaps Updike speaks of himself: while writing his book reviews for the *New Yorker*, he continues plumbing his New England imagination in fiction.) Updike's analogy reminds us that, while sitting down to write something new seems as precarious as setting sail into uncharted waters, criticism too has its perils: sailors must not only follow the shore as reference, they must also avoid the rocks and sandbars hidden under the shallow waves. Good criticism is not a simple outline of what some other sailor has navigated, but a sea log of a voyage that, if the tenets of the rest of this book have succeeded, reaches the destination of the human heart.

Although the short story has obvious merit in the classroom, it is not necessarily a better catalyst for student writing exercises than other genres. In fact, the short story is somewhat problematic because, by its very design, it can offer a sense of closure by which readers may conclude that nothing more need be said. Its brevity gives the impression that the whole has been processed, and, once discussed and comprehended, it can be forgotten. But a good story resists being forgotten, and those moments of intuitive comprehension—sensed first by internally hearing how language may add up to more than the sum of its words—demand contemplation if they are to contribute to personal growth.

Encouraging students to engage in that productive contemplation is necessary, yet difficult. If they are to make personal connections, it will be due to their own central and possibly unresolved issues (conscious or unconscious). Reading strikes at vulnerable places, and a good story will home in on those spots. Put in Gordimer's phrasing, the firefly's flash lights the way, but, when the story ends and darkness once again closes in, relief follows. To write about the story in any meaningful way will entail that the reader engage with sensitive issues more easily avoided. As teachers, then, our job is not only to encourage students to connect to texts but to manage the potentially messy aftermath.

Of course, if students want to ignore the firefly's flash, they will. Establishing a genuine line of thought in response to a story is a frustrating adventure for all of us, an adventure in which there may be dead ends and seemingly pointless side trips. Students write outlines, but outlines don't work when the text doesn't confirm what they want to argue. The encounter with the story is thus necessarily prolonged, but usually this is time profitably spent. To write a heartfelt and analytical essay about a short story demands taking the time to reconstruct a glimpse, giving it a context, a focus, and a meaning that will be "glimpsable" by someone for whom the firefly may have revealed something different. It is as though each student peers at a story through a knothole in the high wooden walls surrounding a construction site. Because the knothole is at the right height and angle, the student can see a great deal. However, boring a knothole that allows other readers to experience the same effect is not so simple. To do that, students must move beyond their personal requirements and sympathies to shareable insights.

Regardless of their particular texts and approaches, the teachers of this book agree that, for students to write authentic, genuine essays, students should always, always begin at a point of contact with the story, a place where the story "gets" to them. At the same time, essays on short stories are not therapy and do not gain by any sort of self-indulgence. The traps are obvious: students either circumvent issues with boring plot summary or obliterate them with uncomfortable personal revelation. In either strategy they avoid real analysis of the story's effect, the one losing the forest for the trees, the other torching the whole thing ablaze. As we read papers in our latest batch of student essays, we can identify either problem almost instinctively. And we wince, knowing that, no matter how well crafted the essay at hand, no real learning has occurred.

In meaningful student response, a point of contact raises a question, which in itself requires clear identification, and a position on how the story answers that question. To help students achieve this focus, teachers often ask students to freewrite so that students can sort and delve, finding what sticks in their craw—what is *not* so easy to explain away. The next step, though, is paramount: teachers push students beyond personal log or journal writing to the question of theme. Theme, it is important to note, is a general statement of meaning, not a generic label ("tragedy") or an abstract noun ("loneliness," "compassion"). If the theme involves the opposition of two nouns ("city versus country"), it demands a position: which is better? As such, students often get at theme through a maxim or truth, a complete sentence with a subject and predicate, and fine-tune from there. In the MGM musical *The Wizard of Oz,* Dorothy does not, we may illustrate to our students, click her heels together and utter, "Auntie Em's House"; rather, she wishes on a theme: "There's no place like home." Getting students to recognize this difference is not as easy as it might seem.

Even when they identify questions, students may find it difficult to decide on a single theme from an intricate and complex story. Happily, the short story answers this problem with its remarkable efficiency—the quality that Flannery O'Connor had in mind when she remarked, "You tell a story because a statement would be inadequate" (96). To support and explain their sense of theme, students marshal story evidence, fitting it into the essay as would a dressmaker, making a tuck here, letting out the material there, adjusting to the reality of the story. They must continually ask themselves, Would someone else draw the same conclusions given these pieces of evidence? Do such narrative aspects as title, tone, character, plot, and the all-important beginning and ending paragraphs fit the theme? In their construction of theme, students learn to be wary of ideas that they do not fully understand and to use their writing as a way to make their own thinking visible to the essay reader.

Analytical and persuasive writing need not follow a prescribed format. Notorious in this vein is the "five-paragraph" essay, in which students state their thesis in the first paragraph and then formulate each "body" paragraph by beginning "First," "Second," and "Third." The result is predictably tedious, form totally eclipsing function. Samuel Johnson, in his "Preface to Shakespeare," suggests a more organic approach: "The work of a *correct and regular* writer is a garden accurately formed and diligently planted, varied with shades, and scented with flowers" (281, emphasis added). Essays that are "correct and regular" will vary in shape from writer to writer, just as gardens vary from gardener to gardener. In this way, essays should express the soul of the person writing the essay, reconstituting what that soul made of the story being described. Whether essays follow a five-paragraph prescription is of no more importance, ultimately, than whether a garden is made square or round, with plants lined up in trim, narrow rows or in wide, cascading terraces—so long as its message is articulate and important. Form responds to function, function to form, as the knowing gardener plants according to taste and terrain. Likewise, for teachers, the ultimate concern is guiding students to take personal responses and make them intelligible, forging a connection that lends itself to what is sometimes called "creative nonfiction," a kind of writing in which personal reflections are skillfully interwoven with analysis.

Given the nature of this book, there remain the tools and voices of literary theorists. Using theory in the classroom, to be sure, is a bit of a gamble; it is all too easy for authority to intimidate students or for students to accept authority indiscriminately. At its best, theory should both encourage and temper students, especially when it complements a student's own thesis. Theory must, however, like those tall neutral plants in the back of the garden, be positioned so that a student's own ideas are foregrounded. Sometimes, in fact, students can take issue with theorists, using critical interpretation as a springboard for a counter line of thought. At such moments, students make the mistake of including too much of a good thing by letting the critics' "authority" override their own, even to the point of eclipsing the story itself. The lesson is valuable: literary theory, like any new tool, is liable to get overworked; when, however, the user achieves dexterity with it, the tool finds its proper spot in the workshop. Our job as teachers is to be sure that our students do not get into ideological ruts and embrace their current theories as laws or certitudes. We must guide them back to their own connections to the stories, and to their own voices in describing those connections. It all starts in helping them hear the full linguistic dimensions of literature so that they can read more fully. In their fuller reading, we know, they become better writers. At that point, their writing tunes their hearing, and, the loop complete, we step back and watch as they become self-reliant learners.

Works Cited

Johnson, Samuel. From the Preface to the Edition of Shakespeare. 1765. *The Selected Writings of Samuel Johnson.* Ed. Katherine Rogers. New York: New American Library, 1981. 261–86.

O'Connor, Flannery. *Mystery and Manners: Occasional Prose.* Ed. Sally and Robert Fitzgerald. London: Faber and Faber, 1972. 87–118.

Updike, John. "Foreword." *Hugging the Shore: Essays and Criticism.* New York: Knopf, 1983.

A Bibliographic Postscript

The available bibliographic materials for teaching the short story range from excerpts of criticism such as those collected in Gale Research's *Short Story Criticism* to monographs like those of the Twayne series, each of which features one author. For a start, teachers and students might consult a general overview like Dean Baldwin and Gregory L. Morris's text, which is organized by reference works, histories, short story theory, and individual authors. Author entries include sections on both general critical estimates and selected titles. For an overview of short story theory, Charles E. May's 1976 *Short Story Theories*, the first serious collection of short story criticism, contains reprints of essays by Edgar Allan Poe, Frank O'Connor, Elizabeth Bowen, and Eudora Welty, along with May's summary of short story criticism in America and an annotated bibliography. May's 1994 *The New Short Story Theories* brings the collection up to date, with contributions that focus on definition and history. In addition, Susan Lohafer and Jo Ellyn Clarey's 1989 *Short Story Theory at a Crossroads* attempts to move short story criticism beyond Poe's "utilitarian" definition to the sphere of recent developments in narrative and reading theories. For a full listing of short story sources, including journal articles, May's annotated bibliography in *Short Story Theories* is quite useful, as are those in both his *The New Short Story Theories* and Lohafer and Clarey's book. For an overview of international stories, especially welcome is Bonnie H. Neumann and Helen M. McDonnell's recent NCTE book *Teaching the Short Story* (1996). Organized by author, each entry provides biographical information, plot summaries, and teaching strategies. Journals such as *Studies in Short Fiction, Short Story Journal*, and *History of Short Story Journal* contain criticism as well as new fiction. Finally, as a complement to literary study in general, Ross Murfin and Supryia M. Ray's handbook, *The Bedford Glossary of Critical and Literary Terms*, provides more than five hundred definitions of literary terms that are both up-to-date and thorough.

There are numerous anthologies of short stories, many quite suitable for classroom use. The best compile stories that can be organized into a coherent course syllabus. Ann Charters's collection, in both its expanded and compact forms, is widely popular because it dovetails stories with relevant commentary. Also popular is James Pickering's *Fiction 100*, now in its eighth edition, which contains many classic stories. May's *Fiction's Many Worlds* contains 142 "highly teachable" stories organized by their focus on reality, fantasy, myth, and story-ness, with an introductory comment for each chapter. Both Norton and Oxford have several fine anthologies of stories. James Moffett and Kenneth McElheny's *Points of View* contains stories especially appropriate for secondary school use. Ron Hansen and Jim Shepard's *You've Got to Read This* is a collection of stories chosen and introduced by contemporary short-fiction writers. The *Graywolf Annual* series arranges stories by theme, with aging, American multiculturalism, family issues, and Italian fiction represented so far. Short story scholars, writers, and readers meet every two years at the International Conference on the Short Story in English for scholarly discussions of short fiction topics and readings by current short story writers.

Bibliography

Baldwin, Dean, and Gregory L. Morris. *The Short Story in English: Britain and North America: An Annotated Bibliography*. Metuchen, NJ, and Englewood Cliffs, NJ: Scarecrow and Salem Presses, 1994.

Charters, Ann, ed. *Major Writers of Short Fiction: Stories and Commentaries*. Boston: Bedford Books of St. Martin's P, 1993.

———. *The Story and Its Writer*. 4th ed. Boston: Bedford Books of St. Martin's P, 1995.

Hansen, Ron, and Jim Shepard, eds. *You've Got to Read This: Contemporary American Writers Introduce Stories That Held Them in Awe*. New York: HarperPerennial, 1994.

Lohafer, Susan, and Jo Ellyn Clarey. *Short Story Theory at a Crossroads*. Baton Rouge: Louisiana State UP, 1989.

May, Charles E., ed. *Fiction's Many Worlds*. Lexington, MA: D. C. Heath, 1993.

———. *The New Short Story Theories*. Athens: Ohio University P, 1994.

———. *Short Story Theories*. Athens: Ohio University P, 1976.

Moffett, James, and Kenneth R. McElheny, eds. *Points of View: An Anthology of Short Stories*. New York: Penguin, 1966.

Murfin, Ross, and Supryia M. Ray. *The Bedford Glossary of Critical and Literary Terms*. Boston: Bedford, 1997.

Neumann, Bonnie, and Helen M. McDonnell. *Teaching the Short Story: A Guide to Using Stories from Around the World*. Urbana, IL: NCTE, 1996.

Pickering, James, ed. *Fiction 100: An Anthology of Short Stories*. 8th ed. New York: Prentice Hall, 1997.

Index

Editors

Carole L. Hamilton is a teacher of humanities at Cary Academy, a private school in Cary, North Carolina. She received her A.B. in comparative literature from the University of California at Berkeley and her M.A. in English from the University of Virginia. Hamilton's scholarly interests are in eighteenth- and twentieth-century literature and drama. She publishes entries on drama for the Gale Research reference series *Drama for Students*. In short fiction, she admires authors Lee K. Abbott for his remarkable use of metaphor, Sherman Alexie for his wit, and Flannery O'Connor for her wisdom. She has recently become a "cyber-teacher," using computer-generated presentation tools to integrate English with art and social studies and to differentiate instruction for gifted learners. In spite of this wide range of interests, her daughter Aubrey and husband Ned are the center of her universe.

Peter Kratzke received his B.A. and M.A. from the University of Washington and his Ph.D. from the University of Kentucky. He presently has a visiting position in the American Thought and Language Program at Michigan State University. Kratzke's scholarship centers on American literary history, and he has published on such authors as Ambrose Bierce, Jack London, and Edgar Wilson ("Bill") Nye. Bierce's call to "write it right," in fact, inspires how he teaches his students the forms and functions of "wordsmithing." In his spare time, he loves sports that range from skiing to tennis to basketball. He would not have much fun, however, if it were not for his wife Jeri and their faithful bassett hound Otto.

Contributors

Janet Gebhart Auten teaches in the college writing and women's and gender studies programs at American University, Washington, D.C., where she received an outstanding teaching award for 1995–96. She has published articles on rhetorical issues in teaching and on using nineteenth-century texts in the classroom, and she is working on studies of antebellum and regional writers and of teacher response to student writing.

Barbara Kaplan Bass has a chapter on Armistead Maupin in *Contemporary Gay American Novelists: A Bio-bibliographic Critical Sourcebook* (1993). She teaches writing and literature at Towson State University in Baltimore. She is director of the Maryland Writing Project.

Susan Berry Brill de Ramirez, associate professor of English at Bradley University, teaches American Indian literatures, folklore, and literary criticism and theory. Her book *The Conversive Imagination: Reading American Indian Literatures Relationally* is forthcoming from the University of Arizona Press, and she is presently finishing *Telling Stories: American Indian Autobiographies*. Her first book was *Wittgenstein and Critical Theory* (1995).

Kelly Chandler is assistant professor in the Reading and Language Arts Center at Syracuse University. Previously she taught English and women's history at Noble High School in Berwick, Maine.

Brenda Dyer teaches English as a Foreign Language through content-based courses in global issues and literature at Tokyo Woman's University and Tsuda College, Tokyo.

Dianne Fallon is the department chair of English and Humanities at York County Technical College in Wells, Maine, where she teaches courses in composition, literature, and technical writing.

Linda L. Gill is associate professor of literature at Pacific Union College, where she teaches literary theory, Victorian literature, the novel, introduction to literature, and English composition.

Tamara Grogan has taught English and French at every level from kindergarten through adult continuing education, and she recently completed an M.F.A. at the University of Massachusetts at Amherst. Her fiction has appeared in journals such as *The Iowa Review, The Massachusetts Review,* and *The Crescent Review.*

Tom Hansen is associate professor of English at Northern State University in Aberdeen, South Dakota, where he teaches composition and creative writing and an occasional novel course. His essays, poems, and reviews appear frequently in literary journals.

Judy L. Isaksen teaches writing, women's studies, and gender studies at Eckerd College in St. Petersburg, Florida; she is also working on her Ph.D. in rhetoric and composition at the University of South Florida.

Sara R. Joranko teaches first-year composition, survey of English literature, introduction to poetry, introduction to short fiction, and writing at John Carroll University in Cleveland, Ohio. She also directs the Writing Center.

Janet Ellen Kaufman is assistant professor of English at the University of Utah and specializes in secondary English education. Her essay came from her experiences teaching middle school and high school in the Washington, D.C., area.

Charles E. May is professor of English at California State University, Long Beach. He is the author of *Edgar Allan Poe: A Study of the Short Fiction* and *The Short Story: The Reality of Artifice* and editor of *Short Story Theories, The New Short Story Theories, The Twentieth Century European Short Story,* and *Fiction's Many Worlds.* He has published over two hundred articles, mostly on the short story, in a variety of journals, books, and reference works, and he developed the software program described in his essay.

Richard E. Mezo teaches introductory and advanced courses in literature and writing at the University of Guam and at the University of Maryland, Asian Division. He is a published writer and has a serious interest in education.

Pat Onion is associate professor at Colby College in Waterville, Maine, where she teaches American Indian literature.

Lawrence Pruyne has taught composition, literature, and writing. He earned his Ph.D. in 1997, and is now an English instructor at Western New England College, outside Boston. In addition, he writes novels.

E. Shelley Reid is assistant professor of English at Austin College in Sherman, Texas. She teaches contemporary and minority American literatures and has published articles on identity and narrative in novels by Amy Tan and Louise Erdrich.

Susanne Rubenstein teaches English at Wachusett Regional High School in Holden, Massachusetts. Her work has appeared in *The Worcester Review, Teacher Magazine, Literal Latte,* and *We Teach Them All—Teachers Writing about Diversity.* She is the author of *Go Public! Encouraging Student Writers to Publish* (NCTE).

Russell Shipp teaches eighth-grade English at Iroquois Middle School in Niskayuna, New York. He has been teaching for thirty years, he loves to write poetry, and he is interested in the pedagogy of writing.

James Tackach teaches American literature at Roger Williams University in Bristol, Rhode Island. His articles have appeared in a variety of academic journals, including *Saul Bellow Journal, The Writing Center Journal,* and *ADE Bulletin.*

Grant Tracey, assistant professor of English at the University of Northern Iowa, teaches college composition, creative writing, and film. He also edits *Literary Magazine Review.*

Jennifer Seibel Trainor teaches literature and writing courses while pursuing her Ph.D. in education at the University of California at Berkeley.

Dennis Young teaches writing and literature at George Mason University in Fairfax, Virginia. His published work focuses on literature and writing pedagogy.

❧

This book was typeset in Palatino and Helvetica.
The typefaces used on the cover were Democratica and Bell Gothic.
The book was printed by Edwards Brothers, Inc.